I0819498

The Bright Edges of the World

The Bright Edges of the World

Willa Cather and Her Archbishop

Garrett Peck

UNIVERSITY OF NEW MEXICO PRESS | ALBUQUERQUE

Printed in the United States of America

ISBN 978-0-8263-6925-3 (cloth)
ISBN 978-0-8263-6926-0 (ePub)

Library of Congress Control Number: 2025945074

Founded in 1889, the University of New Mexico sits on the traditional homelands of the Pueblo of Sandia. The original peoples of New Mexico—Pueblo, Navajo, and Apache—since time immemorial have deep connections to the land and have made significant contributions to the broader community statewide. We honor the land itself and those who remain stewards of this land throughout the generations and also acknowledge our committed relationship to Indigenous peoples. We gratefully recognize our history.

Cover illustration: © Nickolas Muray Photo Archives. Used with permission of the Nickolas Muray Photo Archives.
Designed by Felicia Cedillos
Composed in Galliard

Dedicated to my mother, Elsa Morrison
Who got me started on the Santa Fe trail

Also by Garrett Peck

The Prohibition Hangover: Alcohol in America from Demon Rum to Cult Cabernet
Prohibition in Washington, D.C.: How Dry We Weren't
The Potomac River: A History and Guide
The Smithsonian Castle and the Seneca Quarry
Capital Beer: A Heady History of Brewing in Washington, D.C.
Walt Whitman in Washington, D.C.: The Civil War and America's Great Poet
The Great War in America: World War I and Its Aftermath
A Decade of Disruption: America in the New Millennium 2000–2010

Contents

Acknowledgments

The idea for this book came in 1998 during my first visit to Santa Fe. My mom insisted that I read Willa Cather's *Death Comes for the Archbishop*, and I became hooked on both Cather and Santa Fe. Since then, I have met so many other Cather fans, many of whom helped shape this narrative. As they say, no book is produced in a vacuum.

I am grateful for the work of professors Andrew Jewell and Janis Stout for curating and publishing Willa Cather's letters. I bounced ideas off Andrew more times than I can count, and he was eternally patient with me and enormously helpful. Janis provided crucial feedback on an early draft of this book.

Melissa Homestead, professor of English at the University of Nebraska–Lincoln and one of the nation's leading Cather scholars, pointed the way to the Blue Jay notebook, a crucial source for exploring the backstory behind Cather's novel. And I learned that Melissa and I share an antipathy for interpreting Cather's scribbling handwriting.

Ashley Olson, Tracy Tucker, and Rachel Olsen of the National Willa Cather Center extended wonderful support in reading my manuscript, offering crucial facts (and fact-checking), providing images for this book, and hosting the Willa Cather Spring Conference, which is unbelievably enjoyable.

Josh Caster and other archivists at Archives & Special Collections at the University of Nebraska–Lincoln assisted with a memorable research day in June 2024, providing reams of Cather-related documents and photos. Josh also provided many of the images that you find in this book.

In case you need further proof that archivists and librarians should wear superhero capes, I have a long list of capes to hand out. When I learned that Edith Lewis and Willa Cather had perused books (plural) at the Palace of the Governors in 1925, I contacted the Fray Angélico Chávez Library in Santa Fe to ask what books might have been in the collection in 1925. Heather McClure and the staff dug up a short list of books from their acquisition records, several of which confirmed what I suspected. This was all because Paul Civitelli of the Beinecke Rare Book Room & Manuscript Library at Yale University retrieved Edith Lewis's letters to Mabel Dodge Luhan, one of which included that crucial plural word, "books." And Hannah Abelbeck and Catie Carl opened access to the Palace of the Governors Photo Archives, a treasure trove of images that fill these pages.

Bernadette Lucero of the Archdiocese of Santa Fe Museum and Archives approved the St. Francis Cathedral and other church photographs. Brittany Bratcher at the Harry Ransom Center at the University of Texas at Austin provided publisher Alfred A. Knopf's unpublished memoir. Candace Reilly, the special collections manager at Drew University, retrieved the letters of Louise Guerber.

Jessica Castaño of the McFarlin Library at the University of Tulsa retrieved a crucial letter from Erna Fergusson, while Hector Acosta of the Huntington Library retrieved a letter from Cather to Mary Austin.

Paul Chasen, the librarian-in-charge of the H. L. Mencken Room at the Enoch Pratt Free Library in Baltimore, pulled Mencken's 1927 *Archbishop* review for me. Leah Johanson, reference archivist at the Brooke Russell Astor Reading Room for Rare Books and Manuscripts, New York Public Library, provided several letters from Cather to Mencken.

Karyl Klein of the Denver Archdiocesan Archives provided a crucial 1854 letter from Father Machebeuf that helped establish that Lamy purchased his country farm (now Bishop's Lodge) the year before. Amber Stephenson, the curator of the Jane Pope Geske Heritage Room of Nebraska Authors at the Bennett Martin Public Library in Lincoln, Nebraska, provided a letter from Cather to Alice Corbin Henderson. Matt Perelli, Processing & Reference Archivist at the Boatwright Memorial Library at the University of Richmond, retrieved a Cather letter to Carl Van Vechten.

Here in New Mexico, I owe special thanks to the Santa Fe Public Library staff, especially Esther Rydzik, who ordered so many interlibrary loan articles and books for me that I lost count. Carmella Padilla, Clare Hertel, Mark Bryant, Megan Mulry, and Susan Burks of the Santa Fe International Book Festival opened many doors and are a wealth of encouragement to writers. Frances Zeller, the director of the Belen Harvey House, gave me a personal tour of the museum and provided Harvey Girl images.

The exceptional staff at Bishop's Lodge have been incredibly supportive of this project: general managers Andrea Gates, Angelica Palladino, and John Volponi; Kimber Falkinburg, Rebecca Mascolo, Taylor Gonzalez, Marama Nengel, and the Adventure Team. When I told Rebecca Mascolo that I was visiting Mesa Verde and Walnut Canyon to follow in Cather's footsteps, she bid me a wonderful "Cathercation," a word that still leaves me chuckling. I've taken many Cathercations since then—and I hope readers who wish to follow in the footsteps of Willa Cather will enjoy your own.

Ed Pulsifer, the head of sales and the historian at La Fonda on the Plaza, provided much documentation and images of the historic hotel. The concierges and docents are incredible stewards of the hotel's history, and I give special thanks to John Felix.

The team at the University of New Mexico Press has been fantastic to work with. Michael Millman, acquisitions editor, reached out to me, as he had heard through the grapevine that I was writing this Cather book. He arranged for two outstanding peer reviewers who love Cather as much as I do: author Kali Fajardo-Anstine and Gary Scharnhorst, professor of English at the University of New Mexico. James Ayers and his team designed the cover, oversaw the editorial, and brought in Irina du Quenoy to edit the manuscript. My gratitude to each of you for helping to bring this book to fruition.

And lastly, and most of all, I thank my literary agent, Tom Miller of Liza Dawson Associates.

Introduction

"I seem fated to send people on journeys."

—WILLA CATHER TO MISS MASTERSON, MARCH 15, 1943

WILLA CATHER PUBLISHED THE novel *Death Comes for the Archbishop* in September 1927. She had visited the desert Southwest six times between 1912 and 1926. Her last two trips in 1925 and 1926 were directly related to researching and writing *Archbishop*, which late in life she called her "best book."[1] The novel, an unusual story of two French priests and best friends serving on the American frontier, is loosely based on two actual people, Archbishop Jean-Baptiste Lamy and Bishop Joseph Machebeuf. It is a perennial favorite of visitors to New Mexico.

In 2024 *The Atlantic* published "The Great American Novels" list, choosing the most notable novels from 1924 to 2023. For 1927, the magazine chose Willa Cather's *Death Comes for the Archbishop*, the only Cather novel to make the list.[2]

I first read *Death Comes for the Archbishop* in 1998 before my first visit to Santa Fe. My mom, who came with me, encouraged me to read the book before our trip. I subsequently reread the book so many times and returned to Santa Fe so often that I finally decided to move there during the COVID-19 pandemic. Santa Fe is a tourist town and has been since it achieved statehood in 1912, the year Cather first ventured to the

Southwest. I'm fine with that—I'm a tour guide, and my job is to help guests explore the rich layers of our culture and history. I want every visitor to fall in love with Santa Fe, just as I did, and just as Cather did. The City Different, as we call it, is a magical place.

I lead a tour called Willa Cather's Santa Fe, in which we explore Cather's inspiration to write *Death Comes for the Archbishop* while walking in her footsteps. I call it a "walking seminar," as we explore 1920s Santa Fe with historic images and readings from Cather's articles, interviews, and letters. We also explore characters and themes covered in her novel. So many visitors have read *Archbishop*, and people seem universally impressed by her sparse but beautiful descriptions of New Mexico, descriptions that Cather based on her personal experiences traveling to the Southwest.

A Santa Fean once flippantly referred to Cather as a carpetbagger. Not so, I responded. She was no weekend visitor, but someone who visited the Southwest six times, each time for one to two months. She loved the Southwest and considered buying a second home in the region (alas, she never did). Anyone who travels absorbs the local culture just by being there, meeting the people, hearing the language and customs, exploring the history, and enjoying the food. Cather drew powerful insights from her travels, and she used her linguistic skills to vividly describe places that her characters inhabited—places that she herself had visited. From Cather's six trips to the Southwest came three novels: *The Song of the Lark* (1915), *The Professor's House* (1925), and *Death Comes for the Archbishop* (1927).

"Travel is fatal to prejudice, bigotry and narrow-mindedness, and many of our people need it sorely on these accounts," observed Mark Twain in *The Innocents Abroad*. He added, "Broad, wholesome, charitable views of men and things can not be acquired by vegetating in one little corner of the earth all one's lifetime."[3] Travel builds empathy between cultures and people. Going on a trip requires you to take a step out of yourself and beyond your comfort zone. Often that's where the universe reveals its secrets, when you've shed your routine and are open to possibilities and new perspectives. Willa Cather possessed empathy in abundance and saw differing perspectives through her characters, often real or historical people she met along her journeys.

Historian Flannery Burke called what most visitors to New Mexico engage in "heritage tourism." The label isn't pejorative. People come to explore the ancient human history, stunning landscapes, outdoor recreation, our many cultures, the extensive art scene, and the chile-driven cuisine that make the Land of Enchantment such a distinct place. But they often underestimate how deeply Hispanic, Mexican, and Native American our culture is. We are the only state to place "New Mexico USA" on our car license plates, as many geographically challenged Americans mistakenly think New Mexico is part of Mexico, rather than being the forty-seventh state. We are, as they say, a place apart.[4]

New Mexico has twenty-three federally recognized Indigenous tribes (nineteen Pueblo, three Apache, and the Navajo/Diné), who make up more than 10 percent of our population. Guests sometimes come with romanticized notions of authentic but primitive Indigenous people rooted in the past. I remind people to view Native cultures not just as they *were*, but to experience them as they *are*: modern people rooted in tradition. Going to Bandelier National Monument is fantastic and shouldn't be missed. But if you only visit a historic site without also visiting descendant living pueblos like Cochiti and San Ildefonso, then you've only learned half the lesson. Cather visited both ancestral and living Pueblo communities.

I love reading about a place's history but believe that visiting that place is equally important. Ideally you should do both. You can read about the Battle of Gettysburg, but until you visit that blood-soaked battlefield, you'll never fully grasp its importance to America history and the loss of so many men who "gave the last full measure of devotion," as Abraham Lincoln stated in the Gettysburg Address. You read a book for deeper insight; you visit a historic place to sense what it really means and how you connect to the past. You understand its importance in the present.

This book is not just a history of how Willa Cather wrote *Death Comes for the Archbishop*. It is also a straightening of the historical record and a travel guide. I want you, the reader, not only to explore Willa Cather's novel but also to explore the many sites in her book. They are real places. New Mexico is called the Land of Enchantment for a reason. My goal is to help you see why Cather fell in love with the desert Southwest.

On my walking tours, I remind people that history is like an onion: It has many layers to explore and peeling it back can be so worthwhile. On the other hand, like an onion, history can make you cry for its many tragedies. History is not always pretty. Over the years, I have followed Willa Cather and her partner Edith Lewis's trail throughout the Southwest, visiting hotels, historic sites, national parks, pueblos, towns, and train stations, peeling the onion back (so to speak) to find those deeper insights into Cather's own experiences researching her novel.

Studying history is about understanding context. All too often people judge the past by how they feel about it now. Historians call that "presentism." I intend to gently steer you away from presentism and help you understand Cather and her novel in the context of their time. Importantly, some words we use today didn't exist in Cather's time, such as decolonization, gender nonconforming, genocide, historical fiction, LGBTQ+, mansplaining, overtourism, and settler colonialism.

I approach Cather's novel through a historical and textual perspective, using the book and her letters, articles, and interviews as primary sources. This is a different approach from literary critics and theorists, who often try (and fail) to shoehorn Cather into their ideological frameworks, whether that be anticolonialism, antihegemony, feminism, Freudian analysis, Marxism, modernism, or queer theory. My focus is history, rather than literary criticism, symbolism, or theory. I acknowledge the validity of these approaches, but I don't dwell on them, or as Cather wrote, merely "touch and pass on." This leaves plenty of room for future scholars to explore other facets of *Death Comes for the Archbishop*.[5]

Cather was a lifelong conservative who only desired to write artful stories that she found compelling. She showed little desire to smash the patriarchy or upend the hegemony of white America. She engaged in ethnic and racial stereotyping common for her era and occasionally used racist language. She was a lesbian who showed no interest in carrying the banner of gay rights. She was certainly no Freudian and probably would have never recognized the word anticolonialism. She was uninterested in writing political art to address the Questions of the Day, as the Marxists were. Accordingly, I encourage readers to enjoy *Death Comes for the Archbishop* for its sublime aesthetics. This was Cather at the peak of her writing career. I will guide you through the novel and New Mexico's history, providing deeper context into Cather's research, her travels, and even her feelings.[6]

Another thing to remember is that perspective is everything in a multicultural environment like New Mexico. We all have one. I'm an Anglo, a New Mexican term for non-Hispanic white, which also makes me a permanent outsider compared to the Hispanics who have been here for centuries and the Indigenous people who have been here for millennia. We all live constrained by the limits of our perspectives—and we'd be mistaken to think that ours are the only valid ones. History is never static, but something we must reexamine as new documents, facts, interpretations, and perspectives emerge. A positive trend in interpreting history in the twenty-first century is the increasing tendency to ask, Whose story has been left out? History is becoming more inclusive.

The facts of history are what they are, but *how* we interpret history depends on perspective. The Spanish established the New Mexico colony in 1598. They moved the capital to Santa Fe in 1610. The Pueblo Revolt took place in 1680. Mexico won its independence from Spain in 1821. The United States seized the Southwest in 1846. Archbishop Lamy arrived in Santa Fe in 1851 and began constructing the St. Francis Cathedral in 1869. Those are historical facts. However, cultures have differing points of view about our shared history, and this is where we must respect these different perspectives. What is heroic to one culture (for example, Governor Diego de Vargas reestablishing the Spanish colony in 1692–1693) is controversial to another. There are multiple perspectives about New Mexico's complicated and layered history, and our various ethnic groups are certainly not monolithic in their views.

Let me challenge some assumed perspectives. European settlers called the Western Hemisphere the New World. What's so new about it? Absolutely nothing. Indigenous people have lived here for tens of thousands of years. The idea of the New World is an outdated European perspective, just as the idea of the Old World or Olde Europe is an outdated American perspective.

And just what is the Southwest? I've heard it described as the geography between Durango, Colorado, and Durango, Mexico, and between

Las Vegas, Nevada to Las Vegas, New Mexico. Two American states define the American Southwest: Arizona and New Mexico, though I would more broadly define it both geographic terms as the desert between the Colorado River and the Rio Grande and in cultural terms that are heavily Hispanic and Indigenous. Los Angeles is a southwestern city, though it may lie beyond the region's geographic boundaries (does this claim surprise you?). Southern Colorado and southern Utah are part of southwestern culture, and without a doubt the Chihuahuan and Sonoran deserts of northern Mexico are culturally and geographically part of the Southwest, though they may be beyond the borders of the United States. Hispanics in northern New Mexico continue to call themselves *norteños*. Northerners. This was once a northern outpost of the Spanish Empire, rather than the American Southwest. Again, it's all perspective.

A note on terms, in particular "American Indian," "Native American," and "Indigenous." There is a shift away from "Indian" among many Natives. In New Mexico, the word "Indian" isn't considered pejorative, but it is outdated. "Indians" didn't come from India, just as "Caucasians" (people of European descent) didn't come from the Caucasus Mountains. Some prefer Native American, while others prefer Indigenous, while a great many people still self-identify as Indian. There is no consensus among Natives on this question. But in Cather's time, Indian was the only word available. In this book, I use all three terms. Where I use Indian, it is within its historical context: for example, Indian schools, the Indian Detour program, Indian Territory, Indian Wars, and Pueblo Indian. For most other uses, I employ Native, Native American, or Indigenous.

Among Cather scholars, there are several shorthand methods of referring to her "best book:" *Archbishop*, *Death Comes*, and *DCA*. I've chosen the first of these, simply for brevity. In her letters Cather casually referred to the book as "the Archbishop" or "my Archbishop."

I am indebted to earlier scholarship, including John Murphy and Charles Mignon's scholarly edition of *Death Comes for the Archbishop*, Andrew Jewell and Janis Stout's *Selected Letters of Willa Cather*, and Melissa Homestead's *The Only Wonderful Things*, to name just a few. Homestead made a significant contribution by pulling Cather's partner

Edith Lewis out of obscurity. Like architecture, in this type of scholarship one builds upon the foundations that others have laid. I have also incorporated the results of my own research into this book, including Cather's extensive letters and Lewis's Blue Jay notebook from their 1925 Taos trip.

This is a work for the public: readers who love Willa Cather's novels, as well as visitors who wish to go "a-journeying in New Mexico on the trail of the Archbishop," as Cather wrote.[7] The narrative is both conversational and scholarly. Wherever possible, I let Cather speak for herself, relying on her letters, interviews, and writings. Cather's letters were opened for republication in 2011, among other things providing insight into her creative process behind *Death Comes for the Archbishop*.

How the letters came to be published is a story on its own. Cather explicitly stated in her will that she did not want her letters published after her death. After she died in 1947, her extant letters were deposited in archives, but researchers could not directly quote from them. However, Cather's nephew Charles Cather, who served as the literary executor after Edith Lewis died, passed away in 2011. The Willa Cather Trust, jointly held by a Cather family member, the University of Nebraska Foundation, and the Willa Cather Foundation, stepped in to oversee her intellectual property. Time enough had passed. The trust granted permission for Andrew Jewell and Janis Stout to produce a volume covering a fraction of Cather's letters, which Alfred A. Knopf published in 2013. In addition, the Willa Cather Archive at the University of Nebraska–Lincoln began digitizing and placing Cather's nearly four thousand extant letters online for Cather fans and researchers to access starting in 2018, a National Endowment for the Humanities–supported project known as *The Complete Letters of Willa Cather*. Contrary to popular mythology, Cather never ordered her letters destroyed; however, there were likely isolated episodes of destruction, as when she reportedly destroyed her correspondence with her close friend Isabelle McClung Hambourg shortly after Hambourg's death.

Yes, publishing Cather's letters violated her explicit wishes. And I and many other Cather fans and researchers are grateful that the Willa Cather Trust opened the archives. The letters give us profound understanding of the artist and a sense of her as a person. Jewell and Stout noted that Cather's letters "provide insights into her methods and artistic choices as she worked, and reveal Cather herself to be a complicated, funny, brilliant, flinty, sensitive, and sometimes confounding human being." A huge thank you to Andy Jewell, Janis Stout, and the members of the Willa Cather Trust who made this extraordinary decision. This book wouldn't be nearly the same without this remarkable source.[8]

Fanny Butcher, the noted *Chicago Tribune* book reviewer and Cather fan and friend, wrote in her memoir, "If Willa Cather's other letters resembled those she wrote to me, they could do nothing but add to her stature as a great writer and as a rare human being, both of which she was."[9]

Chapter 1

Miss Cather

"I suppose one's early experiences rather cling to one."

—Willa Cather to Witter Bynner, June 7, 1905

Willa Sibert Cather was born near Winchester, Virginia, in 1873, though as an adult she struck three years off her age. Her father, Charles, had a sheep farm, but a catastrophic barn fire prompted him to sell it and relocate his family to Red Cloud, Nebraska, in 1882, where his father and brother had already settled. Willa was nine years old and deeply disoriented by the move from the green forest of Virginia to the nearly treeless prairie of Nebraska. There was still plentiful prairie grass, though that gradually gave way to the endless ocean of corn and cattle ranches that Nebraska is known for today.

Charles Cather first set up on a farm outside Red Cloud, but after eighteen months he moved the family to town, where he ran an insurance business. His wife Virginia, or Jennie as she was known, ruled the household with an iron fist, and she and her oldest daughter, Willa, often clashed. In contrast, Charles was kind and sweet, and Cather gravitated toward him throughout her life. The Cather family grew to seven children. Willa was closest to her two oldest siblings, her brothers Roscoe and Douglass, and as an adult she would visit and travel with them more than with her other siblings.

The seven years that Cather spent growing up in Red Cloud were the most impressionable and formative years of her life. Uprooted from her childhood home in Virginia, Cather would forever be pulled between seeking a home and being on the road. As an adult novelist, she often wrote about the prairie and of people uprooted to the frontier.

At age fourteen, Cather went to the barber and got a boy's haircut and began signing her name "William," or even "Wm. Cather M.D.," as she was considering becoming a doctor. Cather's identity was evolving. Throughout her life, Cather would often sign letters to family as "Willie," a nickname since childhood. She challenged traditional women's roles and explored different ways of being female, including being ambiguous. To biographer Hermione Lee, Cather's behavior was "the teenage revolt against Red Cloud." It may also have been a rebellion against her authoritarian mother, as Cather challenged both familial and gender boundaries.[1]

Red Cloud lies along the Republican River in south-central Nebraska, just above the Kansas border and twenty miles north of the geographic

Figure 1. Willa Cather's freshman portrait with her boyish haircut at the University of Nebraska–Lincoln. Bernice Slote, Papers, Archives & Special Collections, University of Nebraska–Lincoln Libraries.

center of the lower forty-eight states. It is one of many small farming towns established along the Burlington & Missouri River Railroad that connected Chicago, Kansas City, and Omaha to Denver. Founded in 1871 by Silas Garber, the model for Captain Daniel Forrester in Cather's novel *A Lost Lady*, the settlement was named after a Lakota chief who inflicted a stinging military defeat on the US Army. This led to the Treaty of 1868, which established the Great Sioux Reservation, a sprawling territory that was soon whittled down into seven smaller reservations in Nebraska and the Dakotas.

In 1874 the federal government relocated the Pawnees, whose territory included Kansas and Nebraska, to Indian Territory (the future Oklahoma) after a series of military defeats at the hands of their enemies, the Lakotas. This opened the Nebraska prairie for American and European settlers. Cather knew that Indigenous people had lived in Nebraska, but she largely overlooked that fact in her prairie novels.

Cather did not witness the relocation of the Native population, nor the near-extinction of the bison (who were hunted to deny the main food source for the Plains Indians), but she did see the last of the prairie grass. Sodbusters tore up the native grasses that covered this vast expanse and planted alfalfa and corn in their place. The change made a lifelong impression on Cather. In *My Ántonia*, she lyrically described the prairie in the golden hour before sunset in: "As far as we could see, the miles of copper-red grass were drenched in sunlight that was stronger and fiercer than at any other time of the day. The blond cornfields were red gold, the haystacks turned rosy and threw long shadows. The whole prairie was like the bush that burned with fire and was not consumed."[2]

Red Cloud borders a geographic feature known as the Divide: a plateau between the Republican River and the Little Blue River where European immigrants established farms. The young Cather spent considerable time visiting these communities, and many of the people she came to know ended up in her novels, such as Anna Sadilek Pavelka (Ántonia Shimerda in *My Ántonia*). Today the Divide is easily spotted from a distance: A windmill farm runs along its backbone.

Cather had a great deal of freedom to explore Red Cloud and Webster County. She enjoyed visiting people on the Divide, such as the Sadileks, and made many friends in town, including the Miner family, whom she would correspond with for the rest of her life. A Jewish couple in Red Cloud, Charles and Fannie Wiener, had an excellent library and invited Cather to borrow books.

Cather was intelligent and well-read, and she devoured literature. This was a key part of her self-education. Among her favorites were Virgil, Homer's *Iliad*, John Bunyan's *The Pilgrim's Progress* (a religious allegory published in 1678), Sarah Orne Jewett, and Henry James. She could quote William Shakespeare and Walt Whitman. She was devoted to Leo Tolstoy's *Anna Karenina*. She also came to love live performances. Thanks to the Burlington railroad, traveling theater companies performed at the Red Cloud Opera House. The building is preserved as part of the National Willa Cather Center.

At age sixteen, Cather enrolled in the University of Nebraska in Lincoln. She took a preparatory year, as the Red Cloud school had not adequately prepared her for college. Cather initially thought she would major in science, but after a teacher published one of her class essays in a local newspaper, she became enthralled with the writer's life. She wrote hundreds of articles for the student publication *Hesperian* and the *Nebraska State Journal*. She developed a sharp, opinionated, and often unforgiving voice.

At university she met Dorothy Canfield, the chancellor's daughter, who became one of Cather's lifelong friends. Canfield became a considerable novelist in her own right and was one of the few people Cather could truly bare her feelings and frustrations to, as we see in her letters.

While at college, Cather became infatuated with a young woman named Louise Pound, to whom she wrote in 1892, "It is manifestly unfair that 'feminine friendships' should be unnatural," signing her name with the masculine "William."[3] A year later she wrote another friend about how she was getting along with Miss Pound. "I am pretty well now, save for sundry bruises received in driving a certain fair maid over the country with one hand, sometimes, indeed, with no hand at all," she wrote suggestively. "But she did not seem to mind my method of driving, even when we went off banks and over haystacks, and as for me—I drive with one hand all night in my sleep." It was a candid and frank admission of her sexual orientation.[4]

Cather pursued Pound for two years, but then she wrote a character assassination piece about Pound's brother in the *Hesperian* that ended things. In 1897, she wrote Pound,

> I see you have resorted to designating me by my sex. Do you remember how Tucker used to wail "Alack,
>
> That I have worn so many winters out,
> And know not what name to call myself"![5]

This quote from Shakespeare's *Richard II* was an admission on Cather's part that she didn't easily fit into any bucket. Today we would call her gender nonconforming, but that concept didn't exist in Cather's day. She only knew she was different—and that she was attracted to women but didn't want to be labeled.

Cather graduated in 1895 and returned to Red Cloud while she looked for employment. Thanks to her college journalism, she secured a job with *Home Monthly* and moved to Pittsburgh in 1896, her home for the next decade. After a year, she transferred to the *Pittsburgh Leader*. In 1901, she quit her job as journalist and became a schoolteacher for the next five years.

Cather met Isabelle McClung in 1899, and the two young women sparked. McClung was the daughter of a judge, who headed a prestigious upper-middle-class Pittsburgh family. The McClungs expected their daughter to marry well and make a comfortable home, rather than go to college and have a career, as Cather had done. Cather moved in with their family in 1901. The McClungs set aside an upstairs sewing room as her dedicated writing space. The following year, Isabelle and Willa traveled to Europe for three months—Cather's first trip to the continent—visiting the United Kingdom and France.

Cather lived with the McClungs until she moved to New York in 1906, then often returned to write at their house for the next decade. Were Isabelle and Willa lovers? We don't know. They were certainly devoted and were perhaps more than friends living together in the McClung house. Isabelle became the first of two women Cather lived with as an adult.

In 1903, Cather visited Nebraska and stopped in Lincoln. There she met a pretty twenty-one-year-old named Edith Lewis, and the two quickly hit it off. Lewis was particularly entranced by Cather's radiant blue eyes, and she described Cather as having brown hair and fair skin. Lewis was destined for New York City, and in 1904 Cather visited for a week, staying in Lewis's apartment.[6]

Cather published her first book in 1903, a volume of poetry called *April Twilights*. Two years later, she published *The Troll Garden*, a collection of short stories that included "Paul's Case," widely considered to be a gay story. She wrote and published both books while working as a schoolteacher.

For decades after Cather's death in 1947, biographers, family members, and scholars debated the question: Was she or wasn't she lesbian? Many people simply didn't know, and neither Cather nor Lewis made a public declaration of their relationship or sexual orientation. Today Cather's sexual orientation is a settled question, thanks to the publication of her letters, but it took decades to reach this conclusion, in part because of Cather's desire for privacy. While it's easy for me and countless others to be openly gay in our modern era, her time was different. Homosexuals were considered deviant, and Cather had a growing literary reputation to defend. She was also a conservative, rather than a social activist. Accordingly, Cather was out to much of her family and friends, but not to the broader public.[7]

Cather in New York

In 1906, Cather quit teaching and moved to New York City to work as an editor for *McClure's*. British-born S. S. McClure founded the muckraking magazine, which exposed corruption and the plight of immigrant laborers, all while publishing literature and poetry. The magazine fit squarely into the Progressive Era of governmental and social reform, an interesting paradox for Cather, who was never much of a reformer. In any case she liked it well enough that she recruited Edith Lewis to also work at the magazine.

For the next five years, Cather worked for *McClure's*, learning the business of publishing and the art of skillful editing, along with what made for a compelling story. She discovered the art of nonlinear writing, something that she would later use in *Death Comes for the Archbishop.*

Cather met Sarah Orne Jewett in Boston while researching a story on the Church of Christian Science in 1908. As Jewett would die a year later, it was a brief but important friendship for Cather, for whom Jewett served as a literary mentor. She encouraged Cather not to emulate other people's styles, such as Henry James's, but to write with her own voice and to draw on her experiences. Jewett counseled Cather that the writer needs solitude: "To work in silence and with all one's heart, that is the writer's lot; he is the only artist who must be solitary, and yet needs the widest

Figure 2. A portrait of Willa Cather, taken around 1910. She wore a necklace given to her by Sarah Orne Jewett. Philip L. and Helen Cather Southwick Collection, Archives & Special Collections, University of Nebraska–Lincoln Libraries.

outlook on the world."[8] Jewett noted Cather's tendency to disguise herself in a narrating character, the idea of a "masquerade." Cather often used this technique, typically using a male perspective, such as Jim Burden (*My Ántonia*) or Niel Herbert (*A Lost Lady*).[9]

Cather met one of her most important adult friends in 1910. Elizabeth "Elsie" Shepley Sergeant, a graduate of Bryn Mawr College, came into *McClure's* offices to pitch a story about women immigrant workers in the garment industry. The two women quickly bonded over French culture and literature. Sergeant described Cather's appearance: "Her eyes were sailor-blue, her cheeks were rosy, her hair was red-brown, parted in the middle like a child's." Cather often wore her long hair in a bun, probably for convenience. They became lifelong friends, though their friendship waned during the 1930s.[10]

Another lifelong friend Cather was Zoë Akins, a budding playwright who would meet considerable success, and who often provided Cather with free theater tickets. They maintained an affectionate correspondence for the rest of their lives.

Three years after Cather moved to New York, she and Edith Lewis moved in together near Washington Square. It was the center of Bohemian life in the city and an exciting place to be. In modern parlance, they became domestic partners, also known as a "Boston marriage." Cather and Lewis were a conventional lesbian couple, and they probably considered that there was nothing radical about their relationship. The two lived and remained together until Cather's death in 1947. Melissa Homestead wrote, "Rather than treating their life together as a shameful secret, Cather and Lewis lived together openly for thirty-nine years, their partnership recognized and respected by family and friends."[11]

Lewis, who is less known to the world than Cather, was an accomplished editor and Cather's trusted advisor and collaborator. She would later become her partner's literary executor and posthumous defender. Lewis was present at the genesis of many of Cather's literary ideas, and the two women read proofs together from *O Pioneers!* on.[12]

Publisher Alfred Knopf keenly observed, "Though she never said so right out, I have always suspected the hand of her friend Edith Lewis in much of the copy about her books that she supplied from time to time, for Miss Lewis was an important copy writer." Often mistaken for Cather's secretary, Lewis was a sharp editor, but she never learned how to type, unlike Cather.[13]

Only one complete letter survives from Cather to Lewis, dated October 4, 1936, but it hints at the intimacy and love they shared, their appreciation for nature, and the stars that they so often experienced together. She began, "My Darling Edith," and ended with, "And now I must dress to receive the Planets, dear, as I don't wish to take the time after they appear—and they will not wait for anybody. Lovingly W."[14]

Cather and Lewis spent considerable time apart over their thirty-eight-plus years together, and thus we should expect there to be many more letters than just one. Lewis had an office job, while Cather had the freedom to write wherever she wished. Jan Hambourg returned around six hundred letters between Isabelle McClung and Cather after his wife's death in 1938, which Cather asked Lewis to burn in their apartment building's incinerator. The precedent raises the question of whether Lewis destroyed their correspondence, or if future letters may emerge.[15]

Cather outgrew her tomboy youth. As an adult, she wore dresses—albeit with the occasional necktie. But she also liked adventuring, hiking, riding horses, and living roughly in a Canadian cabin. The ranch attire that she and Edith Lewis wore to Mesa Verde and other Southwestern trips was quite butch. One of Cather's students described her as a "rather mannish young woman," and decades later her violinist friend Yehudi Menuhin wrote about "her mannish figure and country tweediness."[16]

Cather often rode the bus from Washington Square to Central Park, where she enjoyed strolling up to the Reservoir before taking afternoon tea. She kept the apartment full of fresh flowers. Lewis stated that "we went often to the opera, sitting high up, in the cheap seats." Cather never learned to play an instrument, but she loved music and incorporated opera into many of her novels and stories.[17]

While living in Pittsburgh, Cather penned a 1904 short story called "A Wagner Matinée." A young man named Clark took his cultured aunt, who was visiting Boston, to a concert that featured excerpts from Richard Wagner's operas. She had eloped and relocated to an isolated farm in Nebraska, and for decades lived without higher culture, working on the farm and raising six children. After the concert, she cried to her nephew, "I don't want to go, Clark, I don't want to go!" Returning to the farm and living without culture was too much for her. Her nephew empathized with her plight: "I understood. For her, just outside the concert hall, lay the black pond with the cattle-tracked bluffs; the tall, unpainted house, with weather-curled boards, naked as a tower; the crook-backed ash seedlings where the dish-cloths hung to dry; the gaunt, moulting turkeys picking up refuse about the kitchen door." The story reflected Cather's own feelings of not wanting to return to Nebraska.[18]

During World War I, runaway inflation pushed the cost of living skyward. Cather complained to her mother in early 1917, "It is costing us fifty dollars a month more to live than it did last winter, and we have cut out the opera altogether, and most concerts."[19] But the situation proved temporary. In 1920, Cather bragged to her niece, "I go to the Opera a great deal this winter. My old friend Zoë Akins, who made a lot of money on her successful play, 'Declasseé' has season tickets for every Thursday night, splendid seats, near the front, and she comes down in her car for me, and brings me home in her car, so it's little effort, even if I'm tired."[20] By the 1920s, however, Cather wrote less about opera and made no mention of the art form in *Death Comes for the Archbishop*.[21]

After working at *McClure's* for five years, Cather was burned out. S. S. McClure often traveled to investigate stories and find promising writers, and the burden of publishing the magazine fell on Cather, its managing editor. McClure had overextended the magazine's finances, and he lost control of the publication to his creditors in 1911. Stuck in New York City over the hot summer, Cather decided she needed a break. She resigned as managing editor in September with the intention of taking a six-month absence and then returning as a staff member. In fact, she never returned to *McClure's*, save as a freelancer. Her sabbatical prompted Cather to question what she wanted to do next, and the answer was clear: to be a full-time writer.

Freed from *McClure's*, Cather retreated to upstate New York for three months with Isabelle McClung, writing stories and completing the draft of her first novel, *Alexander's Bridge*. McClure had discouraged Cather from writing fiction, but she believed there was something in her driving her in this direction and that she had to try. The novel was published in early 1912 to good reviews but little commercial or literary success. It was too conventional, too contrived, too modeled on the fiction of Henry James. The mixed success only pushed the determined author to try harder.

Cather needed a change of scenery. She left New York on March 7 for Pittsburgh and stayed with the McClung's (Isabelle's mother had suffered a stroke), then journeyed to Red Cloud to visit her parents. In April, Cather ventured to the Southwest for the first time, a trip that would change the direction of her writing career and her life.

Chapter 2

Southwestern Travels

"Now about Arizona: it's good, but New Mexico is better."

—Willa Cather to Elsie Sergeant, April 20, 1912

In early April 1912, Cather began her first journey to the American Southwest. The New Mexico Territory had been formally brought into the union as a state on January 6 of that year, followed by Arizona six weeks later. She was at a turning point in her career with a big decision to make. Should she stay in publishing, or pursue her dream of becoming a full-time writer? She ventured to the Southwest for two months to think it over.

Cather's brother Douglass lived in Winslow, Arizona, working for the Atchison, Topeka, and Santa Fe Railway (better known as the Santa Fe Railway), and she would have a place to stay. Leaping at the opportunity for an extensive getaway, Cather rode the train over the endless prairie to Red Cloud to visit her parents, then set out for Arizona. Her travels took her to Denver on the Burlington line, a route that she knew well, often calling it simply the No. 16. As she crossed the prairie of Nebraska and eastern Colorado, the front range of the Rocky Mountains gradually rose above the western horizon. Snow still covered the summits, the highest of which reach beyond fourteen thousand feet.

From Denver, Cather transferred to the Denver & Rio Grande Western Railroad, which she took due south through Colorado Springs and Pueblo. From the right side of the train, she could view the heavily forested foothills of the Rockies To the left was the prairie, still dormant from winter. As the train approached the city of Trinidad, two breathtaking mountains known as the Spanish Peaks came into view. These were near the southernmost section of the Rockies, the Sangre de Cristo Mountains, which stretched into northern New Mexico.

The train pulled into Trinidad, once a rest stop along the Santa Fe Trail before emigrants crossed the arduous Raton Pass to the south. A Fred Harvey company hotel, the Cardenas, stood next to the depot along the Purgatoire River. Cather must have been wowed by the scenery: The small city is surrounded by mountains. Towering above is distinct Fishers Peak, capped by a basalt mesa that resembles the steps into a Pueblo Indian kiva. In Trinidad she transferred to the Santa Fe Railway, the train that would carry her to Winslow.

Figure 3. A 1907 photograph of Trinidad, Colorado. Fishers Peak, with its basalt steps like a Pueblo Indian kiva, towers over the city. Prints & Photographs Division, Library of Congress.

The Santa Fe train slowly ascended the steep Raton Pass (elevation 7,834 feet) through the Sangre de Cristos, the locomotive belching smoke and steam. A tunnel had opened four years earlier on the New Mexico side of the summit that made the journey smoother; before, a special locomotive pulled trains over the pass via a series of switchbacks. After the mighty effort to haul the train up the mountain, the locomotive rested in the town of Raton to refill its depleted water tank before proceeding on to Las Vegas, New Mexico, the next major destination a hundred miles to the south.

Forty years earlier, Cather's father, Charles, had trekked to the Southwest looking for land, but this was before the train had reached the Rockies. His party crossed the Raton Pass and camped. He met an army wagon train master who reported that five of his mules were stolen and that a stagecoach had been robbed. Deciding that New Mexico was too dangerous, Charles and his party returned to Colorado after just one night. His daughter Willa, born the following year, would explore the Southwest much farther in her travels. She would one day inscribe in his copy of *Death Comes for the Archbishop*, "Hoping my father will enjoy this narrative of the old Southwest, as it was in his young manhood."[1]

Cather's train descended from the Raton Pass to the grassy western edge of the Great Plains where the Comanches, Plains Apaches, and Utes had once hunted bison. She could look up to the Sangre de Cristo range on the right side of the train. The mountains erode into a series of basalt-capped mesas, hinting at their volcanic origins. Cather was smitten by the scenery, as she wrote her friend Elsie Sergeant: "From Trinidad to Las Vegas there is a continuous purple mountain that does tune one up."[2]

The train briefly halted in Las Vegas, the quaint frontier town (not to be confused with the glitzy city in Nevada), where some passengers would dismount to stay at the Castañeda Hotel, run by the Fred Harvey company and adjacent to the depot. The hotel had opened in 1898, and Theodore Roosevelt's Rough Riders staged their first reunion there a year later.

The Santa Fe Railway followed the route of the Santa Fe Trail through Glorieta Pass in the southernmost section of the Sangre de Cristos and passed the massive remains of Pecos Pueblo. Cather would one day visit

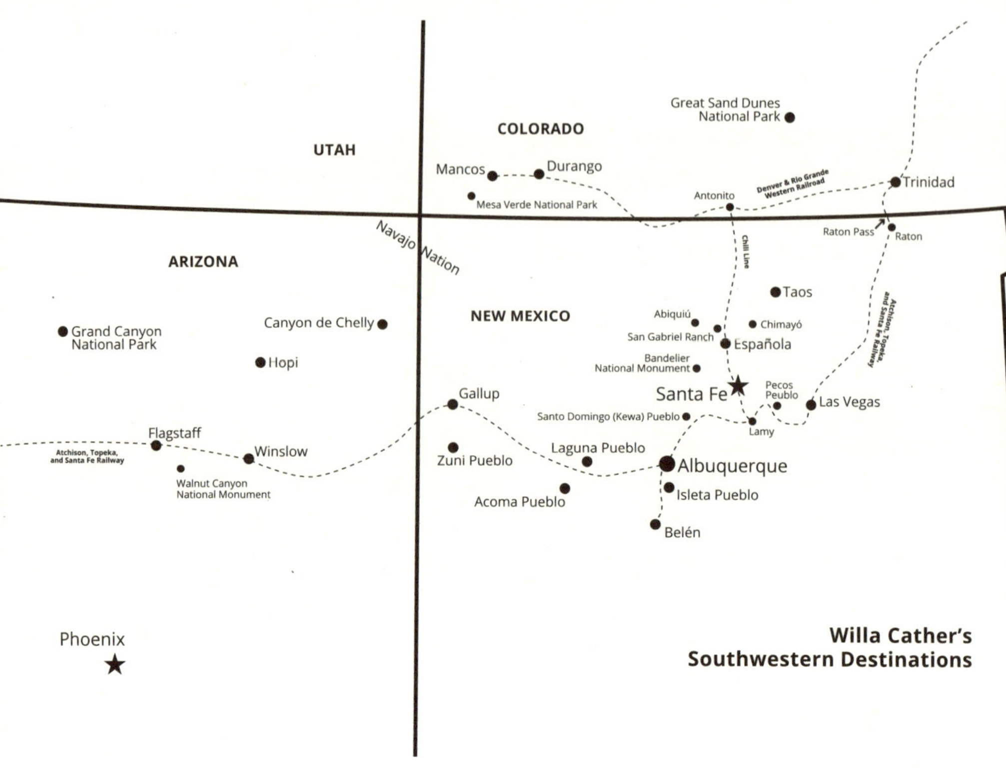

Map 1. Southwest.

the pueblo and include it in *Death Comes for the Archbishop*. Leaving the mountains behind, the train entered the piñon-juniper high desert and briefly halted at the railroad junction of Lamy, named after Santa Fe's first archbishop, Jean-Baptiste Lamy. A boutique Fred Harvey hotel, El Ortiz, stood trackside.

Hours after crossing into New Mexico, Cather's train reached the Rio Grande Valley, where it proceeded south to Albuquerque. Spring was just beginning, and the bright green cottonwood trees that crowded the riverbanks were coming to life. The scenery continued to wow her: "It is in the most beautiful country I have ever seen anywhere, like the country between Marseilles and Niece [*sic*] only much more brilliant. All around it lie the most wonderful Indian villages—not show places, real places, each one built close about its church." She was referring to the southern Pueblo Indian tribes whose lands the train passed through: Santo

Domingo, San Felipe, Santa Ana, and Sandia pueblos. These were ancient agricultural communities that had farmed along the Rio Grande since the fourteenth century.[3]

The Santa Fe Railway had no dining cars, so passengers dined at the numerous Harvey Houses along the route. Several times a day, the steam engine locomotives halted for thirty minutes to refuel with coal and water, and in that short time, the efficient Harvey Girls got everyone off the train, took their drink orders, served their food, and returned them to the passenger cars. Cather experienced the efficiency of the Fred Harvey system numerous times throughout her Southwestern journeys.

The train stopped in Albuquerque to refuel and to feed the passengers at the splendid Alvarado, another Harvey hotel. "There is a strong pull about the place, and something Spanish in the air that teases you. Such color! The Lord set the stage so splendidly there," Cather declared. "I am almost sure I could work at Albuquerque."[4]

From Albuquerque, the train continued west through the high desert, passing through Laguna Pueblo, Gallup, across the Arizona border through the petrified forest and the painted desert, on to Holbrook, and finally to Cather's destination, Winslow. There she met up with her brother Douglass. The siblings planned many adventures during Willa's visit.

Cather was underwhelmed by Winslow, which she described as "an ugly little western town. . . . Only railroad people here, but a good hotel" and the Harvey House restaurant by the depot. "After you cross two miles of tin cans and old shoes the desert is very fine—bright red sand, like brick dust, and the eternal sage and rabbit brush. But the sand storms!" Winslow was Cather's first impression of Arizona, which is probably why she declared, "Now about Arizona: it's good, but New Mexico is better."[5]

Douglass had to work on the railroad for the first two weeks of his sister's visit, so Cather got acquainted with his roommate and fellow railroad man Tooker. Tooker annoyed Cather, being a pedantic man who had the habit, to use a modern term, of mansplaining, largely from knowledge he had gained from magazines. "I've been doing target practice with a pistol, and I know the day will come when I shall let drive at Tooker,"

Cather complained to Elsie Sergeant. "I cannot stand either his information or his nobleness much longer." Douglass also had a British housekeeper. "This cockney housekeeper is good fun, but he is reeling drunk all the time, and he has to be sat upon and sent away," she noted.[6]

Cather would incorporate both Tooker and the alcoholic housekeeper in her novels. Tooker inspired the noble railroad brakeman Ray Kennedy in *The Song of the Lark*, while the Brit became Henry Atkins in *The Professor's House*. Despite the negative first impression, Cather came to appreciate and even like Tooker once they visited the Grand Canyon. "There emerged the real Tooker, the man the sheep camps and the hills made, a very decent sort, strong and active and lots of nerve," she wrote. "We did some really good stunts in climbing. Went down one cliff 150 feet by hand-holds, and it was no joke."[7]

Cather, her brother, and Tooker spent at least five days exploring the Grand Canyon, hiking and horseback riding before returning each day to Bright Angel Camp. Nearby was the fancier El Tovar Hotel, and both facilities were under the management of the Fred Harvey company. Cather called the Grand Canyon "really the most attractive place I have found in this country." She loved that there were no retail outlets, just vast forest, profound silence, and stunning views of the geologic wonder. How things have changed, as the Grand Canyon is now one of the country's top tourist destinations, and the place she stayed is now the bustling Grand Canyon Village.[8]

One of the first places Cather explored in Arizona was Walnut Canyon, just east of Flagstaff, which she visited with Douglass once he returned from railroading. These were the first cliff dwellings that Cather had ever seen, and they made a vivid impression on her. Walnut Canyon forms an omega-shaped loop where the Ancestral Hopi built their stone houses under overhanging cliffs on both sides of the ravine. The interior section is like an island, with visitors circling back to the starting point after exploring the many cliff houses. The Cather siblings had their picture taken in one of the structures.

Tourists began looting Walnut Canyon in the 1880s after the railroad arrived, including using dynamite to blow out the walls to get to the ancient pottery inside. The site became a national monument in 1915 to

Figure 4. Willa Cather with her brother Douglass in Walnut Canyon, Arizona, in April 1912. Philip L. and Helen Cather Southwick Collection, Archives & Special Collections, University of Nebraska–Lincoln Libraries.

Figure 5. Walnut Canyon, Arizona, inspired Willa Cather and her fictional counterpart Thea Kronborg with a new direction for their lives. Cather visited the Ancestral Hopi site in 1912 during her first visit to the Southwest. Photograph by Garrett Peck.

protect its remains, three years after Cather's visit. Douglass later took his sister to another Ancestral Hopi site just north of Winslow, now Homolovi State Park.

In Winslow, Cather met a Catholic priest, Father Thomas Connelly, who was friends with her brother, the first of many priests she would meet in the Southwest. She accompanied him on a several-day trip to the Indian missions he was responsible for and was no doubt impressed by the priests' commitment to their parishes and the vast distances they covered. She explained this to Elsie Sergeant in a Fred Harvey company postcard showing the Hopi village of Mishongnovi, which she probably visited with Father Connelly. The village is sixty-five miles north of Winslow, and to get there they presumably took a horse and wagon.[9]

Back in Winslow, Cather met a handsome young Mexican dancer and singer named Julio, whom Cather seemed to develop a crush on, and who was long used as Exhibit A for those who claimed she was not lesbian. Some scholars believe this episode reflects an inside joke between Cather and Sergeant.[10] Cather spent a day with Julio in the Painted Desert north of Winslow, and "It took several days to get over that," she wrote. "He will drive any number of miles to see flowers or running water, but Cliff Dwellers bore him awfully. 'Why,' he says raising his brows 'do you care for Los Muertos? We are living.'"[11]

After her trip to the Southwest, Cather confessed, "I may still go back for Julio." She attended a Mexican dance with him in Winslow the night before she departed, where she was the only white person (Thea Kronborg would do the same in *The Song of the Lark*). Julio "had a personal elegance of which I've never known the like. . . . he is a very cool and graceful young man who carries his great beauty as lightly as one could." She transcribed the lyrics of a Mexican song he sang to her that was only for a "married lady," then wrote rather romantically, "I wish I could give you Julio's serenade in the Spanish, with the stars and the desert and the dead Indian cities on the mesa behind it." Julio served as the prototype for Spanish Johnny in *The Song of the Lark*.[12]

After their Arizona adventures, the Cather siblings traveled to New Mexico by train, stopping at Laguna, Isleta, and Santo Domingo pueblos and staying in Albuquerque. Willa sent a Fred Harvey company postcard of Laguna's white-washed San José de la Laguna Mission Church to their brother Roscoe in Wyoming. "Douglas [*sic*] and I explored this old Spanish mission yesterday and climbed up to the belfry where José goes to ring the bells. Not one American house in the village." The pueblo built the church around 1706, and an artist known only as the "Laguna santero" painted the exquisite altar.[13]

Several days later, Willa mailed another Fred Harvey company postcard of Isleta Pueblo, just south of Albuquerque, to Elsie Sergeant. "Such a lovely place! My brother and I have spent two days here. Behind the church the priest has wonderful gardens, full of parrots and snow-white doves." The priest, Antoine Docher, was French. Cather would remember the garden full of parrots when she described the fictional priest Jesus de Baca in *Death Comes for the Archbishop*. It was these ancient sacred spaces, not yet crowded with tourists, that so impressed Cather and drew her back to the Southwest.[14]

Cather discovered in the Southwest dramatic desert landscapes populated by Indigenous people who had been there for thousands of years and Hispanics who had settled more than three centuries earlier. The turquoise sky, dry desert air, colorful mesas, and pine-covered mountains were a relief from the flat cornfields of Nebraska, the dark, humid green of the Northeast, and the hustle of New York City.

That first visit to the Southwest was a revelation for Cather. Though the railroad made getting to the new states easier, there were few good roads, and Cather was enchanted by the adobe churches, Mexican villages, and inspiring mountains. She explained what had inspired her to write *Death Comes for the Archbishop* in *Commonweal* magazine two months after the book was published in 1927:

> The longer I stayed in the Southwest, the more I felt that the story of the Catholic Church in that country was the most interesting of all its stories. The old mission churches, even those which were abandoned and in ruins, had a moving reality about them; the hand-carved beams and joints, the utterly unconventional frescoes, the countless fanciful figures of the saints, not two of them alike, seemed a direct expression of some very real and lively human feeling. They were all

> fresh, individual, first-hand. . . . I used to wish there were some written account of the old times when those old churches were built; but I soon felt that no record of them could be as real as they are themselves.[15]

After saying farewell to Douglass, Cather returned to Red Cloud for five weeks, arriving on June 11. She wrote an insightful letter to S. S. McClure the following day that revealed her state of mind. "Those weeks off in the desert with my big handsome brother—six feet four, he is—and his wild pals, are weeks that I shall never forget," she wrote. "They took all the kinks and crumples out. I feel as if my mind had been freshly washed and ironed, and were ready for a new life."[16]

By August, Cather was ensconced at the McClung house in Pittsburgh and reflecting on her time away. She was glad to be back from the West and admitted that it was all so overwhelming.

> Slowly the real meaning came upon me out there of a sentence that I once read carelessly enough somewhere in Balzac: "dans le desert, voyez-vous, il y a tout et il n'y rien; Dieu, sans les hommes." [In the desert there is everything and nothing; God, without mankind.] That sentence really means a great deal. I was sitting mournfully beside the Rio Grande one day, just outside a most beautiful Indian village—Santo Domingo—when I looked up and saw that sentence written in the sand, and it explained what was the matter with me.[17]

Cather was doubtless inspired by more than just the fabulous scenery of the Southwest. It was a cathartic trip for her, a decisive moment when this thirty-eight-year-old woman decided what she wanted to do for the rest of her life. When she returned to New York, she let *McClure's* know that she would not be coming back. It was an enormously brave decision, one she later transposed into the actions of the fictional Thea Kronborg in *The Song of the Lark*, who reached an important life decision at Panther Canyon (Walnut Canyon). In the novel, Kronborg rededicated herself to her career as an opera singer and decided to go to Germany to further study.

About her 1912 trip to the Southwest, Cather later recalled, "The longer I stayed in a country I really did care about, and among people who were a part of that country, the more unnecessary and superficial a book like *Alexander's Bridge* seemed to me. I did no writing down there, but I recovered from the conventional editorial point of view." She went on to write her second "first" novel, *O! Pioneers*. In fact, Cather titled an article "My First Novels (There Were Two)."[18]

Cather returned to New York for a couple weeks, then went back to the McClung house in September to work on *O Pioneers!*, a title taken from a Walt Whitman poem. She often stayed with the McClungs, using their house as a writing retreat. Although she was no longer a *McClure's* employee, the magazine's owners asked her to write stories as a freelancer and return to the office. She begrudgingly accepted, as she needed the income. She also ghostwrote S. S. McClure's autobiography.[19]

On quitting her day job, Cather told her friend Elsie Sergeant, "But one must have simple tastes—to give up a good salary."[20] She had a financial cushion that enabled her to take the plunge. Years later, a friend asked Cather, "In setting aside of sum of money to live on until your writing began to pay, how accurately did you calculate? Was it too much or too little or just enough?"

Cather answered: "Oh, it was far too much—much more than was necessary." She had a rosy-eyed view of the past, perhaps forgetting that she had continued to work freelance for *McClure's* because she needed the paycheck. That said, financial and literary success came faster than Cather expected. She had taken a gamble with her career, and it paid off. It helped that she and her partner Edith Lewis were a two-income family.[21]

Cather and Lewis took a big step forward together in October 1912, when they leased a new and larger apartment on the second floor of 5 Bank Street in Greenwich Village. Cather was excited about their new home, which she called "ideal, the perfect apartment, large old-fashioned, roomy, one flight up; good fireplace, good windows, good woodwork, wide stairs up." The apartment was spacious and quiet, and both women had their own rooms. Manhattan's Greenwich Village, which was then known for its Bohemians and immigrants, as well as the budding gay community, became their home for the next fifteen years.[22]

Finding Her Voice on the Prairie

Sarah Orne Jewett had advised Cather to write about what she knew—and what she knew was the Nebraska frontier, having witnessed the end of the frontier during her childhood. And so she found her voice in writing about her own experiences on the Nebraska prairie. Red Cloud became her gold mine, the setting and inspiration for six of her twelve novels. Though the town names changed (Black Hawk, Frankfort, Hanover, Haverford, Moonstone, and Sweet Water), they were always Red Cloud. And many of the fictional characters she created were based on real people she knew while growing up.[23] She told her friend Elsie Sergeant, "Life began for me when I ceased to admire and began to remember."[24]

Cather idealized the white settlers who overcame the hardships of taming the frontier. She tended to place the pioneers on a pedestal, a common theme throughout her writing career. Biographer Hermione Lee noted that Cather's "subject matter would not be the Europeanizing of Americans, but the transference of European cultures to the American landscape: the survival and reshaping of old orders in pioneer form."[25]

In a poignant letter to Elsie Sergeant, written while composing *O Pioneers!*, Cather described her desire to sublimate herself into her writing: "If only I could nail up the front door and live in a mess, I could simply become a fountain pen and have done with it—a conduit for ink to run through." She dedicated the novel to Sergeant.[26]

Cather completed *O Pioneers!* at the McClung residence in Pittsburgh that fall, so she didn't actually move into the Bank Street apartment until January 1913. The novel was published five months later to fine reviews and solid sales. Cather's writing career was off to a good start.

Her next novel was *The Song of the Lark*, published in 1915, followed by *My Ántonia* in 1918. These three books later became informally known as Cather's "prairie trilogy," and they helped put the author on America's literary map.

"As everyone knows, Nebraska is distinctly déclassé as a literary background; its very name throws the delicately attuned critic into a clammy shiver of embarrassment," Cather wrote. "Kansas is almost as unpromising. . . . But a New York critic voiced a very general opinion when he said: 'I simply don't care a damn what happens in Nebraska, no matter who writes about it.'" She stated this in 1931 after a career writing novels about Nebraska and showing that the state was full of interesting people and stories. Through her writing, Cather nearly single-handedly made Nebraska interesting.[27]

Having committed to her career as an author, Cather quickly took to the writing lifestyle. She was disciplined and stuck to a schedule, as she revealed in a 1921 interview:

> I work from two and a half to three hours a day. I don't hold myself to longer hours; if I did, I wouldn't gain by it. The only reason I write is because it interests me more than any other activity I've ever found. I like riding, going to operas, concerts, travel in the west; but on the whole writing interests me more than anything else. If I made a chore of it, my enthusiasm would die. I make it an adventure every day. . . .
>
> For me, the morning is the best time to write. During the other hours of the day I attend to my housekeeping, take walks in Central Park, go to concerts, and see something of my friends. I try to keep myself fit, fresh; one has to be in as good form to write as to sing. When not working, I shut work from my mind.[28]

Her partner Edith Lewis would later note that Cather wrote her first drafts by hand. Once her ideas were fleshed out, Cather transcribed them on her typewriter. Cather and Lewis would then edit drafts until the story satisfied them. Some books, such as *A Lost Lady*, went through multiple drafts, shifting the narrator's voice from third person to first, and then back to third person.[29]

It is remarkable that Cather achieved so much and in so little time. She typically wrote for about five months each year, spending the remaining time traveling to Europe or to the American West, and later Quebec and Grand Manan Island, though these were sometimes research trips. At her peak in the 1920s, she produced a novel a year.[30]

The 1914 and 1915 Southwestern Trips

Cather returned to the Southwest in September 1914 just after World War I broke out, but this trip remains largely a mystery to scholars. She may have traveled alone. After visiting family in Red Cloud, she mailed a Fred Harvey postcard of snow-covered Fishers Peak to Elsie Sergeant from Trinidad, Colorado, and later that month wrote, "Even when I was up in the Sangree [*sic*] de Cristo mountains I felt rather restless" on account of the war.[31]

The Trinidad-bound train would have passed right through Ludlow, site of a horrific massacre on April 20 of that year. An anti-union Colorado militia attacked a camp of striking coal miners and killed twenty-one people, followed by union retaliation against anti-unionists. President Woodrow Wilson called out the military to quell the violence. The Ludlow Massacre made national news, and undoubtedly Cather was aware of it, but she was not one to take up the cause of the industrial workers.

Cather's letters from the 1914 trip give little hint as to where she specifically traveled in the Southwest. However, the novel that she produced the following year, *The Song of the Lark*, was set in Colorado and included sand dunes on the edge of the fictional town of Moonstone. We may wonder if Cather visited what is now Great Sand Dunes National Park and Preserve, which huddles under the western slope of the Sangre de Cristo range. This may have influenced her return to Colorado the following year.

As the devastating Great War continued in 1915, S. S. McClure wanted to send Cather to Germany to report on the conflict. She was going to take Isabelle McClung with her, but her father objected after a German submarine torpedoed the British ocean liner *Lusitania* on May 7, with great loss of life. Cather canceled her plans and opted to return to the Southwest, this time with Edith Lewis. This was their first vacation together, and Cather's third trip to the Southwest.

Cather and Lewis's destination was Mesa Verde, which had become a national park in 1906. In early August, they traveled by train across the vast expanse of the country to Denver, where they boarded the Denver & Rio Grande Western Railroad, the narrow-gauge railway network

Figure 6. Willa Cather may have visited Great Sand Dunes National Park & Preserve in Colorado during her in 1914 visit to the Sangre de Cristo Mountains. She set the town of Moonstone in *The Song of the Lark* at the edge of sand dunes. Photograph by Garrett Peck.

through the Rocky Mountains. They rode over La Veta pass in the Sangre de Cristo range to Alamosa (Lewis made no mention of whether Cather took her to the nearby Great Sand Dunes). The train continued over the gorgeous San Juan range, the same route the Cumbres & Toltec Scenic Railroad takes today, and on to Durango along a route that straddled the Colorado–New Mexico border and through the Jicarilla Apache and Southern Ute reservations. The route was known as the Whiplash for its many curves through the mountains. The two women rode "sitting much of the way on the open back platform of the little wooden train, where we could see the engine puffing ahead around the curves," Lewis wrote. From Durango, they took another short train ride to Mancos.[32]

Mancos was the gateway to Mesa Verde National Park. The small town lies in a pleasant, irrigated valley with the San Juan Mountains towering

Figure 7. Willa Cather and Edith Lewis rode the narrow-gauge Denver & Rio Grande Western Railroad through the mountains to reach Mesa Verde in 1915. Part of that route today is the Cumbres & Toltec Scenic Railroad. Cumbres & Toltec Scenic Railroad.

to the north. Cather and Lewis had intended to stay only one night but ended up spending six days there, as they enjoyed the town so much. They called on one of the Wetherill brothers, probably Clayton, brother to Richard who had stumbled upon the famed Cliff Palace in 1888 with his brother-in-law Charlie Mason. In fact, many others had visited the remains in the years before Wetherill, but he heavily promoted his find. Richard Wetherill became the genesis for "Tom Outland's Story" in *The Professor's House*.[33]

Although Edith Lewis recalled decades later that her partner did not travel to Mesa Verde and the Southwest "with any express purpose of writing about it—of 'gathering material,' as they say, for a story," more recent evidence suggests that Cather's trip in fact was partly to explore the cliff dwellers for a future novel fictionalizing the Wetherill discovery.[34] While Cather and Lewis were en route to Mesa Verde, they stopped in Denver, and there Cather gave an interview for the *Denver Times*. The journalist reported that Cather was "visiting in Colorado preparatory to writing a book on the cliff dwelling region."[35] David Harrell, the author of *From Mesa Verde to The Professor's House*, believed that "the visit that Cather paid to Richard's [Wetherill] brother was probably a deliberate research venture."[36]

From Mancos, Cather and Lewis hired a driver and a team of horses or a car to take them up to Mesa Verde. The route then passed through the terrifying Knife's Edge along the northernmost point of the mesa. I have hiked a portion of this trail, and not only is it steep on the downhill side, but boulders randomly come tumbling down from above. Once atop the mesa, the vehicle carried them south for miles before reaching some of the most archaeologically significant remains in North America.

Cather and Lewis were nearly the only visitors in the national park. They joined a comfortable tent encampment at Spruce Tree House, where the head park ranger's wife prepared their meals. They spent a week exploring the extensive cliff dwellings, which had intrigued Cather ever since she had visited Walnut Canyon three years earlier. "I recall that we spent a whole day in Cliff Palace, the cliff dwelling with tower, described in the *Tom Outland* part of *The Professor's House*, cooking our lunch there and drinking from the spring behind the cliff house," Lewis later wrote.[37]

The day before they were to depart, their beloved guide Fred Jeep was called away to lead another group, and they were assigned an inexperienced guide named James Rickner (Lewis misspelled his name as "Richnor"). The guide led them down the cliff to Soda Canyon to see an Ancestral Pueblo site. The path down was so steep that they couldn't return that way, and he thought there was another trail up the cliff, but after walking many miles he couldn't find it. He admitted they were lost. They had reached the point where Soda Canyon and Cliff Canyon intersected, and it was getting dark. Rickner believed there was an archaeologist's camp up Cliff Canyon some four miles away, but Cather told him to go on. She had been bruised during the longer than expected hike.

Rickner went to find help, while Cather and Lewis remained behind on a flat rock. Lewis recalled that the hours they spent waiting were the "most rewarding of our whole trip." They sat in silence and watched the moon rise over Mesa Verde. Rickner reached the camp of the lead

Figure 8. Willa Cather at Mesa Verde's Cliff Palace in 1915. She and Edith Lewis had purchased identical khaki outfits that they wore on their southwestern adventures. Philip L. and Helen Cather Southwick Collection, Archives & Special Collections, University of Nebraska–Lincoln Libraries.

Figure 9. Mesa Verde's Cliff Palace, which Cather described as a "little city of stone" in *The Professor's House*. Cather and Lewis visited the national park in 1915. Photograph by Garrett Peck.

archaeologist, Dr. Walter Fewkes, who sent two men to retrieve the women. They found Cather and Lewis late in the evening and assisted them through the broken terrain and massive boulders to the top of the mesa. After they arrived at the camp around 2 a.m., their rescuers retrieved horses and a wagon, then drove them to the Spruce Tree House camp in the dark. Cather and Lewis only had a few hours of sleep after their adventure, as their driver arrived at 8 a.m. to carry them back to Mancos.[38]

Much to Cather's embarrassment, the *New York Times* published a short article about their misadventure: "Miss Cather sustained severe sprains, and both [women] were exhausted by wandering all night in a rocky canon, where they had been conducted by an inexperienced guide."[39]

Even with her bruises, Cather was entranced by Mesa Verde. "I was on my horse again four days afterward, and I want to go right back into that canyon and be mauled about by its big brutality, though all my bruises are not gone yet," she wrote Elsie Sergeant from her parents' home in Red Cloud. "It's a country that drives you crazy with delight, and that's all there is to it."[40]

The trip to Mesa Verde was eye-opening for Cather. As she had experienced in Arizona three years earlier, cliff dwellings revealed that there was a significant prehistoric civilization that existed in this region—not European, but something just as ancient. In January 1916, Cather published a boosterish article for the *Denver Times* that encouraged people to visit Mesa Verde. The national park "stood as if it had been deserted yesterday; undisturbed and undesecrated, preserved by the dry atmosphere and by its great inaccessibility," she wrote. "That is what the Mesa Verde means; its ruins are the highest achievement of stone-age man—preserved in bright, dry sunshine, like a fly in amber—sheltered by great canon walls and hidden away in a difficult mesa into which no one had ever found a trail."

Cather was impressed with Mesa Verde's aesthetics and found the architecture "absolutely harmonious with its site and setting." She went on: "Color, simplicity, space, an absence of clutter, the houses of the Pueblo Indians today and of their ancestors on the Mesa Verde are a reproach to the messiness in which we live." One might notice that Cather's philosophy of the unfurnished novel was emerging.

Cather also appreciated the ritualistic life of the Ancestral Puebloans, who merged agriculture, the seasons, and religion with their environment. "They accommodated themselves to it, interpreted it and made it personal; lived in a dignified relation with it," she explained. Cather noted, "One has only to go down into Hopiland to find the same life going on today on other mesa tops; houses like these, kivas like these, ceremonial and religious implements like these—every detail preserved with the utmost fidelity." The article already suggests how deeply Cather came to deeply admire Pueblo Indians, an admiration that would lead her to incorporate their culture into *Death Comes for the Archbishop* a decade later.[41]

After Mesa Verde, Cather and Lewis retraced the train route east through the San Juans. At Antonito, they transferred to the southbound Chili Line and rode to Taos Junction, New Mexico. From there they caught a ride, probably on a horse-drawn wagon, to Taos, where they stayed at the Columbian Hotel (now the site of Hotel La Fonda) for a week and explored the countryside on horseback as Cather's bruises from Mesa Verde healed.[42]

Taos was the young state's first art colony, home to the Taos Society of Artists. These were largely easterners appalled by industrialization and seeking the authentic and primitive in northern New Mexico. Artists were attracted to the quaint adobe town with the turquoise blue sky and the mammoth snow-capped peaks towering to the north. Another draw was Taos Pueblo, an ancient Indigenous settlement that inspired many of the artists, even as they romanticized Native Americans through their art. Taos's isolation, Indigenous culture, and natural setting may have been what drew Cather and Lewis to visit.

The Fred Harvey Company

Willa Cather mailed a Fred Harvey company postcard to Elsie Sergeant on August 30, 1915: "I have just arrived at Lamy after a glorious week at Taos, a Mexican town 30 miles from the railway. Lovely people there, good riding horses, perfect cantaloupes. Very happy." This was one of Cather and Lewis's several stays at Lamy's trackside El Ortiz, a boutique

Harvey hotel. The postcard was one of many that she mailed over the years, all of them highlighting scenes from the Southwest and advertising the Fred Harvey company.[43]

English-born Fred Harvey followed in the wake of the Atchison, Topeka & Santa Fe Railway, opening Harvey House restaurants to travelers. He was primarily a restaurateur: He wanted to improve the atrocious food that he experienced while riding the rails. After Harvey's death in 1901, his son Ford added hotel management to the company portfolio. Many of the hotels were adjacent to railroad stations: The AT&SF Railway owned the hotels and contracted the management to Fred Harvey.

In *Appetite for America*, Stephen Fried called Fred Harvey "the founding father of the American Service industry." He noted that Harvey "created the first national chain of restaurants of hotels, of newsstands, of bookstores—in fact, the first national chain of *anything*—in America." At its peak, the Fred Harvey company operated over a dozen hotels, mostly in the Southwest, and sixty-five restaurants.[44]

Fred Harvey brought an estimated hundred thousand young women known as Harvey Girls to the desert Southwest. Many of them lived in dormitories above the Harvey Houses. The company had a strict code of conduct and only hired women of good character, and until World War II, most of them were white. Women were expected to remain single for at least their first six months of employment, though many met their future husbands working for Fred Harvey. The women wore spotless black-and-white uniforms and provided excellent service, thanks to a rigorous training program that brought them up to the Fred Harvey standard.[45]

We know from Cather's many letters that she often stayed in Fred Harvey hotels during her travels to the Southwest, as she always traveled by train. These included La Fonda in Santa Fe, El Ortiz in Lamy, and El Navajo in Gallup. She also visited the Alvarado in Albuquerque and stayed at the Bright Angel Camp (now Bright Angel Lodge) at the Grand Canyon. During her travels across the country, she dined at many Harvey Houses while the trains refueled.

Albuquerque was home to the Harvey-run Alvarado Hotel adjacent to the railroad station. Humorist Will Rogers passed through the city in

Figure 10. Two Harvey Girls working at the Belen Harvey House, Madge Pinkerton and Wilma Tinker, posed for the camera in this 1927 image. Belen Harvey House Museum.

Figure 11. The El Ortiz hotel in Lamy, shown in 1930, was part of the Fred Harvey hotel network. Willa Cather stayed there numerous times during her travels to the Southwest. The hotel closed in 1940 and was soon torn down. Prints & Photographs Division, Library of Congress.

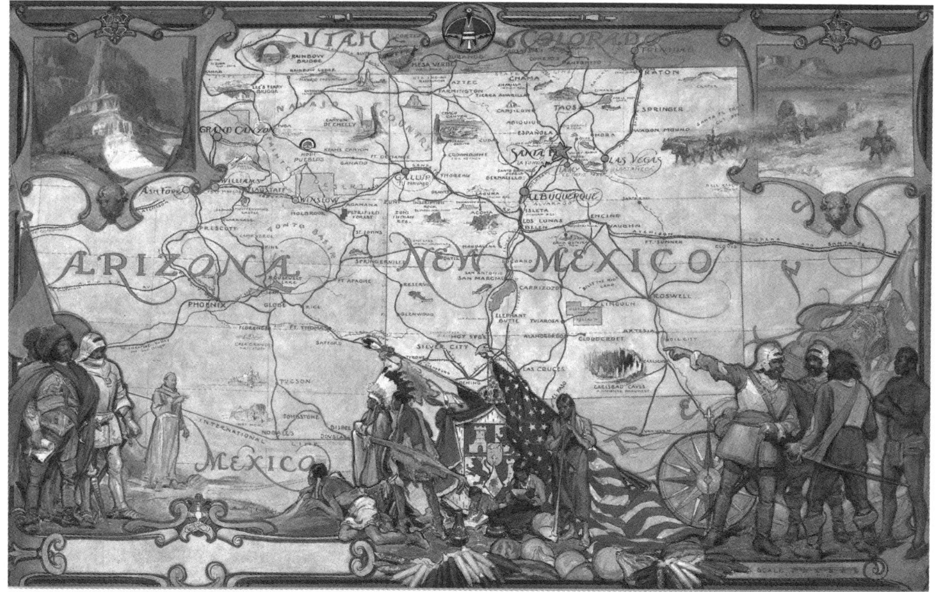

Figure 12. Mary Colter commissioned artist Gerald Cassidy to create this fantastic map showing the state of the tourism market in the 1920s Southwest, highlighting the national parks, Fred Harvey hotels, and the railroads. The map resides in La Fonda's Santa Fe Room. La Fonda Photo Archives.

1924 and observed the Harvey system in action. "Fred Harvey runs a restaurant and department store at the depot, and no matter how big a hurry you may be in to get where you are going, he has the train stopped 40 minutes," he observed with wry humor. "Everybody that didn't buy a lot in Los Angeles, buys a Navajo blanket at Albuquerque. Those who did buy a lot, can only afford a bow and arrow. I don't know why but they all seem to want to spend their last money for a bow and arrow. I suppose an undertaker meets this train in Kansas City."[46]

Back to Taos: 1916

After a week exploring Taos, Lewis returned to New York in mid-September 1915, while Cather visited Red Cloud. "Do you still want a book on the Southwest?" Cather wrote her editor at Houghton Mifflin, Ferris

Greenslet from her parents' home. "I think I could do a good one now." This was to be a work of fiction: "It would be the only reasonably good book on that country ever done," she claimed. Cather was going to call the book *The Blue Mesa*, but she shelved the idea in favor of penning *My Ántonia*. She revisited the idea a decade later through her novel *The Professor's House*.[47]

Cather's third novel, *The Song of the Lark*, was published in October while she was in Red Cloud. She dedicated the novel to her close friend Isabelle McClung. Isabelle's father, Judge Samuel McClung, died a month later. The family sold the house in early 1916, ending Cather's fifteen years at the McClung house. A few months later, Isabelle McClung married Jan Hambourg, a concert violinist.

Cather had sore feelings about McClung's marriage to Hambourg. "Jan and I are not very congenial. He's a strong personality—one likes him or one doesn't," Cather admitted. The loss of the Pittsburgh house as her writing sanctuary and Isabelle's marriage were "a devastating loss to me," and she felt that "a good many doors have been closing."[48] Four months later, Cather wrote her brother Roscoe, "Isabelle has married a very brilliant and perfectly poisonous Jew." Cather had Jewish friends and acquaintances throughout her life but occasionally used antisemitic language. It might also reflect her jealousy toward the man who married her best friend, former girlfriend, and traveling companion. Still, she eventually befriended Hambourg, and she often traveled to visit the couple.[49]

Cather and Lewis returned to Taos for three weeks in July 1916 to go horseback riding, again staying at the Columbian Hotel. Cather wanted to vacation in Wyoming, which she did the following month, but Lewis wanted to revisit Taos, as they only spent a week there the year before. Cather wrote her brother Roscoe, "Taos is a beautiful place, you know, forty dreadful miles across canyons from the railroad; all Mexicans, no whites, wonderful Indian pueblo near the Spanish town."[50]

Lewis recalled that in addition to Taos, they visited Santa Fe and explored the Rio Grande Valley around Española. Travel was difficult, with few hotels and primitive roads. The narrow-gauge Chili Line railroad paralleled the Rio Grande, but to get away from the railroad required hiring a horse and wagon, as there were few cars in New Mexico. A few miles east of Española is Santa Cruz, an early Spanish settlement, and there they met Father Ghislain Haelterman, a Belgian priest who had served that community since 1898. He grew an impressive flower and vegetable garden. "He was a florid, full-bearded farmer priest, who drove about among his eighteen Indian missions with a spring wagon and a pair of mules," Cather later wrote.[51]

After Lewis returned to New York, Cather journeyed north to spend a month with Roscoe in Wyoming. Elsie Sergeant asked Cather for recommendations about the best places to visit, and Cather responded:

> It is awfully hard to advise anyone about places to go in the west unless they have been about in this country a good deal. Then one can say of a new place that it is like such-or-such another place. I think Taos (TAOS) New Mexico, is the best place I know to go alone. . . . The country is glorious—lots of lovely little towns within easy riding distance; all Mexican and Indian, no gringoes. You can get good saddle horses for little money. It's more comfortable than camping. In the South-west, at least, you need a cool, shadowy adobe house after you've been out in that blaze of heat and color. Taos is decidedly the best place I know.

Cather concluded, "This is wonderful enough country up here, but to me, Wyoming and Montana are always tame compared with the Southwest." Sergeant bought a cool, shadowy adobe house in Tesuque, just north of Santa Fe, in 1921.[52]

Cather's Southwestern Fiction

Cather's extensive travels to the Southwest in 1912, 1914, 1915, and 1916 had a significant influence on both her life decisions and her writing. While Edith Lewis observed that Cather "loved the Southwest for its own sake," she transferred so many of her experience into her novels, sharing her love of the region with her readers.[53]

While it may seem logical to think that Cather wrote fiction entirely on her own, the reality was that Edith Lewis had a major influence on her. As Melissa Homestead pointed out, Cather's novels were far more of a collaboration than one might assume. Lewis was a considerable editor—neither a secretary nor a typist—and shared ideas that Cather captured in her stories. "Their multi-layered collaboration—from shared experiences of transformative travel, through generative conversation, up through preparation of text for publication—also produced a sense of joint textual ownership, with Lewis and Cather sharing pleasure in Cather's fiction," Homestead wrote. One should never underestimate Lewis's importance in Cather's writing.[54]

"Cather and Lewis's creative collaboration had the same status as the intimate relationship in which it was imbedded," in novels such as *The Professor's House* and *Death Comes for the Archbishop*, Homestead observed. It was "not a secret but also not explicitly labeled, not hidden but also not part of Cather's public performance of authorship."[55]

This may be surprising, but *Death Comes for the Archbishop* was not Cather's first novel about the Southwest, but rather her last. In fact, she published a short story, "The Enchanted Bluff" (1909), and not one but two earlier novels inspired by her Southwestern travels: *The Song of the Lark* (1915) and *The Professor's House* (1925). Both books featured cliff dwellings, ancient settlements built into cliffsides by Ancestral Puebloans. Cather was fascinated by these ancient builders, and her experiences at Walnut Canyon and Mesa Verde informed how her fictional, white protagonists were reborn and renewed. At the same time, these were historic landscapes bereft of the Indigenous people who lived in them—and by the way, who still lived, though Cather treated them as a vanished race.

Cather's novels about the Southwest were born from her travels. No doubt she thought of her ventures as much more than tourism. Her perspective translated into cultured white fictional creations such as Thea Kronborg, Tom Outland, and Archbishop Latour, even while largely ignoring that Hispanics and Natives already had extensive and distinct cultures (she would more formally address these cultures in *Archbishop*).

Cather published her short story "The Enchanted Bluff" in *Harper's*

Monthly in April 1909. Edith Lewis later called it "an excursion into the future, a tentative foreshadowing of what was to come" in Cather's Southwestern writing. As this was three years before her first trip to New Mexico, Cather had to imagine what the mesa looked like near Acoma Pueblo.[56]

In the story, a group of teenaged boys in Sandtown, Nebraska, discuss their dreams of places they'd like to visit. One of them, Tip Smith, says that he'd like to travel to New Mexico to see the Enchanted Bluff, which he describes as a nine-hundred-foot tall, red granite mesa in the middle of the desert (the actual bluff, known as Mesa Encantado, is sandstone and is about 430 feet tall). "The Indians say that hundreds of years ago, before the Spaniards came, there was a village away up there in the air," Tip says. They were peaceful and only came down a narrow staircase to hunt and collect water, as the mesa offered them protection from enemies.

While the men were hunting, a storm destroyed the stairs, trapping the villagers on top of the mesa. "Of course they never got down. They starved to death up there, and when the war party came back on their way north, they could hear the children crying from the edge of the bluff where they had crawled out, but they didn't see a sign of a grown Indian, and nobody has ever been up there since." Tip explains that he would fire a rocket to anchor a rope atop the mesa, and with that he could climb to the top to explore the ancient village.[57]

In 1897, William Libbey did exactly that, hoisting himself to the top of the Enchanted Mesa in a marine life-saving chair. He declared that he found no remains of human settlement, but later that year Frederick Webb Hodge, an amateur archaeologist, scaled the mesa and found artifacts indicating that people had in fact lived on high. This information was a decade old by the time Cather penned her short story. In her telling, Tip never fulfilled his dream but passed it on to his son. "Bert has been let into the story, and thinks of nothing but the Enchanted Bluff," Cather concluded.[58]

Cather's first novel incorporating the Southwest, *The Song of the Lark*, was her most autobiographical book. She explored how Thea Kronborg, the daughter of Swedish immigrants in Moonstone, Colorado (really Red

Cloud), discovers her remarkable singing voice and transforms from ingénue to internationally renowned Wagnerian opera star. Thea is independent and persevering, and though she lacks money, she finds a way to make her dream come true, usually through adult male mentors.

After Thea takes singing lessons and experiences setbacks in her pathway to stardom, her friend Fred Ottenburg, the third-born son of a wealthy St. Louis brewing family, suggests that she take a break for several months. "I don't think I told you, but my father owns a whole cañon full of Cliff-Dweller ruins," Fred tells her. "He has a big worthless ranch down in Arizona, near a Navajo reservation, and there's a cañon on the place they call Panther Cañon, chock full of that sort of thing." Fred sends Thea to Arizona to recuperate, then later joins her.[59]

Thea's experience at Panther Canyon comes about two-thirds of the way through *The Song of the Lark*. Cather describes Thea exploring the area, rooted in Cather's own memories from her 1912 visit to Walnut Canyon with her brother Douglass: "The Ancient People had built their houses of yellowish stone and mortar. The overhanging cliff above made a roof of two hundred feet thick. The hard stratum below was an everlasting floor. The houses stood along in a row, like the buildings in a city block, or like a barracks."[60]

Thea sets up camp in one of the houses and spends many days there, returning to sleep at the Ottenburg ranch at night. "Thea often felt how easy it would be to dream one's life out in some cleft in the world," Cather wrote.[61] She finds countless pottery remains in the cliff houses and experiences a revelation. "The stream and the broken pottery: what was any art but an effort to make a sheath, a mould in which to imprison for a moment the shining, elusive element which is life itself—life hurrying past us and running away, too strong to stop, too sweet to lose?" Thea observes. "In singing, one made a vessel of one's throat and nostrils and held it on one's breath, caught the stream in a scale of natural intervals." She connects the Ancient People, nature, and her own art.[62]

Kronborg's time in Panther Canyon is a spiritual retreat, echoing Cather's two months in the Southwest in 1912. "She had never been alone for so long, or thought so much," Cather wrote. "The things that were really hers separated themselves from the rest. Her ideas were simplified, became sharper and clear. She felt united and strong."[63]

Thea then makes a profound decision: She would travel to Germany to study singing. Her point of view seems atheistic, that life is only a series of random events, except for the fate that we ourselves choose to pursue: "Only by the merest chance had she ever got to Panther Cañon. There was certainly no kindly Providence. . . . One's life was at the mercy of blind chance." This stands in contrast to the worldview of another Cather hero, Jean Marie Latour, a Catholic priest and man of faith in *Death Comes for the Archbishop*, published twelve years later.[64]

After two months, Fred Ottenburg arrives and quietly pursues Thea romantically, offering to marry her—but without revealing that he was already married. "The past closed up behind one, somehow," she confesses to Fred. "You can't force your life back into that mould again. No, one can't go back." Our lives can only move forward. Published in 1915, *The Song of the Lark* raised the question of a past you can never return to a decade before Scott Fitzgerald more fully excavated the idea in *The Great Gatsby*. For all of its merits, Cather's third novel was overly descriptive and too long. She would come to a more decluttered style in the 1920s.[65]

Cather's second Southwest-themed novel was *The Professor's House*. It contains a story within a story: that of Tom Outland, a young man hired as a cowpoke near Blue Mesa. You may recall that Cather proposed in 1915 to write a book called *Blue Mesa*. It is intriguing that Cather set her novel in New Mexico, though the location she wrote about was obviously Mesa Verde National Park, Colorado. The book is a carefully constructed myth that is only loosely based on the facts.[66] Janis Stout observed that "Tom Outland's Story" was "a staggering accomplishment and an extraordinarily significant product to have come out of a tourist visit."[67]

In the novel, Godfrey St. Peter is a history professor who has difficulty accepting that the world had moved on. He idolizes the past, particularly his friendship with Tom Outland, a brilliant young man killed during World War I. He is no longer in love with his wife, his daughters are grown up and married, and he is depressed. His malaise reflects Cather's as she worked out her feelings in midlife, despite her professional success (she had won a Pulitzer, while Professor St. Peter won the Oxford Prize). Indeed, Edith Lewis observed that "*The Professor's House* is, I think, the most personal of Willa Cather's novels."[68]

The Professor's House includes considerable symbolism. Outland's name reminds us that he is an outsider. St. Peter (in this case, Professor Godfrey St. Peter) was the rock upon which Jesus built his church, and the professor is the steward of Tom Outland's memory. In some ways, the older professor is the disciple of the younger man. St. Peter's two houses symbolize the past and the present. He refuses to give up the past, represented by his old house, and he opposes modernism, represented by his family's new home. Like Cather's fond memories of her childhood attic bedroom in Red Cloud, the professor relishes his antiquated upstairs room; it also resembles Cather's dedicated writing space in the McClung house that she lost when the family sold their home in 1916. And like Cather at the time she wrote the novel, the professor is in midlife.[69]

On the book's frontispiece, Cather included a quote from a character in the novel, Louie Marsellus: "A turquoise set in silver, wasn't it? . . . Yes, a turquoise set in dull silver." This was a metaphor for the novel's structure: "Tom Outland's Story," the middle story in the three-act book, is the bright turquoise set in the dulling silver of Professor St. Peter's ennui. The young man is the spark who returns life to the professor.

The book's story-within-a-story is a flashback to an earlier time before Outland's death. One day while out turkey hunting, the young man finds an irrigation ditch, pottery, and a stone axe, and knows right away that it was an Indigenous farming site. His employer expressly forbids the cattlemen from crossing a river to retrieve lost cattle, but Outland does so anyway, climbing up into a canyon and there to his amazement sees a "little city of stone. It was as still as sculpture—and something like that. It all hung together, seemed to have a kind of composition: pale little houses of stone nestling close to one another, perched on top of each other, with flat roofs, narrow windows, straight walls, and in the middle of the group, a round tower." Here, Cather describes the Mesa Verde cliff dwellings from her own experience, which she had visited a decade earlier with Edith Lewis.

"I knew at once that I had come upon the city of some extinct civilization, hidden away in this inaccessible mesa for centuries, preserved in the dry air and almost perpetual sunlight like a fly in amber, guarded by the cliffs and the river and the desert," Outland recalls (Cather had used similar wording in her 1916 *Denver Times* article). He and his compadres call it the "Cliff City." The actual site is known as Cliff Palace, the best known of dozens of cliff dwellings within Mesa Verde National Park.[70]

Outland and the others explore the site, which is full of pottery, stored grain, and four human remains, one of which they name Mother Eve, and begin amateur archaeological digging and cataloging their findings. He wonders about the people who built the stone city: "But what had become of them? What catastrophe had overwhelmed them? They hadn't moved away, for they had taken none of their belongings, not even their clothes." Father Duchene, a Catholic priest, believes they had been wiped out in a war with another tribe.[71]

Duchene, Outland, and by proxy Cather misunderstood how the cliff dwellers—ancestors to today's Pueblo Indians—lived. The latter had not abandoned Cliff Palace nor gone extinct, which was a common belief in Cather's day; rather, they had migrated eastward toward the Rio Grande before 1300 CE. We don't know why: Was it severe drought, overpopulation, political strife, or a combination of these? Pueblo dwellings are never considered abandoned, as the spirits of their ancestors still reside there, making these living, sacred spaces. Today some two dozen tribes claim descent from Mesa Verde.

Duchene is deeply sympathetic to the people who lived there, as he tells Outland: "Like you, I feel a reverence for this place. Wherever humanity has made that hardest of all starts and lifted itself out of mere brutality, is a sacred spot. . . . They built themselves into this mesa and humanized it." Blue Mesa is an idealized setting: a pristine historical landscape that is perfectly preserved and bereft of people save for the dead.[72]

While Outland travels to Washington, DC, to generate interest in the archaeological remains with the Smithsonian Institution, his partner Roddy Blake sells their artifacts to a German collector, who ships them out of country via Mexico to escape customs. Outland is outraged: "They weren't mine to sell—nor yours! They belonged to this country, to the

State, and to all the people." He feels violated by the fact that something so historic should be sold for profit, instead of being preserved for posterity. He refuses to take his half of the money. Framing the story this way was Cather's means of protesting the looting of Indigenous sites and disregard for Native cultures.[73]

Outland's protest is loosely based on actual events. One of the archaeologist-excavators at Mesa Verde, Gustaf Nordenskiöld, catalogued the cliff dwellings and sent extensive funerary objects, including human remains, back to Sweden. Cather drew extensively on Nordenskiöld's book *The Cliff Dwellers of the Mesa Verde*.[74] After Nordenskiöld died in 1895, his collection made its way to the National Museum of Finland. In 2020, the human remains were repatriated to Pueblo descendants, who reinterred them at Mesa Verde. The museum retained nearly six hundred objects in its collection. Similarly disturbing, when Chaco Canyon was excavated, the massive stores of Ancestral Pueblo pottery and ceremonial objects were carted away to various institutions that sponsored the excavations. The national park retains none of the collection.

On the positive side, we are seeing more Native artifacts and human remains being repatriated. Congress passed the Native American Graves Protection and Repatriation Act (NAGPRA) in 1990. In 2013 a Paris auction house sought to auction off twenty-four sacred masks plundered from the Hopis, and another three sacred objects from the San Carlos Apaches, both Arizona tribes. The Annenberg Foundation stepped in and clandestinely purchased nearly the entire lot at auction for $530,000, then returned them to the rightful owners.[75] In 2019 a ceremonial shield was returned to Acoma Pueblo after a legal battle that lasted several years.[76] In 2022 Congress passed the Safeguarding Tribal Objects of Patrimony (STOP) Act to prevent Native objects of significant cultural heritage from being exported and sold overseas.

Similar to Claude Wheeler, Cather's protagonist in *One of Ours*, Tom Outland was killed during World War I, and that in turn is a cause of the professor's depression. He expresses Cather's criticism of the modern world and wonders what good has science ever done us.

> Science hasn't given us any new amazements, except of the superficial kind we get from witnessing dexterity and sleight-of-hand. It hasn't given us any richer pleasurers, as the Renaissance did, nor any new sins—not one! Indeed, it takes our old ones away. . . . As long as every man and woman who crowded into the cathedrals on Easter Sunday was a principal in a gorgeous drama with God, glittering angels on one side and the shadows of evil coming and going on the other, life was a rich thing. . . . Art and religion (they are the same thing, in the end, of course) have given man the only happiness he has ever had.[77]

Cather may have reveled in Renaissance art but overlooked that the Renaissance was very much about rediscovering science. The arts and the sciences blossomed together. But keep in mind that Cather penned this novel just years after the horrors of World War I. She lost one of her cousins in the trenches, one of an estimated seventeen million people killed by aerial bombings, artillery, machine guns, poison gas, and submarines. Science was unleashed to kill millions. She saw no upside to it.

In an interview with book critic Fanny Butcher, Cather stated that Godfrey St. Peter "was more Tom Outland than he was himself. The book might have been called 'A Man of Fifty Looks at the World,' but he could never have looked at it just as he did without the presence of Tom Outland in his life." She also explained that "this is the first book I've ever written with any irony in it." After Outland's death, his fortune from a scientific invention comes to the St. Peter family and causes much unhappiness and jealousy.[78]

The Professor's House is critical of the materialism that swept the country in the 1920s, in the form of the automobile, cheap gadgets, and home appliances. Guy Reynolds observed that Cather "illustrated the materialist inadequacy of contemporary America by juxtaposing their society against an idealised, earlier civilization," the cliff dwellers of Blue Mesa.[79] Cather was surprised that the novel sold so well. "I thought it a nasty, grim little tale, but the reviewers seem to think it's a cross-word puzzle," she wrote. "It's certainly not my 'favorite' of my own books."[80]

After the 1916 visit to Taos, Cather and Lewis did not return to the Southwest for nine years. In the intervening years, Cather published *My Ántonia*, shifted publishers to Alfred A. Knopf, and won the Pulitzer for *One of Ours*. She developed a writing style that was crisp and more nuanced, and her books got shorter. By the time Cather returned to the Southwest in 1925, her literary ideas had significantly evolved.

CHAPTER 3

A Kind of Freemasonry

"We agreed that no one who had not grown up in a little prairie town could know anything about it. It was a kind of freemasonry, we said."

—WILLA CATHER, *My Ántonia*, 1

IN 1916 WILLA CATHER began working with Paul Revere Reynolds to sell her short stories to magazines, and later serialized versions of her novels. She sold her books to publishers directly and never asked for an advance. Reynolds, who has been called "America's first literary agent," handled sales to periodicals and negotiated payments larger than writers could negotiate for themselves and received a 10 percent commission. He represented about seventy-five writers, including Dorothy Canfield Fisher, Scott Fitzgerald, George Bernard Shaw, Ida Tarbell, H. G. Wells, P. G. Wodehouse, and Willa Cather. Cather was never a major client for Reynolds; however, she was a prestigious one, especially once she won the Pulitzer in 1923.[1]

Over the years, Cather developed a love-hate relationship with New York City. She complained, "I am going to leave that hideous town for good very soon," though she never did.[2] She usually left New York in the summer when it was unbearably hot, and first took refuge at the Shattuck Inn in Jaffrey, New Hampshire, in August 1917. Isabelle and Jan Hambourg were staying nearby and invited her to join them. Cather took a quiet top floor bedroom that gave her a nice view of Mount Monadnock; she befriended the owners, who understood that the author needed quiet and space. She stayed for two months, writing part of her fourth novel, *My Ántonia*, in a tent. The Shattuck Inn replaced the McClung house as Cather's main writing retreat. It became a home-away-from-home, one where she would stay many times in the decades ahead, usually in the fall to avoid the vacation crowds.

Cather repeatedly missed the deadlines for *My Ántonia*. It was supposed to be out in 1917, then spring 1918, and then was finally published in October 1918, shortly before the end of World War I. Fortunately her publisher, Houghton Mifflin, was patient. Cather left out the Germans from *My Ántonia*, though they were the largest immigrant group in Nebraska. Cather astutely recognized that including them would be problematic during the Great War, as the United States was at war with Germany, and instead substituted Bohemian (Czech) immigrants as the center of the story.

My Ántonia begins with a journey that Cather herself experienced: moving from Virginia to Nebraska as a child. *My Ántonia* touched on common themes in Cather's literature: personal experiences, the prairie, and immigrants uprooted to a strange and inhospitable landscape. *My Ántonia* is a fictional memoir, its narrator Jim Burden serving as Cather's stand-in. "We agreed that no one who had not grown up in a little prairie town could know anything about it," Cather observes in *My Ántonia*. "It was a kind of freemasonry, we said."[3]

Cather's friend Dorothy Canfield Fisher wrote in 1933, "The one real subject of all her books is the effect a new country—our new country—has on people transplanted to it from the old traditions of a stable, complex civilization." What is especially interesting is that Cather focused not on English immigrants but rather on minority European immigrants (Bohemians, French, Russians, Scandinavians). She was curious about the outsiders and how they made their way in a new country. In that sense, Cather remains deeply relevant, as the United States is largely composed of an immigrant population that has assimilated into the broader American culture. The frontier was the lens through which she examined a changing American society.[4]

The Nebraska frontier became dotted with farms and small settlements. Small-town life tends to be conservative. Everyone knows everyone, and there are few secrets. It can be gossipy and stifling, as Cather darkly portrayed in *A Lost Lady.* There is a paradox: If you want privacy, then you should live in a city, where people are busier, more tolerant, and less likely to track your personal habits. The 1971 movie *The Last Picture Show*—or the 2013 movie *Nebraska* that seemed like its sequel (both were filmed in black-and-white)—served as an indictment of dying small town life with boarded up main streets and little future. Only the older inhabitants remained, as the younger people moved on in search of bigger opportunities and a life away from farming.

On a farm, the chores are endless. There are no holidays. The cows must be milked and fed. Eggs must be collected. Fences and irrigation ditches must be repaired. Fields must be planted, manured, watered, weeded, and harvested. Bank loans must be secured and paid back, and new equipment and seed purchased. And then everything starts over in an endless cycle. A farmer's work is never done. And some years the weather won't cooperate and a farmer can lose everything.

Nebraska was a place to start over. Virgin farmland was plentiful but required work to break up the prairie grass and turn it into productive fields. Many immigrants came to farm. In Cather's stories, the families were Bohemians, Danes, Germans, Norwegians, Russians, and Swedes. My dad grew up in tiny Hay Springs in the Nebraska Panhandle, and his best friends were the DeCastros (Hispanics) and the Kadleceks (Czechs).

"The only thing very noticeable about Nebraska was that it was still, all day long, Nebraska," Cather observes in *My Ántonia*. The cattle yards and cornfields are endless. It can take you all day to drive across the state along Interstate 80. But she also writes with appreciation for the land that raised her: "There was nothing but land: not a country at all, but the material out of which countries are made."[5]

Mildred Bennett, a South Dakota transplant and Cather's first biographer, started the first Willa Cather Spring Conference in 1955, eight years after the author's death. While her biography largely covered the gossipy details of Cather and Red Cloud, Bennett proved a notable steward of the author's legacy, and she helped establish the Willa Cather Pioneer Memorial, which later became the Willa Cather Foundation.

Figure 13. The National Willa Cather Center takes up nearly an entire block in Red Cloud, Nebraska. Photograph by Garrett Peck.

The foundation opened the National Willa Cather Center in Red Cloud in 2017, stretching nearly an entire block along Webster Street. This small, one-thousand-person prairie town is associated with Cather more than any other place, making tourism a major part of the local otherwise farming economy. Thousands of visitors, known to locals as "Cather people" and "Willa weirdoes," make the pilgrimage to Red Cloud, many coming for the annual conference.

I attended my first spring conference in June 2023, an occasion that focused on *A Lost Lady* and the 150th anniversary of Cather's birth. The following week, Cather's statue was unveiled in the US Capitol. The sculptor, Littleton Alston, was the first Black artist to have a statue in Statuary Hall.

Six miles south of Red Cloud is the Willa Cather Memorial Prairie, a tract of land that has never been plowed. At first glance, you might think the prairie is a monoculture of shaggy grass, but when you look closer, it is a complex ecosystem of grasses, flowering plants, trees, birds, insects, invertebrates, mammals, and reptiles. It is far more complicated than you think. Such is the case for Nebraska. You may think it is just a table-flat landscape of alfalfa, corn, cows, and white people, but you'd be wrong. The state is a gently rolling landscape and is incredibly green. While most of the population is of European descent, they come from many ethnic backgrounds, and there has long been a Hispanic presence. Traveling through Denver on my way to the Willa Cather Spring Conference in 2024, I spotted a billboard advertising Nebraska, showing a couple hikers traversing the hoodoos at Toadstool Geological Park in the northwest corner of the state. "Famous for our flat, boring landscape," the billboard quipped. This was ironic marketing at its best.

"The early population of Nebraska was largely transatlantic," Cather stated in her oft-quoted 1923 essay, "Nebraska: The End of the First Cycle." "The county in which I grew up, in the south-central part of the state, was typical. On Sunday we would drive to a Norwegian church and listen to a sermon in that language, or to a Danish or a Swedish church. We would go to the French Catholic settlement in the next county and hear a sermon in French, or into the Bohemian township and hear one in Czech, or we could go to church with the German Lutherans." She added, "Colonies of European people, Slavonic, Germanic, Scandinavian, Latin, spread across our bronze prairies like the daubs of color on a painter's palette. They brought with them something that this neutral new world needed ever more than the immigrants needed land," that is, their distinct cultures that they contributed to the American melting pot. In the 1910 U.S. Census, more than nine hundred thousand of Nebraska's 1.2 million people were foreign-born. The largest group were Germans.[6]

Although New York City was Cather's home from 1906 until her death in 1947, she frequently traveled to Arizona and New Mexico, to Red Cloud to visit her parents, to New Hampshire to write, and to Grand Manan, a Canadian island off the coast of Maine, where she and Edith Lewis maintained a vacation cottage for two decades in a women-only community. She visited Europe many times and was a Francophile. She was fond of travel and playing tourist. Though Cather often wrote about small town life, there was nothing provincial about the woman.

Cather was a writer who drew inspiration from the past, a past many have interpreted as nostalgia. But she objected to being pigeonholed as a nostalgist. "Please don't use the word 'nostalgic' at me anymore!! Everybody else uses it, so don't you," she complained to Carl Van Vechten in 1937. "Moreover, they use it about every book I write. My God, I am not always homesick!"[7]

Cather's characters were often modeled on real people, whether that was Ántonia Shimerda (Ana Sadilek Pavelka), Marian Forrester (Lyra Garber), or Jean Marie Latour (Jean-Baptiste Lamy). Some call this persona plagiarism or prototyping. It's not a negative concept: Many novelists use this approach. But it made Cather somewhat controversial in Red Cloud, as it was clear she modeled her characters on both deceased and living people and exposed embarrassing secrets, such as Ana Sadilek's out-of-wedlock pregnancy. To this day, many people in Red Cloud have ambivalent feelings about Cather, though doubtless we Cather people are good for the local economy.

While many assume Cather to be a nostalgist and out of touch with modern life (and if so, why do we continue to read her?), she was very much in touch with contemporary culture—and she was critical of it, especially of American materialism. It just so happened that the lens she examined it was through the past.

Despite Cather's themes that explored bygone days, she was unquestionably a modern writer. She highlighted the role of art, examined women's success in a man's world, and criticized American capitalism and consumerism. Her writing style was spare and pared back. She rejected flowery Victorian descriptions and complicated sentences. Her landscape descriptions are stunningly beautiful. Cather seldom used metaphors, though when she did, they were exceptional, such as her description of a Nebraska snowstorm in *My Ántonia*: "The snow did not fall this time, it simply spilled out of heaven, like thousands of featherbeds being emptied."[8]

As Melissa Homestead documented in *The Only Wonderful Things*, Cather's sparse language partly came from Edith Lewis, who helped edit most of Cather's books. As a professional copyeditor and later advertising copywriter, Lewis could reduce a sentence to its most basic and most meaningful. Unsurprisingly, Homestead called Cather and Lewis's relationship a "creative partnership."[9]

Cather's style was to strip a story down to its basics, hinting at layered meanings and nuance, sparsely showing rather than telling. In a 1922 essay for the *New Republic* called "The Novel Démeublé," she wrote, "The novel, for a long while, has been over-furnished. The property-man has been so busy on its pages, the importance of material objects and their vivid presentation have been so stressed, that we take it for granted whoever can observe, and can write the English language, can write a novel." She added, "A novel crowded with physical sensations is no less a catalogue than one crowded with furniture."[10]

Scholars have focused on one key phrase from Cather's essay: "the inexplicable presence of the thing not named," which was her method of hinting toward an idea without explicitly naming it, leaving the reader's imagination to fill in the gap. Think of the scene in *Death Comes for the Archbishop* where Latour insists that Vaillant take their two beloved mules on his Colorado mission. Vaillant's teardrops fell on a piece of paper. Your mind fills in the gap: that Vaillant is touched beyond words, but even more, the mules belong together, just as Latour and Vaillant belong together as friends. Scholars have had a field day with "the thing not named," going well beyond her writing philosophy into a host of Catherly interpretations, for example, applying a gay interpretation to Cather's works, including *Archbishop*.[11]

In a 1925 interview, Cather stated, "Style is how you write, and you write well when you are interested. A writer's own interest in a story is the essential thing. If there is a flash of warmth in him it is repeated in the reader. The emotion is bigger than style."[12] Six years later, she advised, "Unless you have something in you so fierce that it simply pours itself out in a torrent, heedless of rules or bounds—then do not bother to write anything at all. Why should you? The time for revision is after a thing is on paper—not before."[13]

Her style garnered outside appreciation early on. Literary critic H. L. Mencken had admired Cather since she published *O Pioneers!* in 1913. He appreciated her style, as he wrote in a review of *The Professor's House*: "I know of no other American novelist, indeed, whose writing is so certain of its effects, and yet so free from artifice."[14]

In 1920 Cather shifted publishers from Houghton Mifflin to Alfred A. Knopf, at the time a small company founded just five years earlier. She didn't believe that Houghton publicized her work enough, though she remained lifelong friends with the editor, Ferris Greenslet. Knopf never poached Cather; rather, Cather dropped by Knopf's office, introduced herself, and brought him her next book, *Youth and the Bright Medusa*. Knopf would be her publisher for the rest of her life. He noted, "She didn't ask for an advance then—or ever."[15]

After her cousin Grosvenor Phillips Cather's death in the Great War, Cather turned toward a new theme. She penned the novel *One of Ours*, in which the hero, Claude Wheeler (modeled on her cousin), was killed. Critics were divided over it, yet the book won the Pulitzer Prize for the Novel in 1923. Since then, the novel has largely been forgotten. Modern readers are more likely to steer towards Cather's prairie trilogy, as well as *A Lost Lady* and *Death Comes for the Archbishop*. With the fame that accompanies a Pulitzer, Cather was fifty years old and had won the financial and literary success that few writers ever achieve.

Now middle-aged, Cather observed that the world was shifting around her in ways that she did not approve. She looked back at the 1920s in *Not Under Forty*, a book of short essays she published in 1936. She explained the humorous title: "It means that the book will have little interest for people under forty years of age. The world broke in two in 1922 or thereabouts." She pointed out the divide between her generation, which had witnessed the end of the frontier, the Progressive Era and World War I, and the younger, so-called Lost Generation that came of age after the war and believed the older generation had ruined everything. This younger generation included Scott Fitzgerald, Ernest Hemingway, Dorothy Parker, and Sinclair Lewis. They often wrote with deep cynicism about the world they inherited. Cather clearly stood with the older generation, and her writing reflected a more conservative and romanticized view of the past.[16]

Cather's observation about the world breaking in two in 1922 was possibly from personal experience. When she published *One of Ours* that year, critics assailed her (especially men) for writing about a war that she hadn't experienced firsthand, and the younger generation turned its nose up at her. Meanwhile the public loved the book. Cather experienced the emerging generational divide quite consciously.[17] She wrote Dorothy Canfield Fisher, "We knew one world and how we both felt about it. We now find ourselves in quite another."[18]

Cather grew increasingly pessimistic during the 1920s as the nation grew disillusioned after World War I, shedding its progressive idealism. As a person who supported the war effort that would "make the world safe for democracy," she wrote that "It seems to me that everything has gone wrong since the Armistice. Why they celebrate that day with anything but fasts and sack-cloth and ashes, I don't know." Cather's novels of the postwar years—*One of Ours*, *A Lost Lady*, *The Professor's House*, and *My Mortal Enemy*—reflected her dark mood.[19]

With Cather's approval, her literary agent Paul Revere Reynolds began selling the serial rights of Cather's novels to magazines. Serialization earned Cather a quick paycheck, which she sometimes needed before royalties kicked in. Cather portrayed herself as an anti-commercial writer, yet she keenly tracked her book sales and royalties.[20] Generally, Cather was financially successful as an author, able to afford a cook and a housekeeper, as well as pay for her extensive travels. Yet success did not come without a cost: After the critical success of *A Lost Lady*, Cather had countless demands on her time. She hired Sarah Bloom as her secretary in 1923, who worked for Cather until the author's death in 1947.

The New York Times interviewed Cather in 1924, where she famously remarked, "Nobody stays at home anymore. Nobody makes anything beautiful anymore. Quick transportation is the death of art. We can't keep still because it is so easy to move about." She went on to explain the importance of tradition: "Older countries have their wealth of former years to fall back upon. We haven't." She added, "If we have no tradition of years behind us, the people who come to live here have." Cather often wrote about such people, like the Swedish farmers in *O Pioneers!*, the Czech immigrants in *My Ántonia*, and two French priests in *Death Comes for the Archbishop*. The 1920s was a period of anti-immigrant fervor as

Figure 14. Mexican artist Miguel Covarrubias drew this caricature of Willa Cather in 1925. Prints & Photographs Division, Library of Congress.

America locked the gates to new arrivals, but Cather saw the contribution that immigrants had brought to American society. And being a New Yorker, she saw it every day, in a city that was (and still is) awash in foreign accents.[21]

Cather accepted where she came from and embraced the traditions of small-town life, even as she became an urban New Yorker. Cather was a conservative who mined the past as a way of understanding who we are. Her work could be nostalgic, but even then she found ways of telling new stories that felt like they were from another time. Long before she started her writing career in earnest, she penned a letter to poet Witter Bynner in 1905: "I suppose one's early experiences rather cling to one."[22]

After writing a series of books in the 1920s that critiqued the rampant materialism and reflected the pessimism of the era, Cather was ready to move into a new direction. She would expound upon the episodic tales of a saint's life from frescoes she had seen in Europe. Cather would draw deeply upon hagiography developed during Medieval times, updated for a nineteenth-century French bishop in the American Southwest, incorporating her own extensive travels to that very region.

Chapter 4

Mabeltown

"Taos is a beautiful place, you know, forty dreadful miles across canyons from the railroad; all Mexicans, no whites, wonderful Indian pueblo near the Spanish town."

—Willa Cather to Roscoe Cather, 1916

In late spring 1925, Willa Cather and Edith Lewis departed by train for a Southwest vacation that, for Cather, would last more than two months. Their destination was the Grand Canyon and "wild Arizona," and then they planned a week at a dude ranch near Santa Fe where they could ride horses, play cowboy, and review proofs of *The Professor's House*.[1]

The 1925 trip was Cather's fifth visit to the Southwest, and her first since she and Lewis had traveled there nine years earlier. During this vacation Cather would find her inspiration to compose *Death Comes for the Archbishop*. Constructing the timeline of the first half of this trip is not easy, and Cather made no subsequent mention of visiting the Grand Canyon. Her usual modus operandi was to visit family in Red Cloud before venturing further on, but in this case, she visited them during her return trip. We find Cather and Lewis in Lamy, the rail junction south of Santa Fe, on June 12, and then in Santa Fe on June 23. They could have easily made it to Arizona and back in that window of time.

The two women stayed several days at La Fonda, the hotel on the Santa Fe Plaza that stood on the site of the historic Exchange Hotel. Things had sometimes turned violent at the old Exchange. In 1849 gambling house owner Doña Tules was playing a game of monte when a disgruntled man to whom she refused to extend credit fired a gun at her but missed. In 1867 attorney William Rynerson argued with, shot, and killed John Slough, chief justice of the Territorial Supreme Court, in the hotel lobby. And Archbishop Lamy's nephew murdered a romantic rival outside the building in 1879.

The new La Fonda opened in 1922, based on architect Isaac Hamilton Rapp's design, a style known as Spanish-Pueblo Revival that included terraced floors with vigas (wooden roof beams), a faux adobe exterior coated in stucco, and an entrance resembling a Spanish mission church. The hotel is a stunning work of architecture and a Southwestern artistic fantasy. It operated for just two years before going bankrupt. The Santa Fe Railway acquired La Fonda in 1925, then leased it to the Fred Harvey company. And this is what drew Cather and Lewis to stay there in 1925 and 1926, since they often frequented Harvey hotels during their travels. Historian Paul Horgan noted wryly, "Rather like a major power acquiring a colony, the Harvey Company entered Santa Fe to operate La Fonda in a sort of benevolent despotism as the social center of the capital."[2]

In 1925 La Fonda was much smaller than it is today: It now occupies an entire city block, including a well-disguised parking garage with an attractive events space built above it. At the time of Cather and Lewis's visit, the hotel mostly occupied the northwestern corner of the block opposite the Plaza along East San Francisco Street and Old Santa Fe Trail (Shelby Street back then). The hotel advertised itself as "The Inn at the End of the Trail," which was literally true.

While in Santa Fe, Cather and Lewis met up with the writer Mary Austin and her niece, who accompanied them on a day trip to Pecos. Austin and Cather knew each other from New York, and Austin had moved to Santa Fe the year before. Austin had an imperious personality; Cather described her as one who "settles all questions of human conduct and natural history with a word," suggesting someone who does not suffer fools.[3]

Mabel Dodge Luhan, the self-appointed doyen of the art colony in Taos, heard that Cather would be visiting New Mexico and had written her that spring, requesting that she visit Taos. Cather and Luhan were

Figure 15. La Fonda on the Plaza opened in 1922 and soon became the bustling center of downtown Santa Fe. Cather and Lewis stayed there in 1925 and 1926 and the hotel was crucial for *Archbishop's* inspiration. La Fonda Photo Archives.

acquainted with each other from New York City, as both lived in Greenwich Village. Luhan was writing a memoir and sought the Pulitzer-winning author's help. Cather wrote back shortly before she departed New York, "I hardly think my friend [Edith] and I will get to Taos at all, but if there is any chance of our doing so, I'll signal you and ask whether you have a house for us."[4] When Luhan persisted in inviting Cather to Taos, Cather remained evasive: "We'll be at the San Gabriel Ranch near Espanola while I read the proofs of my new book, then will go to the country about Albuquerque. I expect to go to Taos, but we won't be in any one place long enough to take a home."[5]

Cather wrote Elsie Sergeant on June 23 that they were leaving for the San Gabriel Ranch in Alcalde the next day, which would be their home for six days.[6] Carol Bishop Stanley and Roy Pfäffle ran the high-end dude ranch, and there Cather and Lewis reviewed page proofs of *The Professor's House*, rode horses, and played cowboy. Cather later wrote about her time at the ranch, "I have a regular Zane Gray mind; roughneck and low-brow is [the] name for me" (Zane Gray was a popular author of Western fiction).[7]

The Pfäffles offer a fascinating detour into overlapping dude ranch history. Roy was the first manager of the Bishop's Lodge Company (formerly Archbishop Lamy's country retreat near Santa Fe) in 1918, and two years later he and his wife Carol acquired the land that became San Gabriel Ranch. He won the deed to El Rancho de los Brujos (The Witches Ranch) near Abiquiú in a poker game in 1928. His wife recorded the deed in her name and moved there two years later after divorcing her husband, renaming it Ghost Ranch. She turned it into an exclusive dude ranch similar to San Gabriel, but then sold it to Arthur and Phoebe Pack in 1935. The Packs in turn peeled off seven acres for painter Georgia O'Keeffe in 1940.

When Cather and Lewis arrived by train at the San Gabriel Ranch, they discovered that Mabel Dodge Luhan had dropped by earlier that day to secure Cather's visit to Taos. Cather finally relented, writing Luhan on June 26, "While my advice about your manuscript might (possibly) be worth my board and keep, I doubt whether I could stretch my wisdom far enough to cover the keep of two people," meaning her and Lewis. "We would not have more than two weeks, at most, to spend in Taos." She added self-deprecatingly, "I'm sure I don't know why you thought you wanted us—I don't believe we are either of us very exciting visitors."[8]

On June 28, Cather composed a brief note to Paul Revere Reynolds, telling him to forward her mail to La Fonda and adding, "I'm having a glorious trip." Two days later, Mabel Dodge Luhan and her husband Tony Lujan picked up Cather and Lewis at the San Gabriel Ranch and drove them to Taos for an eighteen-day stay.[9]

Cather was not particularly enthusiastic about visiting Taos, but Luhan was persistent and eventually prevailed. This was ultimately to the benefit of generations of readers of *Death Comes for the Archbishop*, as the Taos excursion enlightened the path that Cather would take with her novel. Without the 1925 trip to Taos, there would be no *Archbishop.*

Mabel Dodge Luhan: The Art Doyen of Taos

Taos is located seventy miles north of Santa Fe. Travelers coming from Santa Fe can choose one of two routes today: the more direct route

Taos Pueblo
Arroyo Hondo
Arroyo Seco
El Salto del Agua cave
Paseo del Pueblo Norte
Camino de la Placita
Mabel Dodge Luhan House
Kit Carson Park
Morada Lane
Bent St
Our Lady of Guadalupe Parish
Kit Carson Home
PLAZA
Columbian Hotel
Kit Carson Rd
Ledoux St
Martínez Hacienda
Paseo del Pueblo Sur
Willa Cather's Taos
San Francisco de Asís Church

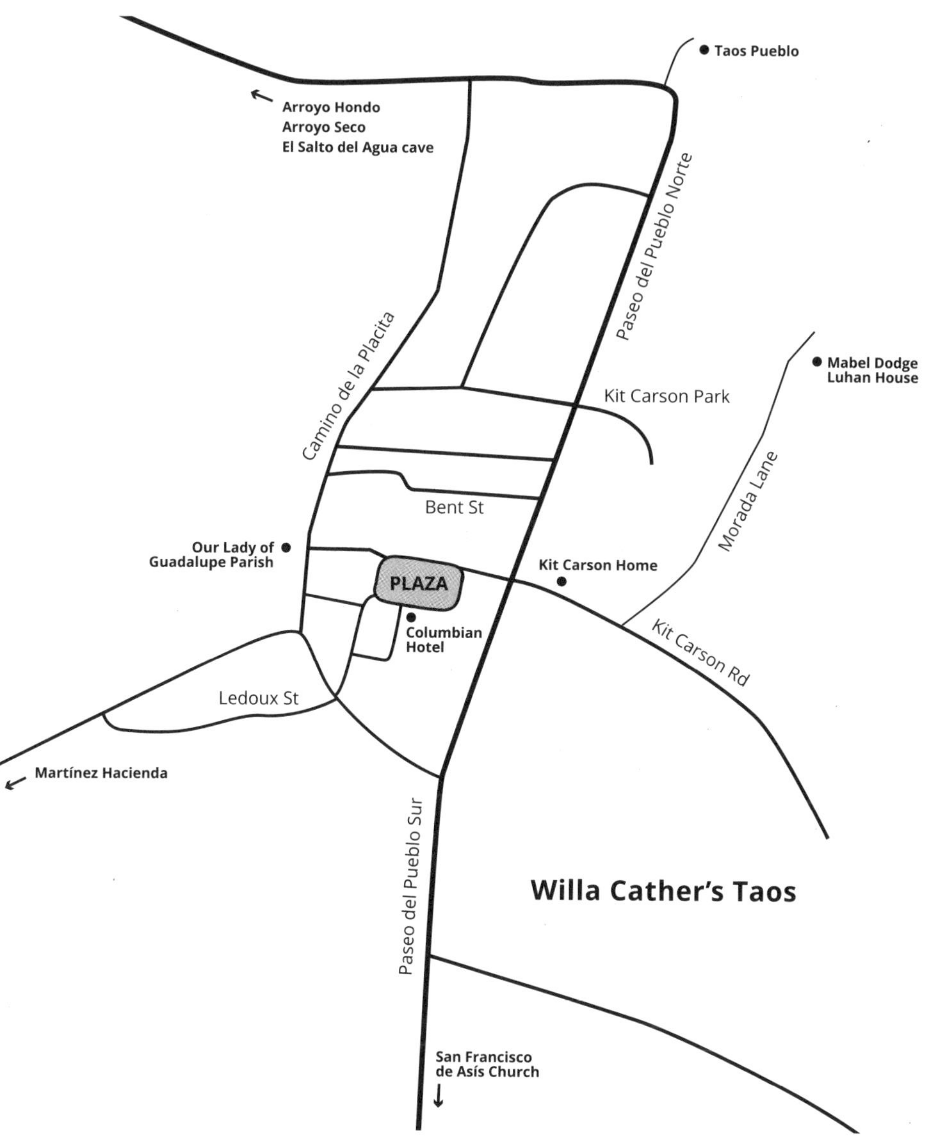

Map 2. Taos.

parallel to the Rio Grande (which Tony Lujan would have driven as he returned to Taos with his wife, Cather, and Lewis) and the High Road to Taos. It is a beautiful drive, passing through the pilgrimage town of Chimayó before ascending the Sangre de Cristo Mountains, leaving the desert highlands behind and entering a thick forest of Ponderosa pines, fir trees, and Hispanic farming villages like Peñasco, Trampas, and Truchas with their ancient adobe churches. Snow-capped peaks tower overhead. Driving through the Sangre de Cristos, you forget that you are in the high desert and can imagine yourself in Switzerland.

Taos is an oasis in the high desert mountains, residing in a D-shaped bowl with the Sangre de Cristos encircling it on three sides, and with the deep Rio Grande gorge slicing through the plain to the west. One geographic feature stands out above all: the massive Pueblo Peak, the sacred mountain of Taos Pueblo. Mountain runoff feeds streams across the valley, and Spanish settlers used irrigation to extend farming deeper into the valley. It was this excellent source of water, in addition to the hunting grounds in the mountains and the trading routes, that made Taos Pueblo a crossroads for many cultures. Canadian fur trappers and American merchants moved into the valley in the 1820s, adding to what was one of the most diverse settlements in New Mexico.

Taos Pueblo is one of the oldest continuously inhabited structures in North America. The Red Willow People, as they call themselves, have lived there since the 1300s. From a distance the pueblo can look like a large, five-story apartment complex, but up close you realize it is two large adobe structures separated by the Rio Pueblo. Unsurprisingly, Taos Pueblo is a UNESCO World Heritage Site.

Well into the twentieth century, there was no such town as Taos (it was incorporated in 1934). Rather, Spanish settlers had established numerous farming and ranch settlements along the outer ring of the bowl-shaped valley near where streams come rushing out of the mountains. Three miles south of Taos Pueblo was Don Fernando de Taos, sometimes referred to as Fernandez, but today simply known as Taos. It is a classic Spanish village with a plaza at the center and a Guadalupe church. A few miles to the south is Ranchos de Taos, known for its famed San Francisco de Asís Church with its curved adobe buttresses, quite possibly the

Figure 16. An expansive early twentieth-century view of the North House at Taos Pueblo, showing the *horno* ovens in the right-center, and the Rio Pueblo or Red Willow River to the right. Beyond the pueblo is Pueblo Peak. Prints & Photographs Division, Library of Congress.

Figure 17. The oft-photographed San Francisco de Asís Church in Ranchos de Taos, probably the most famous church in New Mexico. Cather visited the church in 1925 and set a mass there in *Archbishop*. Photograph by Garrett Peck, with permission of the Archdiocese of Santa Fe.

best-known church in New Mexico thanks to artists like Ansel Adams and Georgia O'Keeffe. Other villages sprouted up to the north like Arroyo Seco and Arroyo Hondo.

During her travels to New Mexico, Cather spent more time in Taos than in Santa Fe. She and Lewis first visited the town in 1915. Their 1916 trip to New Mexico was devoted to Taos: the two stayed at the adobe Columbia Hotel for three weeks. On their return trip in 1925, Cather and Lewis stayed for eighteen days in the Pink House at Mabel Dodge Luhan's Los Gallos estate. This was a separate guest house apart from the larger house. D. H. and Frieda Lawrence stayed in the Pink House in 1922, and Georgia O'Keeffe stayed there on her first visit to the Southwest in 1929.

Taos is much smaller than Santa Fe, but it was once *the* arts center of New Mexico, thanks in part to Mabel Dodge Luhan. Born in Buffalo, New York, in a repressed Victorian household, Mabel was the

Figure 18. The Mabel Dodge Luhan House in Taos, now an inn and conference center. Cather and Lewis stayed in the Pink House, a separate guesthouse, for eighteen days in 1925. Photograph by Garrett Peck.

self-appointed patron of the local Taos arts colony, a wealthy heiress with a small family fortune. D. H. Lawrence sarcastically referred to the scene as "Mabeltown." Her politics were radical leftist, and she hosted salons for the avant-garde in Florence and Greenwich Village while engaging in numerous affairs. She was a sexually liberated woman who was also deeply unhappy, but whose wealth supported a life of leisure.

Mabel moved to Taos in December 1917 on a whim. What began as a vacation soon became permanent. In her memoir, *Edge of Taos Desert*, she wrote that she simply needed a change. "I got it," she wrote. "My life broke in two right then, and I entered into the second half, a new world that replaced all the ways I had known with others, more strange and terrible and sweet than any I had ever been able to imagine." In this she inverted Cather's famous statement, "The world broke in two in 1922 or thereabouts." Clearly she had read Cather.[10]

The bright turquoise sky, the dry air, and the burning piñon that smells like incense have long made an impression on visitors to New Mexico. While serving as the territorial governor in 1879, Lew Wallace wrote his wife Susan, "I am well; how one can be anything else in this climate I do not know. The air is so clear and pure, the sunlight so delicious; no fear of cloudy to-morrows; when one dies away another as bright and as shining comes on. I wish you could fill your lungs with this sweet air."[11]

Mabel had a similar experience when she got off the train in Lamy in December 1917. She immediately noted the smell of incense, which turned out to be piñon wood burning. The scent is delicious and distinctly New Mexican.[12] It made an impression on Cather as well, who described "the smoke of burning piñon logs rose like incense to Heaven" in *Archbishop* (31).

Mabel was immediately enchanted by Taos. There was no electricity, the town was isolated and difficult to travel to, and the ancient Taos Pueblo was just a few miles to the north. This was exactly what she was looking for (she thought Santa Fe too crowded, touristy, and full of outsiders). That said, she found Taos insular with its small population. Some of the Mexicans were *Penitentes* (the Penitential Brotherhood) and one night she hid in the bushes so she could watch their late-night procession on an isolated hill outside of town.[13]

With World War I raging in Europe, Mabel believed that Western society was bankrupt, and she sought renewal in the desert Southwest. Mabel was part of a vanguard of counter culturists who came to northern New Mexico seeking a new way to live. Many of them were privileged—Mabel certainly was. They borrowed symbolically from Anglo, Hispanic, and Native cultures; however, they tended to side with Natives on cultural fault lines, drawing resentment from Hispanics, a trend that continues to this day.

Luhan attracted a long list of artists who idealized Natives while ignoring the poverty, tension, and classism in Taos. Lois Palken Rudnick, Mabel's biographer, noted:

> The New Mexican landscape provided the traditional western myth a new guise. Instead of the lone cowboy going off into the wilderness to prove himself a man by wielding his gun and pitting himself against an unforgiving land on the fringe of civilization, artists pitted their paintbrushes, pens, and cameras against a landscape so overwhelming in its grandeur that it could have easily eclipsed person vision and individual creativity. At the same time, the land beckoned them with the promise that their egos would find a connection to something larger than themselves.[14]

Gossip was a popular pastime in this Mexican village, and Mabel gave people reason to indulge in it. In 1918 she began an affair with Tony Lujan of Taos Pueblo. Tony was unhappily married and childless. Mabel was likewise married, to her third husband, artist Maurice Sterne. After both divorced their spouses, Mabel married Tony in 1923 and agreed to pay Tony's former wife a thirty-five-dollar monthly stipend. Mabel took Tony's last name, although she anglicized it as "Luhan." The marriage created problems at the pueblo, as tribal law forbade marriage with outsiders, and Tony was banned from religious ceremonies, though he remained on the tribal council.

Mabel and Tony had different perspectives—she was a society doyen, while he had little formal education and spoke broken English—but she found a soulmate in his calm and quiet presence. "The thing I discovered quite soon was that the hours took care of each other, and if one lived wholly and well at present the future could truly be left to itself," she wrote. Tony seldom spoke but loved to sing, and he was skilled in both construction and farming. He chauffeured Mabel's guests around Taos.[15]

Unfortunately, Tony infected his wife with syphilis soon after they were married. Syphilis was all too common before penicillin was invented in the World War II era. Three of Mabel's four husbands were infected with the highly contagious disease. There was an outbreak in Taos Pueblo at the time, and Tony had caught it by having sex with the wife of a friend, and then he in turn infected Mabel. They underwent treatment with Salvarsan for years. The couple never had sex again, though they remained together. Theirs was not the perfect marriage that Mabel had hoped would bridge two worlds. They both drank too much, she was prone to depression, while Tony indulged in numerous infidelities.[16]

Still, Mabel found some solace in Taos, being impressed by Taos Pueblo's communitarian ways and thinking them a model for how American society should be. She came to believe that the Natives would save Western civilization and she viewed her marriage as a bridge between Anglo and Indigenous cultures. "It will be the duty of a new interracial Adam and Eve—Tony and Mabel—to bring that light to the Western world," wrote Lois Palken Rudnick. Mabel brought British novelist D. H. Lawrence to Taos in 1922 with the hope that he would write about the pueblo and spread the gospel of Indigenous communitarianism, but Lawrence was not that impressed.[17]

Mabel was capricious, jealous, and prone to meddling in people's lives. She was eccentric, imperious, and could suffocate people with her intensity. Leftist journalist Hutchins Hapgood, who admired Mabel, was well acquainted with her flaws: "Her eager, sometimes graceless searchings, her terrific but formless needs, her occasional sharp unkindness, her extraordinary and otherwise incomprehensible jealousy, her inability to let go of anything even for a moment within her domain: all this seems often ugly and reprehensible. But to me it is not so at all." He recognized in Mabel a fellow traveler who strove for the eternal.[18]

Radical political activist and writer Max Eastman portrayed Mabel as the fictional Mary Kittredge in his 1927 book, *Venture*: "She waged a

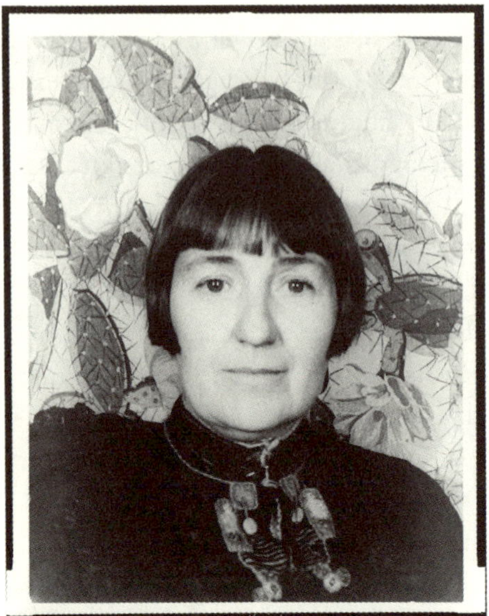

Figure 19. A 1934 portrait of Mabel Dodge Luhan, a wealthy arts patron, center of the Taos art colony, and friend of Willa Cather. Prints & Photographs Division, Library of Congress.

Figure 20. Tony Lujan of Taos Pueblo married Mabel Dodge Sterne in 1923 and was the model for Eusabio in *Death Comes for the Archbishop*. Palace of the Governors Photo Archive (NMHM/DCA), Image 099879.

perpetual war on habit, a war in which she had already routed and driven from the field three husbands, nine lovers, and a half-dozen religions, although she was only thirty-five years old, and as she possessed an enormous fortune, and by right of heredity a certain 'position' in American society, her career and character were well known. She was a public institution."[19]

Mabel helped make Taos a national destination for artists who stayed in one of her five guest houses. As already mentioned, her visitors included D. H. Lawrence, about whom she later published the book *Lorenzo in Taos*. Other guests included authors Aldous Huxley and Carl Van Vechten, painters Mary Hubbard Foote, Marsden Hartley, John Marin, and Georgia O'Keeffe, photographer Ansel Adams, playwright Thornton Wilder, poets Witter Bynner and Robinson Jeffers—and of course Willa Cather and Edith Lewis. Mabel collected people like some people collect art.

Mabel was not homophobic, having had same-sex experiences earlier in her life. She lured her personal secretary, Walter Willard "Spud" Johnson, away from his employer (and lover), Witter Bynner in Santa Fe. Bynner got even by penning a satirical play in 1926 called *Cake: An Indulgence*, which hilariously skewered Mabel. Mabel undoubtedly knew Cather and Lewis were lesbians and undoubtedly approved.

Author Lesley Poling-Kempes wrote that the American West was "where an unmarried woman was able to move about and work relatively free of public scrutiny or societal disapproval." Many middle- and upper-class white East Coast women lived proscribed lives during the late Victorian era, expected to marry and bear children, not earn money or pursue a career. Like so many other women who came to the Southwest, such as Mabel Dodge Luhan, Carol Bishop Stanley, and Georgia O'Keeffe, Cather was not only able to pursue a writing career but lived the life she chose for herself.[20]

Mabel resided in Taos until her death in 1962. Her advocacy for communitarianism influenced the creation of numerous communes around the Taos valley in the 1960s, and actor Dennis Hopper acquired her home during the *Easy Rider* era. Most of the communes closed by the 1970s. Communal living is difficult for most Americans, as we are far too individualistic and seldom willing to yield our personal benefit, property, and wealth for the greater good. Still, even today, Taos has more of a countercultural feel than Santa Fe.

Tony Lujan

Cather met many Native Americans during her travels to the Southwest, and she got to know one in particular: Tony Lujan. Tony was a quiet but influential tribal member. He allied with John Collier, a white advocate for Indigenous rights, to rally the All Indian Pueblo Council to help defeat the 1922 Bursum Bill in Congress that would have stripped the Pueblo Indians of their heritage and land in a misguided quest to assimilate them. Collier would eventually lead the Bureau of Indian Affairs under the Franklin Roosevelt administration.

While Cather and Lewis stayed in Taos, Tony served as their chauffeur. Mabel typically did not join them on these excursions. Lewis later described their time with him in her memoir:

> Willa Cather was very much impressed by Tony Luhan, and felt an instant liking and admiration for him. He was a splendid figure, over six feet tall, with a noble head and dignified carriage; there was a great simplicity and kindness in his voice and manner. . . . Tony would sit in the driver's seat, in his silver bracelets and purple blanket, often singing softly to himself; while we sat behind. He took us to some of the almost inaccessible Mexican villages hidden in the Cimmaron [*sic*] mountains, where the Penitentes still followed their old fierce customs; and from Tony, Willa Cather learned many things about the country and the people that she could not have learned otherwise. He talked very little, but what he said was always illuminating and curiously poetic.[21]

Lewis recognized Tony as the model for the Navajo Eusabio in *Archbishop*.[22] Cather described the fictional Eusabio as "extremely tall, even for a Navajo, with a face like a Roman general's of Republican times. He always dressed very elegantly in velvet and buckskin rich with bead and

Figure 21. Willa Cather on horseback near Taos in 1925, wearing the same adventure outfit she wore ten years earlier at Mesa Verde. She pasted this photo and a nearly identical one of Edith Lewis into her personal copy of *Death Comes for the Archbishop*. Robert and Doris Kurth Cather Collection, Archives & Special Collections, University of Nebraska–Lincoln Libraries.

quill embroidery, belted with silver, and wore a blanket of the finest design. His arms, under the loose sleeves of his shirt, were covered with silver bracelets" (219–20). We see again Cather comparing the stately Navajo to a character from European antiquity, which again underscores Cather's Western perspective.

Cather was quite taken with Tony. When asked why Mabel married the Indian, Cather responded, "How could she help it?"[23] Lois Palken Rudnick noted that strong women such as Mary Austin, Willa Cather, and Georgia O'Keeffe admired Tony because he "offered Anglo women who sought success in male-dominated domains an alternative vision of maleness."[24]

The Blue Jay Notebook

Charles Cather, Willa's nephew, became the second executor of Cather's literary estate after Edith Lewis died. He in turn passed away in 2011, and his estate donated considerable Cather memorabilia (much of which he inherited from Lewis) to the University of Nebraska–Lincoln archive.

One of the most significant objects for our story is a simple Blue Jay notebook, which Lewis purchased to record the 1925 trip to Taos.

Both Cather and Lewis wrote in the notebook, the pages of which show how both women contributed to the novel that became *Death Comes for the Archbishop*. As a primary source, it is a gold mine, as it captured the first ideas that ended up in the book. This included Kit Carson, Padre Antonio José Martínez, the Taos Revolt, El Salto del Agua cave, the Navajo roundup, biographical facts about Lamy and Martínez, a draft story about Manuel Chávez, and even one of the mules (Contento). We'll cover more about Manuel Chávez in chapter 10, "The Cathedral and the Quarry." Reading the Blue Jay notebook is like witnessing the novel's genesis, as you see the creative ideas percolating in its pages.[25]

Few letters have emerged from Cather and Lewis's eighteen-day stay in Taos, but the Blue Jay notebook provides a glimpse into what they explored and who they met. Lewis filled out their itinerary on the first

Figure 22. Edith Lewis's Blue Jay notebook, which she and Cather wrote in to record thoughts from their eighteen days in Taos in July 1925. Charles E. Cather Collection, Archives & Special Collections, University of Nebraska–Lincoln Libraries.

three pages. We learn details about the things the two women did: They often went horseback riding, took numerous cross-country driving trips with Tony Lujan, soaked in Manby Hot Springs not once but twice, visited Taos Pueblo, and explored the ceremonial cave that made an appearance in *Archbishop*.

Thanks to the Blue Jay notebook, we know that Cather and Lewis visited D. H. and Frieda Lawrence on July 6 at their mountain ranch that Mabel had given Frieda in exchange for Lawrence's manuscript of *Sons and Lovers*. They had met in New York the year before and promised to visit. "He and Frieda Lawrence were living very simply and even roughly; they baked their own bread, milked their own cow—Lawrence, I remember, had just been off hunting the cow over a four-square mile pasture," Lewis recalled.[26] Lawrence died of tuberculosis in France in 1930, and his cremated remains were returned to New Mexico. Cather wrote of Lawrence, "He was unquestionably the most gifted writer of his generation, but he let his hates and prejudices run away with him."[27]

The Blue Jay notebook "reveals how inextricably Cather and Lewis's travels in the Southwest intertwined with Cather's creative process," Melissa Homestead observed. "The Archbishop is nestled deeply in the middle of a shared, collaborative travel experience." The proof is in Lewis's copy of *Archbishop*, in which Cather inscribed, "To Edith Lewis, Who discovered the Archbishop with me."[28]

Moments of Inspiration

After eighteen days in Taos, Cather and Lewis said farewell to the Lujans. They returned to Santa Fe by train on July 18, where they stayed four nights at La Fonda. Three weeks of mail forwarded to the hotel caught up with the author. The next day, Cather and Lewis went horseback riding in the Sangre de Cristo Mountains.[29]

Two days after leaving Taos, both Cather and Lewis composed thank you letters to Mabel. Cather's head was buzzing with ideas after learning about Kit Carson, Padre Antonio José Martínez, and the Taos Revolt. "I'm still hard on the trail of my old priests," she wrote. "I found a lot of interesting things this morning which I'll tell you some day."[30]

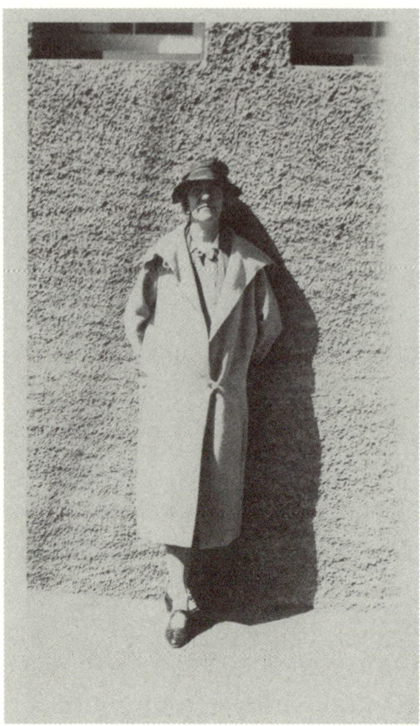

Figure 23. A photograph of Edith Lewis, Willa Cather's partner, in the Southwest in 1925 or 1926. Philip L. and Helen Cather Southwick Collection, Archives & Special Collections, University of Nebraska–Lincoln Libraries.

Lewis wrote, "Miss Cather is still pursuing Father Martinez through all the books in the Museum," referring to the Palace of the Governors, across the Plaza from their hotel. "Each new book tells a new story. We sit up late at night reading about priests. Tomorrow, we are driving to Chimayo, as you suggested, and the next day we go to Lamy," the railhead that would take them to Acoma Pueblo. As we'll explore in chapter 9, Martínez was the priest in Taos whom Bishop Lamy excommunicated.[31]

One of the books Cather came across was William Howlett's *The Life of the Right Reverend Joseph P. Machebeuf, D.D.* Howlett was a Catholic priest who had worked for the Denver bishop (Cather changed Machebeuf's name to Father Joseph Vaillant in *Archbishop*).[32] The book contained numerous letters from Machebeuf to his sister Marie Philomène about his missionary work in America, many of which touched on his work with Lamy, his dear friend. The siblings were both in the church's service, and he often appealed to her for material support in New Mexico

Figure 24. The Santuario de Chimayó is the most significant pilgrimage site in New Mexico, which Cather and Lewis visited in 1925. Photograph by Garrett Peck, with permission of the Archdiocese of Santa Fe.

and later Colorado. "Without these letters in Father Howlett's book to guide me, I would certainly never have dared to write my book," Cather wrote in *Commonweal* in 1927. "Of course, many of the incidents I used were experiences of my own, but in these letters I learned how experiences very similar to them affected Father Machebeuf and Father Lamy."[33]

Edith Lewis noted in her memoir that, from the moment Cather purchased Howlett's book, "it completely took possession of her." She and Edith devoured that and other books during their evenings at La Fonda.[34]

For weeks, ideas about missionary priests in the Southwest percolated in Cather's head. Her copy of the *Life of the Right Reverend Joseph P. Machebeuf* further inspired her creativity. And then one day she hiked up to the Cross of the Martyrs to watch the sunset, and there

Figure 25. Willa Cather and Edith Lewis purchased books at the Palace of the Governors, then known as the Museum of New Mexico, while they stayed at La Fonda in July 1925. A key purchase was William Howlett's *The Life of the Right Reverend Joseph P. Machebeuf*, the first Denver bishop who inspired the Vaillant character in Archbishop. Today the museum houses the daily Native American Artisans Program, the first place that visitors should shop for Indigenous art and jewelry. Photograph by Garrett Peck.

experienced a moment of inspiration that led her to write *Death Comes for the Archbishop.*

> I shall always remember the late afternoon when I was sitting in a very gravelly, uncomfortable spot up by the Martyr's Cross, east of Santa Fé, watching the Sangre de Cristo Mountains color with the sunset. I suddenly, without any questioning, said to myself:
>
> "The real story of the early Southwest is the story of the missionary priests. They all came from France, and came here with a background: cultivated minds and a large vision—and a noble purpose."
>
> From that evening on I began to find out what I could about those missionary priests—and everything I found out about them made me admire them the more.[35]

I might offer a mild criticism of Cather's statement. There was much more to the early Southwest than the French missionary priests, who served during the American Territorial period. Cather overlooked the fact that the Spanish Franciscans arrived hundreds of years before the French and Americans, and the Pueblo Indians had lived there for millennia. But then again, it was Cather's novel, and she had the right to pick the hero for her story.

Cather recalled in a 1931 interview with the *San Francisco Chronicle* how the novel came together while staying at La Fonda.

> But, do you know, I had no idea of writing about those pioneer priests in the Southwest until one night I was reading the letters that Father Macheboeuf wrote to his sister.
>
> Then, before morning, the story was in my mind. The way of it was on the white wall of that hotel room in Santa Fe, as if it were all in order and color there, projected by a sort of magic lantern.[36]

Figure 26. "I shall always remember the late afternoon when I was sitting in a very gravelly, uncomfortable spot up by the Martyr's Cross, east of Santa Fé, watching the Sangre de Cristo Mountains color with the sunset," Cather wrote. The Cross of the Martyrs was erected in 1920, a site that helped inspire *Death Comes for the Archbishop*. Photograph by Garrett Peck.

Figure 27. Santa Fe actually has two Cross of the Martyrs: one from 1920, the other from 1977. The 1970s cross is just east of downtown and is much more accessible to the public. Photograph by Garrett Peck.

Edith Lewis echoed Cather: "There, in a single evening, as she often said, the idea of *Death Comes for the Archbishop* came to her, essentially as she afterwards wrote it."[37]

We can follow Cather's thought process in developing her characters. Because she had spent eighteen days in Taos, she learned of Padre Martínez's historic association with the town. Cather's curiosity to write about frontier priests started with him, and not with Lamy or Machebeuf. The first mention of Martínez was in the Blue Jay notebook and in Lewis's handwriting. In other words, in the epic question about the chicken or the egg, Martínez came first, followed by Machebeuf, and finally Lamy. Given that Cather was a Francophile, it's no stretch to see why she aligned with the French priests.

In his letters, Machebeuf portrayed himself heroically, no doubt to burnish his reputation as a pioneering missionary priest in a hostile land. He embellished numerous accounts, for example his confrontation with

Padre José Manuel Gallegos, and glossed over areas where he didn't look so good, such as his breaking confession, or the fact that he was constantly asking people for money, which annoyed parishioners and other priests. In short, Howland's biography was a crucial source for Cather's novel, but she never examined it critically.

Cather and Lewis's Reading List

Willa Cather and Edith Lewis accessed a wide range of historical works as they researched the story that became *Death Comes for the Archbishop*. Reading Lewis's July 20, 1925, letter to Mabel Dodge Luhan ("Miss Cather is still pursuing Father Martinez through all the books in the Museum"), I keyed in on the word "books"—*plural*. What books might have been available at the New Mexico History Museum in 1925? I reached out to Heather McClure at the Fray Angélico Chávez Library in Santa Fe. She retrieved a short list of histories that the museum acquired prior to 1925. They included William Howlett's *Life of the Right Reverend Joseph P. Machebeuf* (1908) and Jean-Baptiste Salpointe's *Soldiers of the Cross* (1898). We know that Cather and Lewis perused Howlett's book—Cather mentioned it numerous times in interviews and letters. In addition, Lewis copied Spanish quotes directly from Salpointe's book into her Blue Jay notebook, providing evidence that they read that book too.[38]

A thorough reading of both Howlett's and Salpointe's books reveals that Cather relied heavily on both sources. Howlett focused his biography on Machebeuf, while Salpointe's book had far more detail about Lamy, including the details of his country estate, Villa Pintoresca (now Bishop's Lodge), and how he died. It was probably as important a source for Cather as Howlett's work. However, she never mentioned the book in subsequent interviews or letters.

Cather's research didn't stop there. She relied on many other books as she delved into the backstory that would become her *Archbishop*. In 1962 Edward and Lilian Bloom identified additional sources that Cather used: James DeFouri's *Historical Sketch of the Catholic Church in New Mexico*, Ralph Emerson Twitchell's *Leading Facts of New Mexican History*, *The*

Catholic Encyclopedia, and numerous books about the Southwest by Charles F. Lummis, including *Some Strange Corners of Our Country*; *Mesa, Cañon and Pueblo*, to which I would add *The Land of Poco Tiempo*. Other sources Cather tapped into included Hubert Howe Bancroft's *History of Arizona and New Mexico*, Adolph Bandelier's *The Gilded Man*, George Parker Winship's *The Journey of Coronado, 1540–1542*, and Francisco Palóu's *Life and Apostolic Labors of the Venerable Junípero Serra*.[39]

John Murphy, one of the editors of the scholarly edition of *Death Comes for the Archbishop*, added to the list George Anderson's *History of New Mexico: Its Resources and People*, which informed Cather's views of padres Martínez and Lucero. Murphy added John Gunn's *Schat-Chen: History, Traditions, and Narratives of the Queres Indians of Laguna and Acoma* and George James's *New Mexico: The Land of the Delight Makers*.[40]

Thanks to the publication of Cather's letters, we find that she tapped into Horatio Ladd's *The Story of New Mexico* (1891), which provided a general history of the territory.[41] She asked her librarian friend Louise Guerber to compile a list of books on Kit Carson—and Guerber responded with a list of seven books and four magazine articles. We can never know which of these articles or books Cather chose to investigate; however, she did place checkmarks next to three of the book titles.[42]

To this list I would add one more source: Ralph Emerson Twitchell's *The History of the Military Occupation of the Territory of New Mexico*. Twitchell was a prominent New Mexican historian of the early twentieth century. In his 1909 book about the American occupation, Twitchell drafted significant biographical sketches of major figures, including Diego Archuleta and Manuel Cháves, both of whom appear in the "Party at Oteros" story in the Blue Jay notebook. Cather's details about Cháves neatly align with Twitchell's essay on the man.[43]

"*Death Comes for the Archbishop* is more than any other Cather narrative a product of research, the fusion of an astounding array of sources that would be disparate if not combined within its text," John Murphy concluded. Many of the episodes Cather wrote in her novel were not based on her imagination, but rather emerged from her detailed research of actual events and people, though she sometimes changed names and even the timeline and relied upon histories largely written by white men that rarely included Hispanic or Indigenous perspectives.[44]

Cather and Lewis departed Santa Fe on July 22 to visit Acoma Pueblo, an ancient site that would inspire an entire chapter in *Archbishop*. It was monsoon season, the summertime thunderstorms that provide the bulk of the Southwest's rain, and the women got stuck in Lamy for three days from a washout near Trinidad, Colorado. They stayed at the Fred Harvey hotel El Ortiz and had plenty of time to explore the area, including the Lamy quarry that provided the ochre-colored sandstone for the St. Francis Cathedral, whose construction Cather covered in chapter 8 of *Archbishop*.

Once the train tracks reopened, Cather and Lewis traveled to Laguna Pueblo, some twenty miles from Acoma, which was only reachable by wagon. Days of monsoon rains made the roads impassable, and they had to stay in Laguna at a filthy hotel for three extra days, a time that gave Cather time to think quietly with little distraction and helped her further develop the story. "There was a cloud-burst every afternoon," she wrote Mabel Dodge Luhan, "But we met very interesting people and didn't mind the delay a bit."[45]

When the rain finally stopped, they hired a Laguna man named Walter Saracino to transport them through the muddy roads to Acoma. "As we passed the Mesa Encantada (the Enchanted Bluff) we stopped for a long time to look up at it," Lewis remembered. "A great cloud-mesa hung over it. It looked lonely and mysterious and remote, as if were far distant in time—and thousands of years away." Cather finally saw the mesa that she had written about in 1909. Lewis provided no description of Acoma Pueblo, noting only that Cather's description in *Archbishop* was accurate.[46]

After Acoma, Cather and Lewis traveled to Denver on July 31 to meet Cather's mother, who was staying at the Olin Hotel. Lewis returned by train to New York three days later, as she had to return to work, while Cather's brother Roscoe and his family joined them from Wyoming. Cather wrote Mabel Dodge Luhan, "My weeks with you in Taos stand out as the fine reality of the summer."[47]

Cather frequented the Denver Public Library as she continued pursuing her story of the New Mexican priests, a gossipy fact reported in

Figure 28. A portrait of Willa Cather taken in Denver, probably in 1925, while researching *Death Comes for the Archbishop*. PHO-4-W689-1128, WCPM Collection, Willa Cather Foundation Collections & Archives at the National Willa Cather Center in Red Cloud, Nebraska

Bookman.[48] She befriended a young assistant librarian, Louise Guerber, and took her to tea. A few days later, Cather invited Guerber to join her family for dinner. The librarian wrote in her diary, "As for me if I had not already completely lost my mind, my heart, my soul to Willa S. Cather I made a thorough job of it that evening." Guerber continued, "She was just full of her new book and fathers Macheboeuf [*sic*] and Lamy and she told us a great deal about the Southwest, the mission churches and about the old days." Cather had acquired jewelry during her travels: "She showed us her ring: a 'turquoise set in silver', a square setting and a necklace of turquoise—very lovely."[49]

Cather was likewise quite fond of the young woman. She inscribed a copy of *The Professor's House* to Guerber (Guerber's "turquoise set in silver" was from the novel's frontispiece), and she would send the young librarian signed book copies for the rest of her life. Guerber signaled that she would be happy to help Cather's research, and the author obliged, writing from Red Cloud to ask about various dates when the railroad arrived in Santa Fe. She asked another favor of Guerber: "You may not know that in the Sovereign State of Nebraska it's illegal to sell cigarettes." As Cather was staying on longer in Red Cloud than expected, she asked Guerber to send her Lord Salisbury Cigarettes. "I enclose a dirty dollar for this low purpose." Guerber soon moved to New York City, where Cather helped get her settled. Guerber continued to help Cather's research from her new job at the Metropolitan Museum of Art.[50]

That fall, Cather returned to the Shattuck Inn in Jaffrey, New Hampshire, to write, as she had done since 1917. There, she drafted ideas for *Death Comes for the Archbishop.* According to Lewis, Cather composed the novel's introduction, the prologue "At Rome," in one day.[51]

Cather had found her story. The eighteen days in Taos had sparked ideas about the role of missionary priests in the Southwest, as had Howlett's biography of Machebeuf. These ideas percolated while Cather and Lewis stayed at La Fonda, leading to her moment of inspiration to write the novel. But Cather had not spent much time in Santa Fe and knew she would have to return to further research Archbishop Lamy, the subject of her book. She planned to return to the Southwest the following year.

CHAPTER 5

Indian Detour

"We are most comfortable here, but the Indian Detourists abound and the motor horn is the worm that dieth not. . . . Somehow, I'm awful glad to be back in this country."

—WILLA CATHER TO MABEL DODGE LUHAN, JUNE 5, 1926

WILLA CATHER WROTE HER brother Roscoe just after Christmas 1925, asking him, "Do you think you could bring your ladies," his wife and three daughters, "down to New Mexico in the car in June and run about for a couple weeks with me?" They planned a family reunion for the upcoming summer in Santa Fe, where they would all stay at La Fonda.[1]

On May 15, 1926, Cather and Lewis journeyed west for the book that was fourteen years in the making. This was Cather's sixth and final trip to the Southwest. She was fifty-two years old. It was a working vacation: Cather intended to spend much of the time researching the Santa Fe angle of her novel. Before she set out, she submitted a new, shorter introduction for *My Ántonia* to Houghton Mifflin. Alfred Knopf had printed the proofs for *My Mortal Enemy*, due out that fall, and Edith Lewis would have to return to New York early for her day-job as an advertising copywriter.[2]

Cather and Lewis first took the train to visit Willa's parents in Red Cloud for two days, as her father had requested her presence. From there they journeyed to Denver, then on to Lamy, where Cather penned Louise Guerber that they were venturing to Gallup, the gateway to the Navajo Nation. They planned to explore Canyon de Chelly by horse.[3]

Fresh off the train in Gallup and ensconced at El Navajo, a Fred Harvey hotel, Cather wrote Mabel Dodge Luhan. "Oh Mabel, we rode from Lamy to Gallup on the same train with Rin-Tin-Tin," the German shepherd rescued from a World War I battlefield and now a Hollywood star, "and had the pleasure of meeting him during the half-hour at Albuquerque. I never was so excited about any celebrity before!"[4]

The two women visited Zuni Pueblo on May 27, though they had to wait for Lewis to recover from a cold before they could venture to Canyon de Chelly.[5] "I'm feeling awfully fit, except that the sun on the sand and blazing sandstone rock simply burns my eyes out, and I'm staying indoors for a couple days to get over the inflammation," Cather complained to Blanche Knopf. "We've had blinding sand storms, also cloud bursts, all within four days."[6]

While waiting for Lewis to recover, Cather conducted some business. Before setting out on her Southwest trip, Cather had written Paul Revere Reynolds to explain her intentions for *Death Comes for the Archbishop*, as he wanted to sell the serial rights to a magazine. She noted that the book was well underway and had provided him a draft that he could use.

> It is concerned with the picturesque conditions of life in the Southwest, just at the time that New Mexico was taken over from Old Mexico, and with the experiences of two Catholic missionaries who were sent there to bring order out of the mixture of Indian and Spanish and Mexican superstitions. The real hero of the story is Father Latour (his real name was Lamy) the young Frenchman who was made Bishop of New Mexico at the age of 37, a man of an old and noble family in Puy de Dom, a man of wide culture, an idealist, and from his youth hungry for the world's frontiers. He was finally made an archbishop, and died in Santa Fe in 1886 [actually 1888]. In other words, he went there in the days of the buffalo and Indian massacres, and he lived to see the Santa Fe railroad across New Mexico.
>
> As I told you, I had the good fortune to come upon a great many letters written by the Bishop and his Vicar to their families in France, so that I have not had to depend upon my own invention for the

> reactions of these two French priests to the conditions they met there. Many of the incidents are invention, some of them are used almost literally as they happened, such as the chapter called "The White Mules."[7]

Reynolds offered the serial rights to *Archbishop* to several top magazines for fifteen thousand dollars, but they all declined. He slashed the price to three thousand and offered it to *Atlantic Monthly*. The magazine's editor, Ellery Sedgwick, was interested, though he disliked Reynolds. He bypassed the agent and wrote Cather directly. She wrote back from Gallup: "I never have felt much interest in the serialization of my books,—I've never cared a bit whether they were serialized or not. It's Mr. Reynolds who likes to serialize! And that matter is entirely up to him."[8]

With this lukewarm response, "Sedgwick then returned the manuscript to my father with a letter stating that 'in view of Miss Cather's attitude,' he would not buy it," according to Paul Revere Reynolds Jr. The agent instead sold the serial rights to *Forum*.[9]

Once Lewis had sufficiently recovered, the two women hired a driver, Frank Allen, to drive them to Canyon de Chelly. "He lost his way in the midst of a vast plain encircled by great mesas, and was several hours finding it again," Lewis wrote. "Then his car broke down, and for a while it looked as if we might have to spend the night there in the open." In 1935 Allen was driving Anna Ickes, wife of Secretary of the Interior Harold Ickes, from Taos to Santa Fe when his car overturned near Velarde, killing Ickes and injuring the other passengers.[10]

Canyon de Chelly is about one hundred miles north of Gallup, and the roads were difficult, so the two women likely stayed several nights in the canyon or in the nearby town of Chinle while they took guided horseback rides. The canyon is a cultural center point for the Navajo Nation, and many of their stories radiate from its steep sandstone walls. Cather and Lewis took several photographs, including of an Ancestral Pueblo cliff dwelling called White House. They doubtless heard stories of Kit Carson's siege of the Navajos in 1864, the Long Walk to the Bosque Redondo, and the humanitarian disaster that followed. Cather called Canyon de Chelly a "thrilling trip."[11]

Cather and Lewis returned to Gallup to reunite with the train, then

Figure 29. An iconic photo of the American West, taken by Edward Sherriff Curtis in 1904, shows Navajos riding through Canyon de Chelly in Arizona. Prints & Photographs Division, Library of Congress.

arrived in Santa Fe on June 4.[12] They checked in to La Fonda, the hotel where they had stayed the year before. This would be Cather's home for the next month as she researched her novel. From the hotel she could walk directly across the street to the St. Francis Cathedral and Lamy's statue. "Somehow, I'm awful glad to be back in this country," Cather penned Mabel Dodge Luhan.[13] She also wrote Paul Revere Reynolds and told him to forward her mail to La Fonda until July 1. She planned to travel to Taos on July 3 for a two-week visit with Luhan.[14]

The City Different

There are few American cities where the past is so relevant to the present

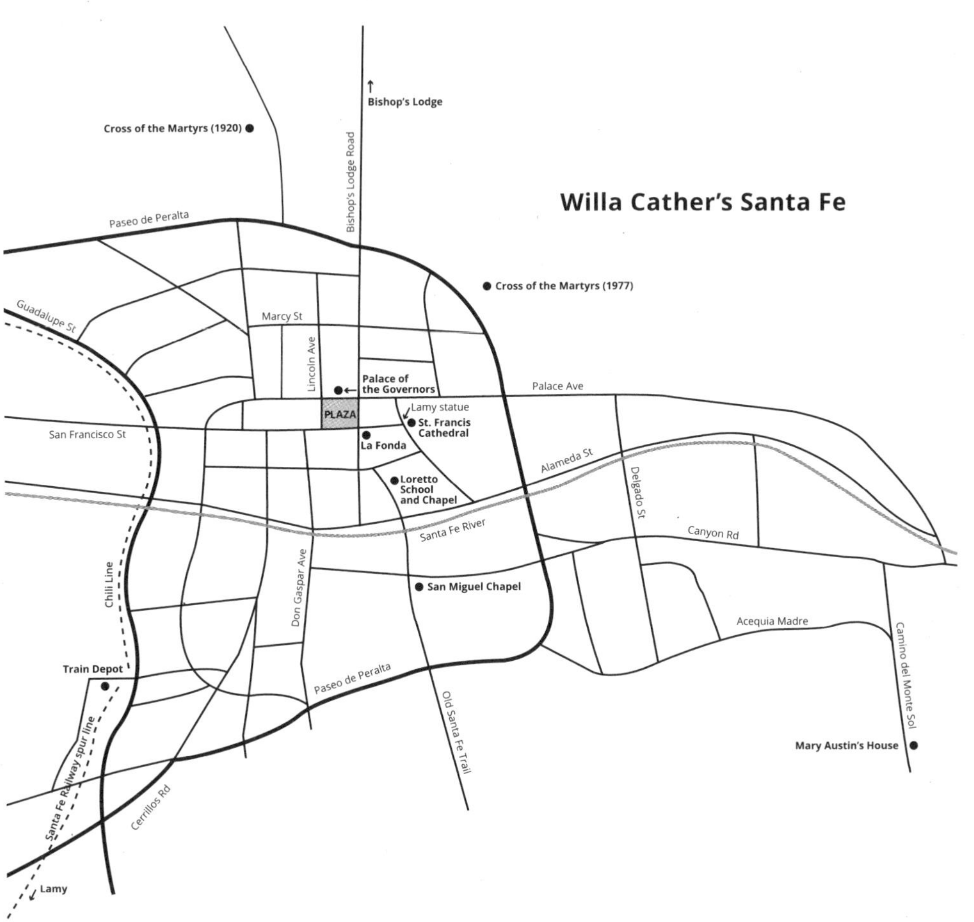

Map 3. Santa Fe.

as Santa Fe. It is the oldest state capital in the country, dating to 1610, and also sits at the highest elevation at seventy-one hundred feet, a quarter mile higher than Denver. The city is set in the piñon-juniper desert at the foot of the Sangre de Cristo Mountains. The elevation and forested landscape surprise visitors, who often expect something more like Phoenix and aren't prepared for our cold winters. We have neither saguaros nor sand dunes. Santa Fe is a mountain city.

American schools tend to teach a British-centric view of our colonial history, often forgetting that the Spanish colonized the Americas more than a century before the British. The Spanish conquered the Aztec Empire in 1521, the Inca Empire ten years later, sent an expedition under

Coronado to find the nonexistent Seven Cities of Gold in 1540, and established the colony known as the Kingdom of New Mexico in 1598. The Spanish relocated the capital to what is now Santa Fe twelve years later, attracted by a year-round water supply, the Santa Fe River. They named the settlement La Villa Real de la Santa Fé de San Francisco de Asís, or The Royal Town of the Holy Faith of St. Francis of Assisi. Santa Fe literally means Holy Faith.

The Santa Fe area has seen human habitation for thousands of years. Paleoindian hunters-gatherers first inhabited the area some three thousand years ago. Tesuque Pueblo ancestors lived there from around 1300 CE to the early 1400s, then migrated to their current location along the Rio Tesuque. In the Tewa language, the Pueblo people called their home O'gha Po'oge Owingeh, translated as White Shell Water Place for the limestone beds with fossilized bivalves dating back to three hundred million years ago when this land was under the ocean. The Spanish built their settlement atop the Ancestral Pueblo site that sprawled on both sides of the river.

When Cather and Lewis visited Santa Fe in 1925 and 1926, it had about seventy-five hundred residents, most of them Spanish American, as they called themselves at the time, and Spanish was still widely spoken. The city was compact and easy to walk around. At the center was the Plaza, the public gathering point, and the destination for trade caravans. American merchants had taken over the Plaza after the Santa Fe Trail opened in 1821 from Independence, Missouri. There were numerous hotels catering to lawmakers and visitors. The budding artist colony resided on the east side near Canyon Road, drawn there by inexpensive rents, and there were numerous small family farms in the area.

The city was slowly growing into the desert south of the Santa Fe River. Modest adobe bungalows were springing up near the state capitol, and a new neighborhood was emerging near the railroad depot. Santa Fe was a small-town capital of a poor state. Most of the roads were dirt, and many houses didn't have plumbing or running water yet. People cooked and heated their houses with firewood, which they purchased on Burro Alley, two blocks west of the Plaza. They burned piñon, which gave the city its distinct incense-like smell. And above, plentiful sunshine and the

Figure 30. A view of San Francisco Street in 1926 looking east toward the St. Francis Cathedral. The Plaza is the tree-covered expanse to the left, and La Fonda can be seen as the lighter structure on the right. Palace of the Governors Photo Archives (NMHM/DCA), Image 051869.

ever-present turquoise sky from the clean mountain air, high altitude, and low humidity.

Santa Fe is a deeply Catholic city. It wasn't uncommon in the early twentieth century to see nuns and priests walking about. The Catholic Church had a significant presence downtown. St. Francis Cathedral stands a block east of the Plaza, and just to the south were two Catholic parochial schools: Our Lady of Light Academy, the girls school known to most as the Loretto Academy, and St. Michael's College for boys.

The city also hosted two schools that worked to assimilate the Native population. The US Department of the Interior ran the Santa Fe Indian School, while the Catholic Church ran St. Catherine's Industrial Indian School. These were just two of forty-three such schools in New Mexico. Richard Henry Pratt, the man who founded the Carlisle Indian Industrial

Figure 31. Cars navigate the hairpin turns down La Bajada, the five-hundred-foot volcanic escarpment south of Santa Fe. Palace of the Governors Photo Archives (NMHM/DCA), Image 008225.

School, summarized the government's position in 1892: "Kill the Indian in him, and save the man." They almost succeeded—but not quite.

Travelers approaching Santa Fe by automobile from the south had to climb the steep volcanic escarpment known as La Bajada (the descent). Since colonial days, the Camino Real traversed the five-hundred-foot face through a series of twenty-three hairpin turns, making it a hair-raising adventure for any traveler. The US Army Corps of Engineers straightened part of the route in 1923 for automobiles and buses, and once Route 66 opened three years later, it traversed this road. Interstate 25 was later built several miles to the south, avoiding the switchbacks altogether.

Visitors coming by train reached Santa Fe by an eighteen-mile railroad spur line off the main trunk of the Atchison, Topeka, and Santa Fe Railway, which opened in 1880. Yet between 1880 and 1890, Santa Fe's population declined from 6,635 to 6,185 people. Albuquerque was attracting newcomers, while Santa Fe stagnated. The spur line hadn't jump-started commerce as hoped. The city needed something to market itself. It found the solution in tourism.

The Santa Fe Railway promoted New Mexico as the Land of Enchantment, a nickname that stuck. It was designed to sell passenger tickets and bring visitors to the territory. And as we have seen, the Fred Harvey company followed in its wake and built hotels and restaurants to support railroad-based tourists, such as Cather and Lewis.

Another major draw was the city's two tuberculosis sanitoriums. The bacterial infection wreaked havoc on people in humid climates such as on the East Coast and it was often a source of death. While today tuberculosis is treated with antibiotics, at the time of Cather's visits this remedy did not exist. Instead, people known as "lungers," including many artists, came to the Southwest for the dry air that would allow their lungs to heal.

From its founding, Santa Fe had a distinct look based on adobe architecture. The Spanish introduced adobe to the Southwest, but they acquired the technique from the Moors, who ruled Spain for nearly eight centuries. "Adobe" comes from the Arabic word *al-tüb* and is a prehistoric Mesopotamian method of mixing mud with sand and straw to create molded, unbaked bricks. Once assembled into a structure, adobe bricks are plastered over with mud for protection, which must be reapplied often, as the rains gradually wash it off. Maintaining adobe is labor-intensive. The advantage is that adobe houses keep cool in the summer and retain heat in the winter.

There is a surprising amount of Arabic and North African influence in New Mexico. The rule of the Moors—Muslim North Africans whose name came from the Roman province of Mauretania—added richly to Spanish culture and its vocabulary. The Moors introduced *acequias* (irrigation ditches) and adobe, along with silver smithing. We wouldn't have *alcohol* or *algebra* without Arabic science, nor the Spanish province of Andalusia (*Al-Andalus*) or the gorgeous Alhambra without the Moors, and Arabs named many of the stars we see at night, such as Alcor, Aldebaran, and Altair. If it weren't for the Arabic numbering system (1, 2, 3, 4, 5), we'd be stuck using Roman numerals. The term Our Lady of Guadalupe has Arabic origins: it comes from the North Africa Arabic *oued* or *wadi*, meaning dry river valley, and the Latin word for wolf, *lupus* (the River of the Wolf). The Spanish colonists in turn brought their Moorish-influenced culture to the Americas. The *naja*—an upside-down crescent often used by Navajo jewelers—originated with the Moors, which the Navajos in turn copied from the Spanish, who adorned their horses with the design.

Before the Spanish arrived, Ancestral Puebloans constructed their houses with stone, though they also used puddled mud and sometimes mud balls to build walls. The Pueblo Indians gradually converted their structures to adobe after the Spanish introduced the building material. At Taos Pueblo, you'll see that most of the buildings now are built of adobe bricks, as well as *hornos*, the Moorish beehive-shaped ovens that the Spanish introduced.

Santa Fe has mostly flat roofs because of pueblo buildings. The Pueblo people laid out a series of parallel logs known in Spanish as *vigas* as the foundation for the roof. They overlayed these with perpendicular juniper or willow branches called *latillas*. Above that they layered corn husks and other refuse, then plastered the top with mud to seal the roof. Voilà, a four-layered, flat roof.

Historic pueblos were constructed like a stacked-up apartment building without any doors or windows. They could be up to five stories tall. To enter the structure, you climbed a ladder to the roof, then descended another ladder through a hole in the ceiling into one of the houses. This was partly defensive: When an Apache, Comanche, Navajo, or Ute raiding party attacked the pueblo, the inhabitants could simply pull up the ladders, making the pueblo unassailable. But this could leave their crops and livestock vulnerable, and the attacking tribe could burn or trample the cornfields and steal the horses and sheep. Most pueblos now have doors, but those are Western features that were added in the nineteenth and twentieth centuries.

Anglo merchants and settlers disliked adobe. Sister Blandina Segale, who arrived in Santa Fe in 1877, was not impressed with the primitive town: "'Antique' to the first degree," she described it. The adobe houses looked "like piled brick ready to burn, to enter which, instead of stepping up, you step down onto a mud floor; rafters supporting roof made of trunks and trees, the roof itself of earth which they were told had to be carefully maintained, else the rain would pour in; door openings covered with blankets; the whole giving you a prison feeling."[15]

Figure 32. A 1903 image of Zuni Pueblo highlights the layered structures and ladders common to historic pueblo buildings. Note the adobe bricks, which the Spanish introduced, and the cutout in the roof and ladder to access a room. Prints & Photographs Division, Library of Congress.

Adobe houses and buildings were gradually torn down and replaced by multi-story brick Italianate structures, such as the 1891 Catron Block on the east side of the Plaza. One exception was the historic Palace of the Governors, though that was replastered and scored to resemble granite blocks. Brick became the favored building material, and Victorian architecture came to dominate the city.[16]

Archbishop Lamy thought adobe primitive and beneath European architecture. Most of the church or school buildings he erected were Neogothic, Romanesque, or Second French Empire. You see this in the Loretto Chapel, the St. Francis Cathedral, and the St. Michael's College dormitory (now the Lamy Building). They were built of sandstone, which at least matched adobe in color. The Guadalupe Sanctuary was rebuilt in

1881–1882 along the lines of a New England Congregational Church, complete with spire, though at its core it was still an adobe building.

When New Mexico won statehood in 1912, this coincided with the era of the City Beautiful movement that sought to improve urban spaces. Santa Fe nicknamed itself as the City Different. One key problem was that downtown Santa Fe looked like any other Midwestern city with its French Second Empire and Italianate buildings. The 1912 City Beautiful Plan sought to revive the city's historic adobe architectural style, which visitors expected to see. The Chamber of Commerce encouraged building owners to retrofit their buildings in Spanish–Pueblo Revival style, invented by the Rapp brothers in 1913, or in the earlier Territorial Style with its brick coping along the roofline and symmetric windows, Santa Fe's version of Greek Revival.

European-style buildings were torn down or retrofitted. The *portales* (porches) removed decades earlier to widen downtown streets were now rebuilt for local charm and summertime shade. The Museum of New Mexico, which underwent renovation starting in 1909 under Edgar Lee Hewett, restored the Palace of the Governors to how it might have looked in Spanish colonial days.

Although today's downtown Santa Fe looks ancient, it's mostly an illusion. Most buildings you see were retrofitted in the early twentieth century in Santa Fe Style as the city capitalized on tourism. Chris Wilson wrote in *The Myth of Santa Fe*, "In a world infatuated with maintaining historical traditions and ethnic identities, Santa Fe has created an unusually successful illusion of authenticity." He cynically called it the "invention of tradition."[17] That said, every tradition begins somewhere. We didn't always have Christmas and Easter, or Fourth of July barbecues or Thanksgiving family gatherings, or mid-century modern architecture. Santa Fe's unique architecture is a product of the early twentieth century as locals embraced pretend adobe ("fauxdobe") buildings that are largely built of brick, covered with stucco, and painted brown. It's part of what makes the City Different unique, even though some refer to downtown as the "Adobe Disneyland."

By the time Willa Cather and Edith Lewis visited in 1925 and 1926, the conversion of the Plaza area to Santa Fe Style was well underway. It didn't look much different than it does today. The city embraced this look as it grew into the twentieth and twenty-first centuries. Architectural building styles were encoded in 1957, in part to retain the city's appeal to visitors.

New Mexican culture is often described as a fusion of Anglo, Hispanic, and Indigenous cultures. It is a hybrid culture, as all three groups have brought something to the table. This is also referred to as the "tricultural myth," a vast oversimplification of the state's complicated and layered cultures.

Where did this mythology come from? It emerged in part from the tourism industry, which portrayed New Mexico as an exotic destination, especially once the railroad arrived and visitors could be here in a matter of days, rather than months. Edgar Lee Hewett, who headed the Museum of New Mexico beginning in 1909, was a key proponent of the tricultural myth. He revitalized the annual Fiesta de Santa Fé in 1919 as a tricultural celebration. It's true: New Mexico is beautiful, exotic, and historic. We've earned our nickname as the Land of Enchantment. But the tricultural myth does our state and its citizens a disservice.[18]

It does so through holding that Anglos, Hispanics, and the Indigenous exist as distinct and separate cultures. Cather played into this when she wrote in *Archbishop*, "The Mexicans were always Mexicans, the Indians were always Indians" (284). In contrast to Cather, and to the myth, I hold that race is an artificial construct that has nothing to do with biology. What we have are multiple cultures that arose from different ethnicities, and we are far more interconnected than anyone can imagine, as DNA testing has shown. We are all one human family.

The early Spanish settlers who came up from Mexico, who were largely a creole and mestizo population, intermixed with the pueblos, creating an even more mixed population. And once the Americans began arriving in 1821 with the opening of the Santa Fe Trail, there was much intermarriage between Americans and Mexicans. The mixing of these different ethnic groups continues to this day, and I think that's a good thing.

Particularly problematic, the tricultural myth mislabels many people. Anyone who isn't Hispanic or Indigenous gets lumped into the Anglo category. Fathers Lamy and Machebeuf, who were core to Cather's Santa

Fe story, were French (Gallic), but from the point of view of the tricultural myth they were Anglos. The same applies to the Spiegelbergs and Staabs, German Jewish merchants who came down the Santa Fe Trail starting in 1844. These people had roots in France and Germany, rather than the British Isles, so how can they be Anglos?

New Mexico has far more than three cultures. The tricultural myth isn't inclusive and marginalizes many people. Where do our African, Caribbean, South Asian, and East Asian populations fit within this model? Are whites and Hispanics monolithic cultures? Not at all. New Mexico has twenty-three Indigenous tribes, each with its own distinct culture and subcultures. The myth also paints over cultural fault lines between these groups, privileging a mythical past where everyone got along, though the historical record indicates otherwise. The fault lines are still there, paint or no paint.

In 1923 Willa Cather's friend Elsie Sergeant warned that tourism could ruin New Mexico's authenticity and make things worse for its Indigenous population. She wrote for *The Nation*, "If the picturesque features, like Indian villages and Spanish missions, become as in California merely tourist attractions played up by hotelkeepers and chambers of commerce, the last fate of the Indian will be worse than his first and the rare distinction of the State will vanish away."[19]

Fortunately, that has not come to pass. There remains much authenticity in New Mexico. Santa Fe is in Tewa Country, and the city leans in on Indigenous sovereignty more than most cities. Native Americans aren't some abstraction—we Santa Feans live among them, and they among us.

Cather and Lewis Return to La Fonda

On May 15, twenty days before Cather and Lewis arrived at La Fonda, the Fred Harvey company launched its signature tourist program, known as the Indian Detour. These were one to three-day chauffeured trips aboard Harveycar buses to Pueblo Indian sites, including Isleta, Pecos, Puye Cliff Dwellings (a Harvey rest house was built there that now serves as the visitor center), San Juan (now Ohkay Owingeh), Santa Clara, Santo Domingo, and Tesuque. Westbound passengers riding the Santa Fe Railway detrained

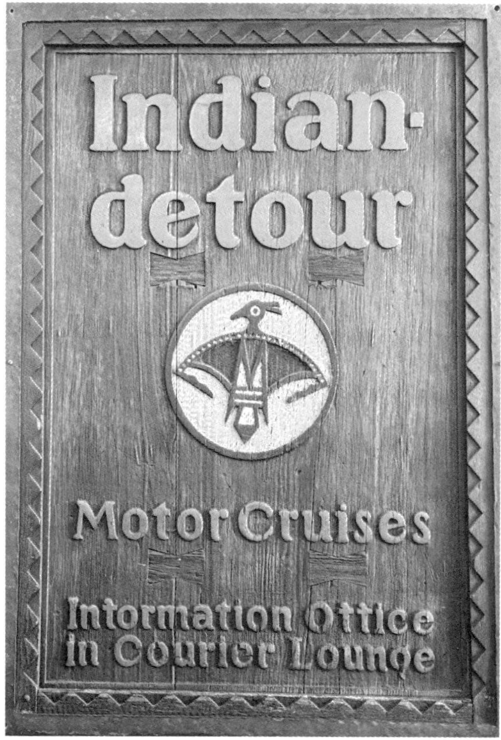

Figure 33. The original Indian Detour sign from the 1920s at La Fonda on the Plaza. La Fonda Photo Archives.

at Las Vegas for a three-day Indian Detour adventure, spending two nights at La Fonda while exploring pueblo sites during the days, and on the third day rejoined the train at Albuquerque. Eastbound train passengers did the same in reverse. The initial cost was forty-five dollars per person, and before the program formally launched it already had five thousand people booked for that summer. At its peak in 1930, the Indian Detour offered eight different tourist programs around the Southwest.[20]

A Scotsman and World War I veteran named Hunter Clarkson conceived the Indian Detour after running Fred Harvey programs at the Grand Canyon. He brought in Erna Fergusson, an Albuquerque native who earned a master's degree in history at Columbia University, and who cofounded Koshare Tours in 1922, which took train-based visitors on multiday excursions around New Mexico by car. Her guides were all women.

Fergusson was an independent and pragmatic woman who had served with the American Red Cross in New Mexico during World War I. Her grandfather, a German immigrant, built Huning Castle in Albuquerque. Her father had served in Congress, while her brother Harvey was a well-known novelist. She loved traveling and became a promoter of the state's culture through tourism and her numerous history books, becoming known as "New Mexico's unofficial first lady."[21]

Fergusson had much experience with the details and logistics that surround a tour. Any guide worth their salt prepares for contingencies and maintains a smile even when the unexpected happens. "When we arrive at your door in a big car with a spade on behind for possible mud, a lunch kit for the inevitable famine, huge thermoses for probable thirst, a strong man for emergencies and an expectant group of tourists in the back seat, don't get the idea that it just happened," Fergusson mused to *Sunset Magazine*.[22]

Fergusson oversaw the hiring and training of the Indian Detour guides. These were well-educated young women known as couriers who dressed in Bohemian art colony attire with an abundance of Navajo jewelry, while the drivers were men called cowboys. The program staged Pueblo Indians in regalia at the various stops, who sold blankets, jewelry, and pottery, and occasionally offered a dance. The couriers interpreted archaeology, geology, Pueblo culture, and the region's history.[23]

Barring someone finding the hotel register from the time, we can't be certain what rooms Cather and Lewis stayed in during their visits to La Fonda—but we do have clues. We know that Cather complained about the noise from the Indian Detour Harveycars, which assembled along East San Francisco Street. Lewis also snapped a photo of Cather sitting along the edge of the second-floor terrace with the St. Francis Cathedral in the background. This may indicate they stayed on the north side of the hotel, facing the street.

I ran a fun experiment, asking the La Fonda concierge, John Felix, if I could replicate Cather's photo on the terrace. He took me to the hotel general manager's office, where we crawled through a window and out onto the terrace to photograph me standing roughly where Cather posed in 1926.

Figure 34. Four young women guides known as Couriers for the Fred Harvey company's Indian Detour program. The women had extensive knowledge of New Mexico's Native cultures, and though they largely visited Pueblo Indian reservations, they wore Navajo jewelry. La Fonda Photo Archives.

Figure 35. Two Indian Detour Harveycars are shown parked in front of La Fonda. The tourist program began in May 1926, just weeks before Cather and Lewis arrived at the hotel. Cather was irritated at the noise from the buses and tourist clamor. La Fonda Photo Archives.

Figure 36. Willa Cather in 1926 on the La Fonda balcony with the St. Francis Cathedral in the background. Philip L. and Helen Cather Southwick Collection, Archives & Special Collections, University of Nebraska–Lincoln Libraries.

Figure 37. Author Garrett Peck near where Cather posed on the La Fonda balcony in 1926. Photograph by Garrett Peck.

Thanks to the success of the Indian Detour program, La Fonda needed to expand, and the hotel hired architect John Gaw Meem. He tripled the hotel in size in Spanish–Pueblo Revival style to 160 rooms. Meem designed the bell tower at the hotel's southwest corner modeled on San Estevan del Rey church at Acoma Pueblo. Designer Mary Colter furnished the hotel interior in Southwestern style and added to its growing art collection. The expansion commenced in 1927 and was completed two years later.

Sometime during Cather and Lewis's sojourn in Santa Fe, they visited Bishop's Lodge, four miles north of downtown. It was Archbishop Lamy's country retreat, acquired by the Thorpe family in 1918 and turned into a dude ranch and resort. Cather accurately described Lamy's adobe house and an ancient apricot tree on the property in *Archbishop.*

Cather and Lewis worked at La Fonda for ten days, proofreading *My Mortal Enemy* and researching *Archbishop.* As comfortable as the hotel was, La Fonda was a distraction, what with construction, street noise, and tourists. Cather complained to Mabel Dodge Luhan a day after they arrived, "We are most comfortable here, but the Indian Detourists abound and the motor horn is the worm that dieth not."[24]

Santa Fe historian Paul Horgan, who later won Pulitzers for his histories of Archbishop Lamy and the Rio Grande, was nearly twenty-three years old when Cather and Lewis visited Santa Fe. Years later, he recalled intruding on them as they worked at La Fonda in June 1926.

> One morning quite idly I went through a heavy paneled door leading to one such porch and knew at once that I must go away.
>
> In the deepest corner of the porch were two steamer chairs, and upon them reclined two ladies whose concentration I disturbed. They were busy with papers and pencils. I have an impression of many accessories—notebooks, opened volumes, steamer rugs against the vagrant breezes which feel cool to someone out of the sun in Santa Fe, perhaps a thermos jar containing hot bouillon, possibly a fly whisk, and what else? If I invent it, it is because I have forgotten, and if I have forgotten it is because the nearer of the two ladies turned upon me a light blue regard of such annoyance and

> distaste at my intrusion that I was gone too quickly to take more than a sweeping impression of where I had been. But I was there long enough to recognize that it was Miss Willa Cather whom I had interrupted at work with her secretary, and I was already so devoted to her work that my chagrin rose equal to my respect. . . .[25]
>
> When I saw her that day—it was the only time I ever saw her and I always regretted that I never had the opportunity to tell her how sorry I was for my transgression—she was working only a hundred yards from his [Lamy's] cathedral, whose humble beauties she was the first to recognize. I remember the eagerness and excitement with which I awaited my first edition copy of her Lamy novel in the following year, 1927.[26]

Because of Santa Fe's small size, most everyone knew one another—and what notables were visiting. Cather's 1925 visit to Santa Fe drew no attention in the press, unlike her 1926 visit. The *Santa Fe New Mexican* falsely noted on June 14 that Cather was in Taos and coming to Santa Fe for a monthlong visit: "The art and literary colonies of Santa Fe are on tip-toes awaiting Miss Cather's arrival." In fact, Cather had already been in town for ten days.[27]

Though Cather was well traveled, her experience was from an era other than ours: She came by train, and while this was much faster than a Conestoga wagon rolling across the prairie, it could still take days to reach a destination. The airplane was invented, but air travel was still in its infancy. But one transportation mode was becoming more affordable and widely available in the 1920s, thanks to Henry Ford: the automobile. While Edith and Willa traveled by train, Cather's brother Roscoe and his family came by car from Wyoming to join them. Driving by car was more modern and would help spell the demise for the railroad-driven tourist industry like the Fred Harvey company.

Roscoe Cather, his wife Meta, and their three daughters arrived on June 14 for the long-planned family vacation. They took several family photos, including of Cather with her twin nieces at the cathedral and the Lamy statue. "They will have only a week, so I expect to lead a busy life until they're gone," Cather wrote Luhan.[28] Roscoe's family stayed ten days.

Figure 38. Willa Cather with her twin nieces Elizabeth and Margaret at the Archbishop Lamy statue in Santa Fe. The photo is dated June 14, 1926—the day that Cather's brother Roscoe and family arrived. Philip L. and Helen Cather Southwick Collection, Archives & Special Collections, University of Nebraska–Lincoln Libraries.

Cather mentioned nothing in letters about where the family visited; however, we do have clues. She picked up a tourist map of the Santa Fe area and probably used it either to plan their sightseeing ventures or record the places where they visited. Cather noted ten sites with heavy pencil hashtags; they were concentrated around Lamy and Pecos; the Cerrillos Hills where turquoise was mined; Tesuque Pueblo; and Bandelier National Monument and nearby San Ildefonso Pueblo. These are day trips from Santa Fe. One clue is in *Archbishop*, where Cather wrote, "Holes of that shape are common in the black volcanic cliffs of the Pajarito Plateau" (128), the plateau above Bandelier National Monument that is home to Los Alamos. The rock walls are made of soft volcanic tuff out of which Ancestral Puebloans carved out cave dwellings and storage areas known as cavates. But they are pale orange or white, rather than black. We have

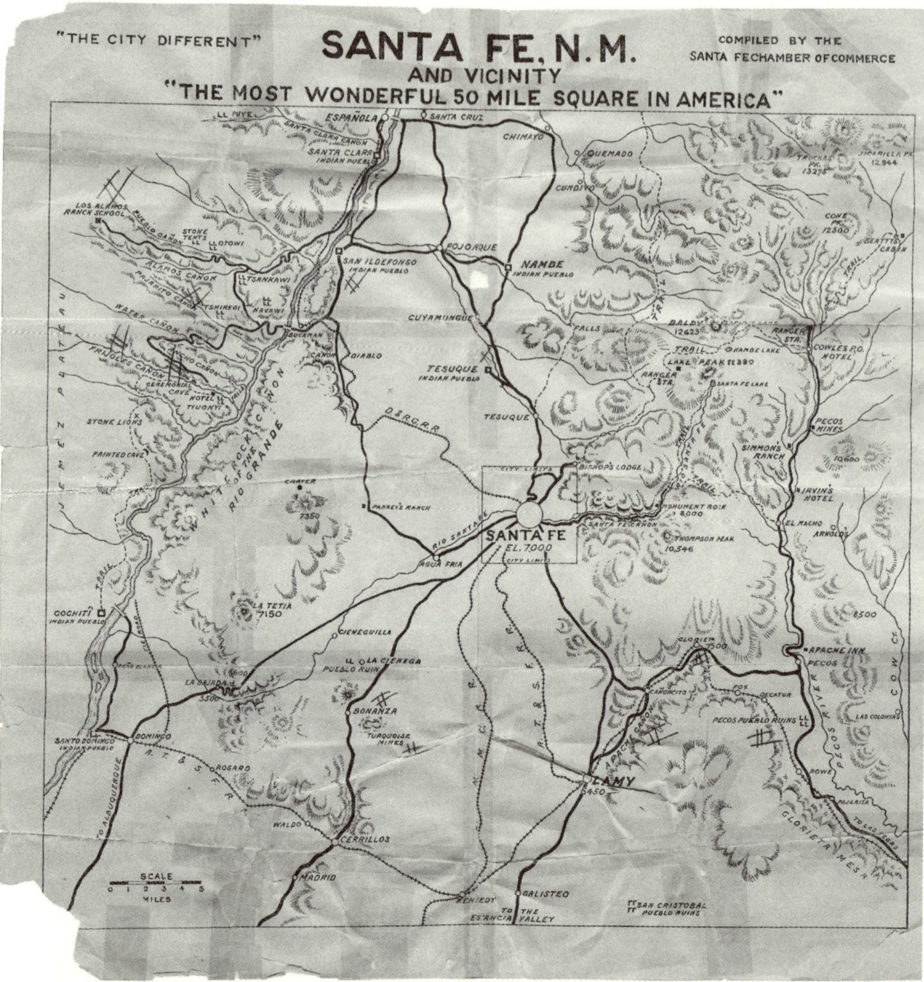

Figure 39. Cather acquired a tourist map of the Santa Fe area that may have helped her plan the vacation with her brother Roscoe's family in June 1926. Ten pencil hashtags indicate places that they may have visited. OBJ-50-4001. Southwick Family Collection. Willa Cather Foundation Collections & Archives. National Willa Cather Center in Red Cloud, Nebraska.

few photos from these day trips, though the archives contain photos of Santa Clara Pueblo and San Juan Pueblo (now Ohkay Owingeh Pueblo), which Cather and Lewis could have been taken in either 1925 or 1926.

Did Cather and her family take any Indian Detour excursions? Many of the sites the program visited were on Cather's hashtag map. We don't know, but I'm skeptical. She was not the type to take a bus tour, and besides, they had Roscoe's automobile, though it would have been a challenge squeezing seven people into it. None of the tourist photos they took showed Indian Detour people or vehicles. My hunch is that the Cather family made their own day trips.

Sadly, the family vacation came to an end. Edith departed first, taking the train back to New York on June 23, while Roscoe and his family left the next day. Willa was finally by herself. She got back to work on her *Archbishop*.[29]

Writing is unquestionably a solitary activity. Cather needed a quiet place to work, and she found that in the home of author Mary Austin, who was in the hospital and offered Cather the use of her Casa Querida, or Beloved House.

Cather walked to the quiet home on Telephone Road (now Camino del Monte Sol), about a mile from her hotel, for a week starting June 24. She wrote her brother Roscoe, "I went right up to Mrs. Austin's house to work that morning as soon as you left, and found my Bishop there waiting for me. I have worked every day since then."[30] Cather penned a gracious thank-you letter to Austin, calling the house "the most restful, quiet, sympathetic place to work in" and noting that she sat in a "dear little blue plush chair in that corner of the library" to draft her book, her paper resting on her knee.[31]

After several days by herself, Cather was lonely. She wrote her mother on June 28: "Edith went back to New York the day before Roscoe's party left, and I have been plenty lonesome, I can assure you. I have been working every morning up in Mary Austin's new house. She has gone away for an operation and was kind enough to leave me the key of her house and big library so that I could write there. But I am getting rather homesick and tired of being in Santa Fe alone." She also expressed hope to one day buy a vacation home in the Southwest.[32] Three days later, she sent a Fred Harvey company postcard of Isleta Pueblo to Roscoe and Meta's daughters with a single sentence, "If I build a little house in a town like this, will you come and visit?" Cather never built that vacation home, but rather focused on the Grand Manan cottage that she and Lewis began building that same year.[33]

Figure 40. After vacationing with her brother Roscoe's family in Santa Fe in June 1926, Cather sent his daughters a Fred Harvey company postcard that showed Isleta Pueblo. She wrote: "If I build a little house in a town like this, will you come and visit me?" Roscoe and Meta Cather Collection, Archives & Special Collections, University of Nebraska–Lincoln Libraries.

Cather's host, Mary Austin, had visited Santa Fe for years and was a leading fixture in the local arts and an early champion of historic preservation. She founded the Santa Fe Community Theater in 1919, which she incorporated as the Little Theatre three years later and which is now the Santa Fe Playhouse. She finally moved to Santa Fe in 1924, built her home the following year and helped found the Spanish Colonial Arts Society. She spent the last ten years of her life in the City Different, fighting for architectural and cultural preservation. She even led a campaign against the Daughters of the American Revolution, which wanted to erect a Madonna of the Trail statue along the Santa Fe Trail in 1927. Austin believed that the real pioneers were the Spaniards, not Americans. She was a white progressive who took up the cause of minority rights.[34]

The Mary Austin House Controversy

The fact that Willa Cather wrote part of *Death Comes for the Archbishop* in

Figure 41. Mary Austin was a noted author and environmentalist who accompanied Cather and Lewis to Pecos in 1925 and opened her Santa Fe home to Cather in 1926. Here she poses with Ernest Thompson Seton at her home in 1927. Palace of the Governors Photo Archive (NMHM/DCA), Image 014248.

Mary Austin's house in Santa Fe later proved controversial. Austin did not know what Cather was writing about until the author forwarded a signed copy of *Archbishop*. Being a champion of Spanish arts and culture, Austin was cross. "I was very much distressed to find that she had given her allegiance to the French blood of the Archbishop; she had sympathized with his desire to build a French cathedral in a Spanish town," she wrote in her 1932 memoir, *Earth Horizon*. The cathedral "was a calamity to the local culture. We have never got over it."[35]

Now it was Cather's turn to be upset, and she downplayed the role of Austin's house in her writing *Archbishop*. She wrote Mabel Dodge Luhan, "You know why I went to the house for a few hours every day for about a week—merely to be polite. I had two perfectly good rooms at La Fonda." Perhaps Cather had forgotten how noisy it was at the hotel, which was the reason why she decamped to the quiet residence. She likewise grew defensive about her subject: "And how the devil could I help it that the first archbishops of New Mexico were French? As I don't wear a Spanish comb in my hair I didn't mind it a bit that Bishop Lamy was a Frenchman."[36]

Likewise, Cather fibbed to her friend Elsie Sergeant, claiming that she hadn't written any of *Archbishop* at Mary Austin's house. "She had left her manuscript in a vault in New York when she went to New Mexico," Sergeant reported. Cather claimed that she walked to Austin's just to write a few letters. If that were the case, she could have written those from La Fonda.[37]

Twenty years after penning *Archbishop*, and shortly before her own death, Cather continued to restate her version of events. This was prompted in part by Mary Cabot Wheelwright (that "mad woman," the author called her), who purchased Austin's home and told people that Cather had written *Archbishop* in the house.[38] "In truth, the book was written in the course of one year, most of it was written in a house near Jaffrey, New Hampshire," she wrote literary critic E. K. Brown in October 1946.[39]

Memory is a funny thing. We can have false memories, or we can remember things differently than how they happened, sometimes to better support our version of events. Austin's criticism stung Cather, especially since it was in print, and being a private person Cather was deeply wounded. She sought to downplay Austin's role, yet Austin's house was undoubtedly important for Cather's writing, as she inscribed in Austin's copy of *Archbishop*: "For Mary Austin, in whose lovely study I wrote the last chapters of this book. She will be my sternest critic—and she has the right to be. I will always take a calling-down from my betters."[40]

The cathedral was far from a "calamity to the local culture," as Austin wrote: Many families regularly attend services at the St. Francis Cathedral and generations of people have been confirmed into the Catholic Church there. It is a top site for visitors. No doubt there are holdouts who wish the cathedral had never been constructed, or who wish the old adobe Parroquia it replaced still stood, but the cathedral is widely recognized as part of the historic fabric that makes up Santa Fe.

Cather would not have known it at the time, but Santa Fe was eclipsing Taos as the leading art colony in the state. It was attracting more artists, in part because it was more accessible by train than Taos, and it had infrastructure that attracted ailing artists: tuberculosis clinics. As the state capital, Santa Fe hosted the Museum of Fine Arts, built in 1917 (now the New Mexico Museum of Art). And Santa Fe had a secret weapon that Taos lacked: the Fred Harvey company, which ran La Fonda and the Indian Detour program. The company knew how to promote the Southwest to tourists.

Erna Fergusson observed the changes to Santa Fe in the early twentieth century as white artists flocked in and turned the city into an artistic haven.

> New Mexico had been discovered by a hitherto unknown race, who used unfamiliar words with accents very strange. They spoke of Amerindian culture, of colonial arts, of racial rhythms, and of such color that even a native began to see red, white, and blue in a muddy ditch. Some painted pictures, some wrote books and poems, and they all went nuts about something: ruins or Indian dances, old Mexican plays, or tin sconces. Their women appeared in men's pants and cowboy hats; their men wore velvet blouses and Navajo jewelry.[41]

And we still do. At first glance, you may think the cowboy boot and hat–wearing crowds, adorned with Indigenous jewelry, are cowboys. They are not. They are Bohemians.

A minor controversy was underway at the time of Cather's 1926 visit to Santa Fe. Advocates, including the chamber of commerce and the Texas Federation of Women's Clubs, were championing a Chautauqua-like cultural colony to be built near Sunmount Sanitorium, a health resort for people suffering from tuberculosis. Having seen other cultural colony concepts with their temporary buildings and part-time occupancy, activist Mary Austin declared, "The effect is always the same and always disastrous."[42] Waldo Twitchell, a historian and former Santa Fe resident, wrote, "Can an absent Santa Fean become a member of the Keep-Santa-Fe-as-It-Was Association? If so, put me on?"[43] Pulitzer-winning author Sinclair Lewis, who was fond of the "unspoiled beauty of Santa Fe," called the colony idea a "ghastly misfortune," one that would turn the city into a "flimsy fair-ground." The opposition steadily built from numerous civic groups and prominent citizens.[44]

The *Albuquerque Journal* and *Santa Fe New Mexican*, the state's leading newspapers, asked Cather for her opinion of the proposed cultural colony. She waded into the controversy. She had seen similar experiments in Nebraska, and they did not end well, leaving behind ghost towns. "It would be too bad for Santa Fe ever to get a suburb of that kind," she told the reporters. "I have never known that kind of colony to be a success." The cultural colony project was eventually shelved.[45]

A *New York Times* reporter, Robert Duffus, visited Santa Fe in 1929 and observed that the small city "was more interested in maintaining its quality than increasing its size," even as it recognized how dependent it was on tourism. "Santa Fé may be off the trunk line of the railway but it is on the main line for any one making a cultural tour of America," he wrote. Duffus addressed the Chautauqua controversy and why it had failed three years earlier: "But some proponents of the plan thoughtlessly let fall the argument that Santa Fé needed culture and that the Chautauqua would bring it. At this the lid blew off entirely." Santa Fe already had plenty of culture.[46]

Completing the Novel

For her 1926 trip to New Mexico, Cather had planned to visit Taos first, staying at Mabel Dodge Luhan's, but Mabel's husband Tony was hospitalized in Albuquerque. Cather delayed her visit to Taos until July. She planned to travel to Taos on July 3 and stay with Mabel for two weeks, but she had to cancel that portion of her trip.

Cather's mother was feeling ill and had requested her presence, so Cather hurriedly traveled to Nebraska. Cather sent two letters from Denver, both dated July 4, as she waited for the train to Red Cloud. "So I've broken my time in New Mexico right in two," she wrote Zoë Akins. "I hated to do it." After visiting her family, Cather returned to New York by mid-July.[47]

Cather met with Paul Revere Reynolds, who sold the serial rights for *Archbishop* to the magazine *Forum*, which would publish three-fourths of the novel in six installments beginning in January 1927. The New York summer was frightfully hot, and so Cather decamped to a private cottage at the MacDowell Colony in Peterborough, New Hampshire. She stayed there for about a month in what is now the Irving Fine studio, working on her novel during most of August and into early September. It was her one and only stay at MacDowell, though she enjoyed the company of her fellow "colonists," one of whom was then-unknown playwright Thornton

Wilder.[48] Cather relocated to the Shattuck Inn in nearby Jaffrey around September 8, where she stayed for the next seven weeks. "There at the inn, sociability was skin-deep, and she could be as aloof as an oyster," her friend Elsie Sergeant observed.[49]

While Cather worked on her manuscript, Lewis traveled to Grand Manan Island to buy a piece of property and contract for a builder to construct a cottage. The two women had vacationed on the Canadian island several times and decided to make it their second home. This ended Cather's dream of owning a house in the Southwest, though she wrote Mabel Dodge Luhan that she was still considering building or buying a home in Taos.[50]

Two weeks after arriving at the Shattuck Inn, Cather promised Blanche

WILLA CATHER (SEATED) AND EDITH LEWIS (STANDING)
ON LAWN AREA NEAR OLD MEETING HOUSE - 1926

Figure 42. A rare photograph of Willa Cather and Edith Lewis together in Jaffrey, New Hampshire, in fall 1926, where Cather completed *Death Comes for the Archbishop*. Photograph by Mrs. Josiah Wheelwright, from Theodore Jones, "Willa Cather in the Northeast (A Pictorial Biograph), 1917–1947," masters' thesis, University of New Brunswick, 1968. Archives and Special Collections, Harriet Irving Library, University of New Brunswick.

Knopf that she would submit the *Archbishop* manuscript in November, then later moved the date up to October 29.[51] In fact, she finished composing the novel by late September, and soon felt the absence of her fictional archbishop. She wrote Louise Guerber on October 2 that she "missed the old fellow's society. It's always dismal to have an old friend go away or to finish a book. The thing that gave one pleasant excitement for so long is simply gone and done with—like a squeezed lemon."[52]

Five days later, Cather sent the novel's first installment to *Forum*. She liked to be involved in the design of her books and how they were promoted, and in this case suggested promotional copy for the serialized version:

> Miss Cather's new narrative, Death Comes etc, recounts the adventures of two missionary priests in the Old Southwest. Two hardy French priests find themselves set down in the strange world at the end of the Santa Fé trail, among scouts and trappers and cut-throats, old Mexican settlements and ancient Indian pueblos. The period is that immediately following the Mexican War, and the story is a rich, moving panorama of life on that wild frontier.[53]

With the novel completed, Cather spent her time hiking on Mount Monadnock near the Shattuck Inn and handling business related to *My Mortal Enemy*, due out October 26. She departed Jaffrey and spent several days traveling back to New York, arriving home on November 4 or 5, and then turned in the manuscript to Knopf about a week after she had promised, followed by the second installment to *Forum*.[54]

Cather wrote her niece Virginia Cather (whom she nicknamed "West Virginia") to be on the lookout for the serialized version of *Archbishop* in *Forum*. "You must write me as soon as you read the first number of The Archbishop. He is my real Christmas present to my nieces, and all my dear family. You can't buy him over the counter—you have to have a real foxy aunt who can make him, or go without."[55]

That winter, Cather reviewed the novel's proofs, which any author can attest is attention and time-consuming, as she admitted to her niece Mary Virginia Auld. "Nothing in particular to make me feel blue, except that I

Figure 43. A portrait of Willa Cather taken by Edward Steichen and published in the July 1927 edition of *Vanity Fair*, two months before *Archbishop* was published. Edward Steichen, Vanity Fair, © Condé Nast.

don't see my way to beginning a new story as Archbishop right now, and reading proofs is dull work after writing." She added, "You can have a new adventure, but you can never have the same one over."[56]

A year after Roscoe Cather's family joined Willa in Santa Fe, she visited them in Casper, Wyoming, in June 1927. They explored the Big Horn Mountains for three days by car, then Cather looped back to Red Cloud to visit her parents in July.[57] While she was there, her father Charles suffered his first heart attack. Once his health stabilized, Cather returned to New York in August to help Lewis clear out their 5 Bank Street apartment, as their building was to be demolished. They put their goods in storage and lived like vagabonds for the next five years. Lewis observed, "I think Willa Cather did her happiest writing in the fifteen years we lived there."[58]

Cather had planned to travel to France just before publication of *Death Comes for the Archbishop* in September but canceled the trip on account of her father's health. Two weeks before her new novel was published, she wrote Dorothy Canfield Fisher, "I've almost forgotten I ever wrote the Archbishop,—so much has happened since then."[59]

The 1926 trip was Cather's last visit to New Mexico. Though *Death Comes for the Archbishop* would give her—and New Mexico—ever greater fame, she had no time to return, as she dealt not only with her successful literary career but also with her aging parents and the loss of her home. "The great disadvantage about writing of the places you love is that you lose your beloved places forever—that is, if you are a quiet person who doesn't like publicity," Cather wrote in 1943.[60]

Chapter 6

My Best Book

"I think that 'Death Comes for the Archbishop' will stand the wear and tear better than the others."

—Willa Cather to Mr. Meromichey, 1931

Alfred A. Knopf published Willa Cather's ninth novel, *Death Comes for the Archbishop*, on September 2, 1927. He observed, "I think she cared more for Archbishop Lamy's story than for any other book of hers we published. She never asked for an advance and, I feel certain, would have regarded publishers who offered them (all publishers did and do) and authors who accepted them as equally immoral." Cather asked for an additional 1 percent in royalties for *Archbishop*, meaning that she would get 16, rather than 15 percent, of the $2.50 sales price, or $.40 per copy.[1]

Cather was often involved in the design of a book cover, as she had a good understanding of how these helped sell books to the public. She was particularly involved in *Archbishop*'s first and second editions. Explaining the novel's look and feel to Knopf in 1934, Cather wrote, "But you see I wanted the 'Archbishop' to look as if it were printed on a country press, for old people to read."[2]

Once *Archbishop* was published, Cather had little chance to enjoy it, as life intervened. Having cleared out their Greenwich Village apartment and put most of their belongings in storage, Cather and Lewis regrouped at the Shattuck Inn in Jaffrey. Lewis's mother had experienced a stroke in nearby Springfield, Massachusetts, and both women needed a break. Cather remained in Jaffrey through late October.[3]

Knopf noted that by mid-September the book had sold nearly thirty thousand copies. "She was at Jaffrey, New Hampshire, where she wrote she was walking six or eight miles a day and doing nothing else," he recorded. That wasn't entirely true: Cather was inundated with fan mail, and she attempted to respond to much of it. On September 17, she wrote six letters in one day.[4]

Her friend Carl Van Vechten purchased an early copy and wrote Cather about how much he enjoyed *Archbishop*. "Your letter gives me a fine glow of satisfaction," Cather responded in rather highbrow fashion. "In this book I tried to be as self-less as the good missionary, to make the country my existence as it was his. I suppose one could very properly use that country as a decor, a setting, for a story of human emotions. But it most appeals to me as a thing big enough and beautiful enough to drink up all personal entanglements—almost personality itself!" It was clear how much Cather enjoyed sublimating herself into this story.[5]

James Thorpe, the president and owner of Bishop's Lodge in Santa Fe, wrote Cather to ask for a publicity photo and for her publisher to send fifty copies of the novel to sell at the resort. He added, "I cannot thank you enough for this book, as it means so much to me and to the Bishop's Lodge guests. It is charming, awfully well done, and entirely to my taste."[6] Cather directed her publisher to send a copy of her 1924 studio portrait taken by photographer Nickolas Muray. That portrait hangs in the resort's reception today.[7]

Cather wrote Ida Tarbell, the progressive investigative journalist who wrote a muckraking history of Standard Oil, a month after *Archbishop*'s publication. "The writing of that book was the most unalloyed pleasure of my life—and it keeps on bringing pleasures,—letters from priests in remote deserts and mountains that melt my heart," Cather wrote. "The rector of the Cathedral in Denver writes me that he <u>still</u> uses father Joseph's chalice and the vestments made by Philomène and her nuns! He knows every inch of the ground and he really loves the book. He is an old man, and he wrote me a letter like a school boy's." She continued, "These letters do help me to bear the trials of this hour," the eviction from her

Figure 44. Willa Cather's 1924 studio portrait, taken by Nickolas Muray. She asked her publisher to send a copy to Bishop's Lodge after Archbishop was published. PHO-4-W689-771. WCPM Collection. Willa Cather Foundation Collections & Archives at the National Willa Cather Center in Red Cloud, Nebraska. © Nickolas Muray Photo Archives. Used with permission of the Nickolas Muray Photo Archives.

New York apartment and her father's declining health. "Of course I miss my 'Archbishop' awfully, working on him was almost like working with him, it was so happy and serene a mood."[8]

Cather kept her eye on the reviews and how those might be leveraged for advertising purposes, forwarding favorable snippets to Blanche Knopf.[9] She was thrilled to see positive reviews in the Catholic press, and many of the fan letters she received were from Catholic readers. She explained to Louise Guerber, "I feared nothing so much as seeming a sort of stage Catholic." The fan mail and reviews assuaged her fear of imposter syndrome.[10]

Cather's partner, Edith Lewis, noted how concerned Cather was about this question. "It would have deeply hurt her pride if her representation of Catholic thought and feeling had been considered by them inaccurate or superficial or misleading," she wrote. "Not being herself Catholic, it had been an enterprise of considerable boldness to write a narrative of French Catholic priests from their own point of view." Cather had been criticized for writing about the experiences of World War I that she had not personally had when she published *One of Ours* in 1922, and that must have weighed on her in writing *Archbishop*.[11]

The Catholic fan mail grew to such proportions that Cather penned an open letter explaining her intentions for the book, published in the Catholic magazine *Commonweal* in November 1927. She wrote Fanny Butcher, "The Catholics have been so broad-minded and handsome about this book."[12] According to Mildred Bennett, Cather's first biographer, Father William Howlett (the author of the Machebeuf biography that Cather extensively used as a source) wrote Cather, as she hadn't credited him. She in turn wrote the *Commonweal* letter, where she acknowledged the debt to Howland, and she sent him an autographed copy.[13]

Cather's *Commonweal* article is a significant primary source, as she answered many questions about how she wrote the novel. Many fans assumed she was Catholic, but she wasn't—in fact, she was confirmed in the Episcopalian Church in Red Cloud in 1922. Yet it was clear she sympathized with the church. Cather felt that Archbishop Lamy "had become a sort of invisible personal friend. . . . I never passed the life-size bronze of him which stands under a locust tree before the Cathedral in Santa Fé without wishing that I could learn more about a pioneer churchman who looked so well-bred and distinguished."[14]

Figure 45. The bronze statue of Archbishop Jean Baptiste Lamy, installed in 1915, stands in front of the St. Francis Cathedral. He holds a scroll that reads in Latin, Fides et Opera, or Faith and Works. Cather noted how much the statue influenced her novel. Photograph by Garrett Peck, with permission of the Archdiocese of Santa Fe.

Figure 46. Hans Holbein the Younger produced a satirical series of woodcuts known as the *Dance of Death* in the 1520s. In this image, a skeletal Death triumphantly marches off with an abbot. The hourglass in the tree signals that time is up. Metropolitan Museum of Art.

While you might mistake the novel's title for an Agatha Christie murder mystery, the title *Death Comes for the Archbishop* derives from German Renaissance artist Hans Holbein the Younger's satirical wood engraving series *Dance of Death* from the 1520s. Cather would have seen these at New York's Metropolitan Museum of Art. Each woodcut shows a tableau of death interacting with a soon-to-be dead person. Cather wrote an episodic novel of tableaus, each telling a parable from the priests' lives or from her own. She brought these scenes to life through her descriptive writing and sparse but telling emotion.[15]

Cather further explained, "I had all my life wanted to do something in the style of legend, which is absolutely the reverse of dramatic treatment. Since I first saw the Puvis de Chavannes frescoes of the life of Saint Geneviève in Paris's Panthéon in 1902 in my student days, I have wished that I could try something a little like that in prose: something without accent, with none of the artificial elements of composition." She likely saw the artist's frescoes in the Boston Public Library as well.[16]

Legend is different than myth; legend has truth behind it. Cather's novel addressed legendary and real historical figures from New Mexico's history: Archbishop Lamy, Bishop Machebeuf, Padre Martínez, and Kit Carson. She left out the state's arguably most legendary figure, Billy the Kid, but then again, she composed a book about frontier priests, not gunfighters.

Cather concluded her letter to *Commonweal*, writing, "I did not sit down to write the book until the feeling of it had so teased me that I could not get on with other things. The writing of it took only a few months, because the book had all been lived many times before it was written, and the happy mood in which I began it never paled." It actually took her longer to write this book, as she had returned to New Mexico in 1926 to complete her research.[17]

After two months in Jaffrey, Cather returned to New York, where she and Lewis rented a suite of rooms at the Grosvenor Hotel, an apartment hotel they disliked. She complained of post-publication drudgery to Harriet Fox Whicher, a professor of English at Mount Holyoke College. While Cather may have enjoyed writing advertising copy, she did not particularly like publicizing her books.

> I'd love to see you all, but I must get away from New York as soon as I can and escape the tiring and time-consuming consequences of having a new book out. The "Archbishop" was all pleasure in the making, but now he brings the dreary aftermath of dinners I won't go to and letters I can't answer. The letters from old priests are lovely, though,—I do answer those. The Catholics have been lovely about the book. They write such stirring things about it and <u>don't</u> ask me to speak at dinners like a mayor or a governor.[18]

Cather intended to visit Arizona in January 1928, which would have been her seventh trip to the Southwest. She arrived in Red Cloud on December 5 to celebrate her parents' fifty-fifth wedding anniversary and stayed into the new year, while Lewis remained back in New York. Cather fibbed to Blanche Knopf, writing that she was in "inaccessible deserts," when she was still in Red Cloud. On January 21, she wrote that she was on her way to Arizona but was still with her parents. Cather's father suffered a second heart attack in late January, and she continued postponing the Arizona trip until late February, when she gave up and returned to New York.[19]

Charles Cather died on March 3, and Willa raced back to Red Cloud. She arrived early in the morning before the family woke and sat with her father's remains. "He looked so happy, so contented, so at home—his smooth fair face shaved—everything as it always was," Cather wrote. "He was such a sweet southern boy, and he never hurt anybody's feelings, not even in death." While her brother Douglass took their mother to California, Cather remained at her parents' house and oversaw renovations. She deeply grieved the loss of her father, her favorite parent.[20]

Cather suffered from arthritis in her right shoulder, which made it uncomfortable to write. In April, she spent several weeks undergoing treatment at the Mayo Clinic in Rochester, Minnesota. She was exhausted after her father's death, as she confessed to Mary Austin: "This is the first time in my life that I have ever felt absolutely tired, through and through, and I am simply going to rest for a while." Returning to New York, she caught the flu and was sick for two weeks.[21]

"I'd get more rest if the Archbishop were not so popular," she complained to her mother in April. She complained to her again six months later about how she could not keep up with all the demands on her time: "I'll never be able to write any more books unless people let me alone. I've been owing the President of Bohemia a letter for two months—I never feel energy enough to thank him for his beautiful letter about The Archbishop. His name is [Tomáš] Masaryck he reads English perfectly and writes it fairly well." The Czechoslovak president had become a Cather fan after reading about Bohemian settlers in *My Ántonia*.[22]

Death Comes for the Archbishop spawned copycats, which annoyed Cather to no end. "About once a week I get a letter from some puppy who tells me he has done a story of sophisticated easterners in a New Mexico background," she complained to Mabel Dodge Luhan. "I wish to God I could have put the Archbishop in Kansas or Nebraska—not many sensitive artistic natures have the grit to follow you there. It's a great advantage to work in a part of the country that is distinctly déclassé—it rids you [of] superficial writers and superficial readers."[23]

In a 1931 interview with the *San Francisco Chronicle*, Cather admitted making a minor mistake in *Archbishop*: "I never should have said that the painting—the masterpiece that had strayed from the Old World to far New Mexico—was a painting by El Greco. Why, I had dozens of letters from readers of the novel, and they were sure they had found that 'missing El Greco' in their attics. They would ask me what art dealer they should send it to, and some of them thought their fortunes were made. The next time I mention a painting, I'll invent a name for the artist."[24]

Cather admitted that another painting inspired the book's prologue, which is set in Rome in a scene where Catholic prelates discuss assigning a bishop to New Mexico.

> French painter, [Jean-Georges] Vibert, once did a precise piece of work in the manner of his day called "The Missionary's Return."
>
> It showed a gorgeously furnished room with cardinals in scarlet, sitting at ease with their wine and speaking to them, telling of the hardships and glories of missionary work in some far part of the world, a pioneer priest, his garments dull and worn out, but his face all alight.[25]

The painting, acquired by New York's Metropolitan Museum of Art in 1924, is actually named *The Missionary's Adventures*. It shows a group of six prelates in their colorful robes relaxing on couches in a grand, art-filled room while a simple missionary in black robes sits on a stool and intently tells them of his works. The cardinals and bishops are sipping coffee and look downright bored or distracted. One of the prelates seems more interested in a begging dog. Another appears to be asleep with a cigar in his hand. It is quite a contrast between the worldly prelates and the simple missionary, or in Cather's perspective, a visual juxtaposition.

Cather confessed to the *Chronicle* that she left a chapter out of the book: "I tried to put into *Death Comes for the Archbishop* what I thought was the best chapter I had written for that story, but it didn't fit. I left it

Figure 47. Jean-Georges Vibert's 1883 painting *The Missionary's Adventures* inspired the Prologue in *Death Comes for the Archbishop*. Metropolitan Museum of Art.

out. A novel should be like a symphony, developed from one theme, one dominating tone. That chapter was out of tone."[26]

Cather and Lewis visited Quebec City during the summer of 1928, and now it was Lewis's turn to experience the flu. The women remained in the city for ten days while Lewis recovered. There Cather found the idea for her next book, *Shadows on the Rock*, which explored French Catholic life on the Canadian frontier in the late seventeenth century. After Quebec, Cather and Lewis traveled to Grand Manan for their usual summer visit before returning to New York in the fall.

In December, Cather's mother suffered a debilitating stroke in Long Beach, California, that left her paralyzed and unable to speak. The twin blows of Charles Cather's death and Jennie Cather's stroke left Cather depressed and unmoored. "I've lost my bearings and can't write except as bitterly and desperately as I feel," Cather confessed to Dorothy Canfield

Fisher in one of her darkest letters.[27] When Fisher's mother died in 1930, Cather wrote a letter meant to console, but revealed her profound sense of loss: The death of friends and family "have such an impoverishing effect upon those of us who are left—our world suddenly becomes so diminished—the landmarks disappear and all the splendid distances behind us close up. These losses, one after another, make one feel as if one were going on in a play after most of the principal characters are dead."[28]

Cather relocated her mother to a Pasadena sanitarium, which she paid for, and she maintained a cottage on the property to reside in while visiting. Cather's playwright friend Zoë Akins was now living in Los Angeles and the two women visited. Cather was not able to publish her next book, *Shadows on the Rock*, until August 1931—four years after *Archbishop*. It proved a major commercial success, though critics complained that it lacked conflict. Cather's mother died a month later. She did not attend the funeral. Cather traveled to Red Cloud for Christmas that year, and never visited her hometown again.

After Cather learned of the death of Zoë Akins's husband in 1932, she wrote, "It's a brutal fact, Zoe, that after one is 45, it simply rains death, all about one, and after you've passed fifty, the storm grows fiercer."[29]

Publication History

Publishers weigh consumer demand in deciding how many copies of a book to print, and in planning how to promote the book. In the case of Willa Cather, she was one of the best-recognized authors in the United States with an international following, and *Death Comes for the Archbishop* could anticipate a welcome reception. Cather's name recognition and book reviews, in addition to selective advertising, would do the work of generating sales.

Little effort was required of an author to market a book in the 1920s. The author wrote it; the publisher promoted it. Cather's publisher, Knopf, did most of the promotional work, sending out review copies, paying for advertisements, and occasionally asking Cather to sign books. There were no national book tours, and Cather was one to refrain from book talks or lectures. She was in France in 1923 when *A Lost Lady* came out and had intended to be in France again for *Death Comes for the Archbishop* in 1927 (her father's heart attack sidelined the trip). She sat for the occasional interview, signed Knopf's deluxe editions of the book, and penned an essay for *Commonweal*, but beyond that expected Knopf to do most of the promotional work.

Prior to the book's September 2 publication, publisher Alfred Knopf ordered three printings of *Archbishop* totaling 40,225 copies thanks to strong pre-order demand. He ordered a fourth printing of 5,500 copies in October, and a fifth printing of 1,500 copies in December. Here Knopf erred, not realizing how strong the demand would be around the holidays, when there were widespread shortages of the book. In his memoir, Knopf noted that *Archbishop* had sold 52,000 copies by December 1927. He blamed the book shortage on distributor Baker & Taylor, which had cut its order of 5,000 books in half. Knopf ordered five more printings that month alone, and an eleventh and twelfth printing in January and February 1928. By 1934, Knopf had ordered thirty-four printings of the first edition, totaling 105,000 copies.[30]

The reviews for *Archbishop* were largely positive, and it was soon clear that the book was a success—so much that the publisher had difficulty keeping up with demand. Five months after the book's publication, Cather complained to Knopf, "The demand for the Archbishop seems a mixed blessing, as even now there seems to be no very adequate method of satisfying it. As I telegraphed you last night, the dealers here and in all the little towns about have been trying to get books from McClurg, Chicago, to fill the orders of a few patient friends who were not able to get the book for Christmas." She had been in Red Cloud for two months, and still no books were available. It was an embarrassment to Cather in her hometown. "I've had so many complaints from Catholics all over the country that I'm afraid there has been the same difficulty in getting books, East and West," she added before taking a swipe at Knopf: "I don't think you've given the Archbishop a flattering show of your interest and attention," since the book seemed already out of print. This exchange revealed Cather at her flintiest. Her book sales and literary career were on the line.[31]

For the book's fourteenth printing in June 1928, Cather corrected several textual errors about the Catholic Church, replacing "surplices" with "cassocks" and "Sacrament" to "Sacrifice," and changed the geographic location for the Colorado gold rush from Cripple Creek to Cherry Creek.[32]

Because of *Archbishop*'s success, Knopf decided to publish a special illustrated edition in time for Christmas 1929. This is considered the book's second edition. Knopf hired Harold von Schmidt for the images. Cather was often involved in the design of her books, and she was livid at the publisher's draft copy jacket.[33] "She was more upset about this than I ever found her to be about anything in her dealings with us," Knopf confessed, "and insisted that she assume full responsibility for this jacket text and that we print exactly what she gave us. She said, wisely, that a jacket should tell the public that they want to know, something that they write authors letters about—something about how and why the book was written." Knopf deferred to Cather. Following the author's guidance, the team at Knopf produced a gorgeous book with antique typesets and unusual blocking, and integrated Schmidt's illustrations into the text.[34]

Schmidt had provided the illustration for the dust jacket of *Archbishop's* first edition, which showed a heroic Latour on a mighty horse, his cloak billowing in the wind, and had drafted the images for the serialized edition in *Forum*. These were bulkier images than one might expect for such a nuanced novel. Cather worked closely with Schmidt on the images, which illustrated the lives of her protagonists in New Mexico. Knopf complained that the artist "was extremely slow in delivering and did not keep to promised dates."[35] Schmidt observed years later:

> I worked for two years on these sixty-odd drawings for Willa Cather's beautifully written story of old New Mexico. She had insisted with her publisher that I do the illustrations, and my dealings were all with her directly. I made pencil roughs, and we talked over the approach to take. We disagreed on some things, but I felt that her characters were so well realized in words that it would be a mistake for me to depict them too and possibly confuse the reader whose interpretation of her words might be different from mine. So I did the pictures as decorations that would set the background for the story and help the audience to get to know the old New Mexico as she knew it and as I knew it.[36]

Figure 48. Harold von Schmidt designed about sixty illustrations for the second edition of *Death Comes for the Archbishop.* Shown from Cather's personal copy of the book is his illustration of the St. Francis Cathedral in Santa Fe. Archives & Special Collections, University of Nebraska–Lincoln Libraries.

Cather confessed to Alfred Knopf in 1933, "I should really have thanked him [Schmidt] for the work he did on the illustrated 'Archbishop', you know,—and I never did thank him. I like his drawings much better now than I did at first."[37] Cather eventually expressed her gratitude to Schmidt about six years after their collaboration when he received "a letter from her thanking me for insisting on doing it the way I wanted."[38]

The second edition was Cather's favorite. Her personal copy, now in the University of Nebraska–Lincoln archives, was a 1930 printing of the second edition for the British market. She used her copy as a scrapbook. Cather inserted a color block print of a pueblo building by an as-of-now unknown artist, possibly a souvenir from her travels. She pasted into the book a letter from Agnes Thompson, dated January 31, 1928, and enclosed a carte de visite of Kit Carson, whom her father had met. On the contents page, she posted a photo of herself on horseback. On the pages before

"The Vicar Apostolic" (book 1), she pasted in mirror image photos of her and Edith Lewis on horseback in Taos from 1925, as if to suggest that she and Lewis were Latour and Vaillant, the fictional friends of her novel.[39]

In 1931 Cather agreed to a cheaper Modern Library reprint of the book's first edition. The sixty-five thousand copies printed from 1931 to 1936 earned her six cents per copy, which Cather soon regretted, though it earned her considerable royalties just as *Shadows on the Rock* was being published. "I certainly believe that a book of this sort is absolutely ruined for young readers by an introduction and explanatory notes," she complained to her former editor, Ferris Greenslet. This statement obfuscated the real reason why Cather disliked inexpensive reprints.[40]

"Because she was confident that the success of *Death Comes for the Archbishop* and *Shadows on the Rock* would increase the sales of her other titles, her objective was not to attract more readers, but to maximize the amount that each reader would spend," observed Lise Jaillant.[41] By 1932 Cather was working to halt cheap reprints, believing they had cost her money, though having more copies in circulation would secure a larger audience and ensure her long-term literary reputation. The author wrote, "My whole preference is to sell a few books and to make a dignified royalty on them; to have fewer readers and better readers." That is to say, she sought the interest of those who could afford the more expensive copies, a challenge for many people during the Great Depression. Cather presented herself as a literary elitist, rather than a writer for everyday people, deflecting the cultural gatekeepers of the 1930s such as the leftist critics and the emerging academics who were defining American canonical literature. She resisted being represented by the popular Book of the Month Club (BOMC) until publishing *Shadows on the Rock* in 1931, though BOMC had recommended several of her titles to its readers.[42]

The Reviews and the Critics

Having won the Pulitzer for Fiction in 1923, Cather was considered among the top American writers, and therefore her new book *Archbishop* was reviewed by dozens of publications around the country. The reviews were largely positive. Henry Longan Stuart prominently reviewed the book on the second page of *The New York Times Book Review*. "From the riches of her imagination and sympathy Miss Cather has distilled a very rare piece of literature," he wrote, calling it a "truly remarkable book." He offered one reservation: Cather had so fundamentally changed the facts about Archbishop Lamy's life that he called it "a little disquieting." Stuart concluded that *Archbishop* was "not so much as an historical novel, as a superimposition of the novel upon history."[43]

Another review appeared in *Commonweal*, which as a Catholic publication appreciated Cather's dedication in writing about two Catholic priests. "Willa Cather is one of the few American artists who has perceived the great treasures lying in wait for art in the Catholic tradition of the United States," critic Michael Williams wrote. "I know few books so deep, even so profound, in subject matter, which are expressed in so simple a vocabulary. . . . A child could read this book without effort; artists, philosophers and priests, may and will ponder it profoundly." He called the book "Willa Cather's masterpiece."[44]

The Milwaukee Journal Sentinel praised the author for creating a new style of historical fiction: "Miss Cather has built a vivid, finely conceived book, a book which is a splendid example of the sort of things towards which modern playboys at history are striving."[45] *The Omaha World Herald* described the book as "page after page of compelling description, illuminating portraiture." The paper celebrated her as a fellow Nebraskan who showed that great art could emerge from the prairie. "She is our defense against the pointing finger which accuses us of Main streetism and Babbitry," a reference to Minnesota native Sinclair Lewis, a contemporary Lost Generation author who satirized small-town values and conformity.[46]

Rebecca West published the longest, most highbrow, and the floweriest of all the reviews in *The New York Herald Tribune*. "This, perhaps the most delicate legerdemain man has ever practiced on his senses, falls in to our comprehension as lightly as a snowflake into the hand because of Miss Cather's complete mastery of every phrase of the process," she wrote—and yes, much of the review reads just like that. She added, "Great is her accomplishment."[47]

Cather's writing style might seem sparse, wrote Fanny Butcher in the

Chicago Tribune. "And yet there is no one writing in America today who has a purer, clearer, more beautiful style than Miss Cather." She added, "Anyone who doesn't read it will miss one of the fine books of the year." Butcher's review was reprinted in *The Seattle Daily Times* a week later.[48]

Robert Ballou of *The Chicago Daily News* noted that "Willa Cather has written another western novel," then humorously supposed what most people expect Westerns to be: "Ride, ride, ride, shoot, shoot, shoot, ride, shoot, ride, shoot, ride, marry the girl." Instead, Cather wrote a book of "beautiful quiet prose." He opined, "Her prose is fashioned after the older traditions of writing in which speed (or I believe the later word is pace) is of little consequence. It is restful and satisfying."[49]

"The story has charm and atmosphere, without excitement or suspense," wrote Lillian Ford in *The Los Angeles Times* (a review that was reprinted in *The Santa Fe New Mexican* with the exciting title, "A Santa Fe Novel!"). "Miss Cather seems to know every landmark in the country in which she writes and to appreciate all the complex elements out of which the New Mexico of today developed."[50]

"*Death Comes for the Archbishop* is an epic in which to rejoice," wrote William Whitman in *The Independent*. "Against the feverish backdrop of current literature, this romance enjoys the quiet of permanence and the benediction of understanding."[51] Dorothy Foster Gilman wrote succinctly in *The Boston Evening Transcript*, "it is one of the most superb pieces of literary endeavor this reviewer has ever read."[52] And Robert Morss Lovett of *The New Republic* called *Archbishop* an "unquestionable masterpiece" and an "American classic."[53]

H. L. Mencken had reviewed many Cather novels since *O! Pioneers*, but *Death Comes for the Archbishop* was his last review of a Cather book. He was more impressed with the sidekick character, Joseph Vaillant, and thought Cather should have focused her story on him rather than the sedate Latour. "But of the story that is told there is little complaint to be made," Mencken observed in *American Mercury*, noting that sometimes "her narrative drops to the level of a pious tale." He remained impressed with her writing skills and concluded, "She has done stories far richer in content, but she has never exceeded *Death Comes for the Archbishop* as a piece of writing."[54]

Mencken's review was positive, yet it stung Cather because it was a double review with novelist Harvey Fergusson's *Wolf Song* (Fergusson was the brother of Erna Fergusson who helped establish the Indian Detour program), and Cather felt her book should have stood alone. Mencken penned a 1931 entry in his diary, "She complained to Knopf that I should not have bracketed her with Fergusson. I told him that I was not prepared to consider her wishes in such matters—that if she tried to influence me through him I'd bar her from the magazine altogether. This I have done ever since."

Mencken added pejoratively, "Her recent writing, of course, would not fit into the magazine. She has succumbed to Catholicism, and both 'Death Comes for the Archbishop' and 'Shadows on the Rock' have been widely read and praised by Catholics." Mencken was an atheist and regretted seeing religion in literature.[55]

Despite the strong praise for *Archbishop*, Cather believed the book was not well received among critics. It was perhaps her internal negative feedback loop that listened more to the small critical voice rather than the broader praise. Cather read the reviews and assumed they were worse than they were. The one that struck the deepest was the criticism that *Archbishop* wasn't a novel. She wrote Mary Austin in exasperation:

> This book is just one too many for the poor reviewers. They complain about it, and say "it is almost impossible to classify this book", as if I had put over something unfair on them. They feel so bitterly because Knopf calls it a novel; I, myself, wanted merely to call it a narrative. I'm not sure that I know just what a novel is, and I'm not sure that the reviewers do.[56]

Cather made a similar observation in other letters and her *Commonweal* article: "I am amused that so many of the reviews of this book begin with the statement, 'This book is hard to classify.' Then why bother?"[57]

Just as the book was published, Cather wrote Fanny Butcher. "I've always wanted to try something in the style of a legend, with a sort of New Testament calm, and I think I succeeded fairly well," Cather explained (she made a similar statement in her *Commonweal* article). "I had a glorious year doing it, and working in that new form with no solid drama," an acknowledgment that the book lacked conflict.[58] After Butcher published her positive review—one that stated that Cather had written about folklore, Cather wrote back, "I said legend, didn't I, not folk-lore? There's such a difference. Folk-lore is unarticulated—detached. But legend is a sort of interpretation of life by Faith." She added, "You did nobly by me in your review."[59]

Over time, the negative comments lost their sting, or at least they should have, seeing how well the public took to the book: It was an artistic, commercial, and literary success. Still, Cather couldn't quite let it go. She wrote her mother in 1931, "When the 'Archbishop' first came out, all the reviews were unfavorable and many of them savage. Now those same newspapers call it a 'classic.'"[60]

The literary and popular success of *Archbishop* confirmed Cather's status as one of the country's leading authors. She won the William Dean Howells Medal for the novel in 1930. That same year, *Good Housekeeping* magazine began publishing a series of profiles covering what its readers considered the twelve most significant American women alive. Willa Cather was included in the list, which also included Jane Addams, Carrie Chapman Catt, and Helen Keller. Her profile was published in September 1931—the same month that critic Granville Hicks published his dismissive article calling Cather a "minor artist" (we'll get to him shortly). Cather also earned numerous honorary doctorates, including from the University of California, Columbia, Michigan, Princeton (she was the first woman to receive an honorary degree there), Yale, and of course her own University of Nebraska. Cather was honored with the gold medal of the American Academy of Arts and Letters for fiction in 1944.[61]

Cather was especially fond of the story called "December Night," a section within "The Great Diocese" chapter. The imagery is particularly lovely, the silence of the falling snow, the weeping slave woman Sada and Latour's kindness toward her, their midnight prayers at the altar, and Cather's profound statement that "Only a Woman, divine, could know all that a woman can suffer" (217). Knopf published this section as a standalone booklet for Christmas 1933 with Harold von Schmidt's illustrations.

In 1935 an agent approached Cather and Alfred Knopf on behalf of a client to ask if they could dramatize *Death Comes for the Archbishop*. She had agreed to sell the film rights for *A Lost Lady*, and two film adaptations were produced. The first was fairly faithful to the novel, but Cather was aghast at how Warner Brothers bastardized her story in the second production. She instructed Alfred Knopf to reply, "On no account does Miss Cather permit dramatization of any of her books, and Mr. Knopf also would refuse to grant his permission." Knopf noted her repeated rejection of Hollywood agents who wanted to adapt her novels for the screen.[62]

By February 1942, two months after the Japanese attack on Pearl Harbor, Knopf reported that *Archbishop* had sold 178,000 copies.[63] World War II in turn led to the Armed Services Editions (ASE), small paperbacks designed to fit into a sailor or soldier's pocket. The ASE included many of the leading American novels that the Pentagon considered appropriate for troops to read. Thousands of copies of *Archbishop*, along with *O Pioneers!* and *My Ántonia*, were distributed for free to American men and women in uniform.[64]

During the war, *The Saturday Evening Post* reported on the impact of the ASE and how the service members eagerly read these stories, including one wounded soldier who read Cather: "Huddled in a muddy foxhole on Leyte with a hole in his ankle, Corp. Erwin Rorick spent the hours before help came reading Willa Cather's Death Comes for the Archbishop. He had grabbed it the day before under the delusion that it was a murder mystery, but he discovered, to his amazement, that he liked it anyway."[65]

As the 1930s and the Great Depression progressed, Cather earned a new batch of critics: left-wing intellectuals and Marxists. Many American intellectuals of the era became enamored with the Soviet Union as they recognized the failings of capitalism; only later did they learn of the human catastrophe as Comrade Stalin starved millions to advance the union's material economy and sent perceived enemies of the state to Siberian gulags. The dictatorship of the proletariat turned out to be just another dictatorship.

Left-wing critics admired Cather's writing craft but despised the fact that she wouldn't join their cause to uplift the industrial workers of the world, and so they turned against her. And indeed, she was a conservative who had no interest in making political art.[66] Biographer Hermione Lee put it succinctly: "She was a writer who worked, at her best, through indirection, suppression, and suggestion, and through a refusal to be enlisted."[67]

Clifton Fadiman, a leading intellectual who became a radio and television personality in the 1950s, wrote that Cather offered moral courage "acting in harmony with convention. It never takes up arms against the social order."[68] Columbia University English professor and literary critic Lionel Trilling tut-tutted, "Miss Cather has gone down to defeat before the actualities of American life."[69] Marxist critic V. F. Calverton (née George Goetz) made the ultimate of radical insults, calling Cather "petty bourgeois."[70]

Harlan Hatcher, who later became the president of the University of Michigan, was the most positive of these critics toward Cather. "She had comforted the hearts of millions who revered her because she had written a realism which could be read in schools and women's clubs where Theodore Dreiser and Sherwood Anderson would have caused a panic," he wrote. He concluded, "In a bewildered age whose uncertainties and preoccupation with fundamental problems of economics and government suggest nothing to challenge her fine pen, she has become the most talented of our escapists."[71]

One of these leftist critics drew Cather's ire: Granville Hicks. He published a mean-spirited review of *Shadows on the Rock* in *Forum* in September 1931. He opened his broadside with an attack on Cather herself by dismissing her as a "minor artist." What Hicks exposed was his own bias against Cather's gift for nostalgia and sparse description: "Like most of her books, it is elegiac, beguiling readers with pictures of a life that has disappeared, and deliberately exploiting the remoteness of that life in order to cast a golden haze about it." Cather was from an earlier generation of writers, and Hicks believed that her time had passed. "To-day, perhaps even more than in the past, it takes stern stuff to make a novelist," he penned. "Miss Cather, one is forced to conclude, has always been soft; and now she has abandoned herself to her softness."[72]

Every author gets a bad review now and then, but this review deeply hurt Cather's feelings, which seemed an ad hominem attack on her, rather than on her work. "It is possible to say uncomplimentary things in a courteous and even a respectful way," she protested to Henry Leach, *Forum*'s editor. It was a double betrayal, as Leach had published *Archbishop* in serial form in 1927, and Cather had always considered him friendly to her writing. "But the tone of this article is sarcastic and contemptuous throughout." She took strong exception to Hick's phrase "deliberately exploiting" and scolded Leach, "This is the first letter of protest I have ever written an editor concerning a review, and I am very sad that it is to you I am addressing it."[73]

The following spring, she responded to Leach's two apologetic letters for Hicks's review. "The review about which I wrote you was the only review that ever gave me a case of hurt feelings; and my grievance was entirely a personal one," she wrote. "I mean by that that I was hurt as a person, not as a writer." She concluded the letter with a casual dismissal of Hicks: "Please let us have tea together and drink to Mr. Hicks—if that was his name." In this exchange Cather demonstrated her flintiness; her usual thick emotional skin could be pierced.[74]

Hicks was not done with Cather. He continued his campaign in a 1933 essay called "The Case Against Willa Cather." He decried "the political conservatism that is in all her works." He went on, "Miss Cather has never once tried to see contemporary life as it is; she sees only that it lacks what the past, at least in her idealization of it, had." Cather was guilty of "supine romanticism" and nostalgia.[75]

Hicks took aim at *Archbishop*, calling it "highly episodic." He wrote, "At first one is charmed, but soon questions arise. One asks what unity there is in these various episodes, and one can find none except in Miss Cather's sense that here, in the meeting of old and new, is a process of rare beauty." He admired Cather's considerable skill as a writer, but he rejected her perspective. He concluded damnably, "Miss Cather, we see, has simply projected her own desires into the past: her longing for heroism, her admiration for natural beauty, her desire—intensified by pre-occupation with doubt and despair—for the security of an unquestioned faith."[76]

When leftist critics accused her of escapism, Cather responded in a 1936 letter to *Commonweal*, "What has art ever been but escape? . . . When the world is in a bad way, we are told, it is the business of the composer and the poet to devote himself to propaganda and fan the flames of indignation. But the world has a habit of being in a bad way from time to time, and art has never contributed anything to help matters except escape." She then launched an oblique attack on Marxist critics like Hicks and the nihilist writers of the Lost Generation: "They were to bring about a renaissance within a decade or so. Failing this, they made a career of destroying the past. The only new thing they offered us was contempt for the old."[77]

Another negative critique came from John Randall, who called *Archbishop* a "poorly organized book" in his 1960 overview of Cather's writing, published thirteen years after her death. But is that a fair criticism? Just because Cather shuffled the timeline doesn't mean the novel has no organization. From a linear perspective, the narrative may appear unconventional, but from an emotional perspective, the novel builds toward a conclusion of loss and acceptance. Cather knew what she was doing.[78]

Randall disliked the novel's lack of conflict, a valid criticism. Cather "asks us to admire the Bishop as both a pioneer and a deeply religious man, whereas in the book he is neither. Pioneers have to struggle, but the Bishop lets Father Vaillant do his struggling for him. Religious men have to face the problem of evil and suffering, but this too is carefully avoided." Fair enough. But what of Cather's sparse language that conveyed the desert landscape of the Southwest? "Some beautiful description of landscape and a well-conceived minor character or two" was all that Randall was willing to credit her. He concluded damningly that Cather "has given us four walls and left the passion out" and that "it is not a good book." Randall was quipping on Cather's own words, as she was fond of quoting Alexandre Dumas's principle that a great drama only needed one passion and four walls.[79]

As the United States has become more aware of its historic role as a European colony that expanded into a continental empire, more recent critics have addressed the questions around America as a colonial power. These critics view the world through a postcolonial lens and the impact of colonialism on Indigenous peoples and minorities. Some opposed

Cather's views of Latour as the redemptive colonizer, her simplification of the Hispanic population, and her portrayal of Natives as antediluvian. Patricia Clark Smith described it as Cather's "colonial attitude" and denounced *Archbishop* as "an astonishing document of colonialism." Historian Ray John de Aragón criticized Cather for using "fictional and bigoted material" in how she portrayed the novel's antagonist Padre Antonio José Martínez. E. A. Mares called the novel "badly flawed by her cultural parochialism and narrow and ugly ethnic perspectives." These critics viewed Lamy as unsympathetic to Hispanic traditions and insensitive for building a European cathedral in Santa Fe.[80]

But these are the outliers in the world of Cather critics. Many more critics, as well as readers, have come to appreciate the novel. She considered it her finest book, and it remains one of her most popular works. She wrote a fan in 1931, "I think that 'Death Comes for the Archbishop' will stand the wear and tear better than the others."[81]

E. K. Brown published an "Homage to Willa Cather" in *The Yale Review* in fall 1946, reviewing her writing career at age seventy (she was in fact seventy-three, having altered her birth year to seem younger). "'Death Comes for the Archbishop' is her great book, the most beautiful achievement of her imagination; in it at last her craftsmanship and her vision are in relation, and that relation is complete," he wrote. "The length of her unconscious preparation to write it had served her well indeed."[82]

The Unfurnished Novel

In 1922 Cather described decluttering a house as a metaphor for writing. Her intention was to strip away extraneous and irrelevant material, leaving just four walls and passion. *Death Comes for the Archbishop* reflects this style. Cather's prose in *Archbishop* is deceptively simple, and it conveys a sense of living people, faith, breathtaking landscapes, and above all profound friendship.[83]

In the novel, two French Catholic priests meet at seminary, became best friends, and decide to become missionaries in the United States. The characters are Jean Marie Latour and Joseph Vaillant. Vaillant is torn between his devotion to serving God and his duty to his widowed father.

Latour encourages Vaillant to take the voyage with him to America, and later to join him in New Mexico, where he is appointed bishop shortly after the American conquest of the Southwest following the Mexican-American War. The novel unfolds as New Mexico transforms from frontier to American territory, symbolized by the arrival of the railroad.

Cather created two leading characters who were opposites in personality: one reserved, the other outgoing. She gave them symbolic names: Latour (the tower) and Vaillant (valiant). The tower established the orthodoxy of the church and upheld its traditions, while the valiant one rode from mission to mission, bringing the gospel to people who had not seen a priest in years.

As we saw, Cather did not refer to *Archbishop* as a novel, but rather as a "narrative." In modern day parlance, we'd call it historical fiction. But other than the basic facts of Bishop Lamy's life, Cather's Latour was a profoundly different person from the real Lamy. One must read the book with the understanding that it is fiction with a historical background. Cather wrote in *Commonweal* in 1927, "I followed the life story of the two Bishops very much as it was, though I used many of my own experiences, and some of my father's," recalling Charles Cather's trip to the Southwest in 1872.[84]

The four novels that Cather published in the 1920s before *Archbishop*—*One of Ours*, *A Lost Lady*, *The Professor's House*, and *My Mortal Enemy*—have dark themes. Biographer Janis Stout called them "metaphors for the world's larger brokenness." The first deals with a young Nebraskan unhappy with his life and his marriage, and who fights and dies in World War I. In the second book, an upper-middle-class woman loses her fortune and status; in the third, a professor experiences a midlife crisis and realizes he is no longer in love with his wife; and in the fourth, a wife comes to find contempt for her husband as their lives spiral downward. In *Death Comes for the Archbishop*, however, Cather took a more uplifting tone, exploring faith, friendship, and a life well lived.[85]

Despite Cather's lifelong conservatism and her unwillingness to engage in the issues of the day, there are several unexpected things about *Archbishop* that stand out. In Cather's day, American literature was synonymous with white literature, but *Archbishop* is a multicultural novel that reflects the diversity of New Mexico's people, and she composed the novel with characters that reflected that diversity. True, her narrative focused on two European male characters, Fathers Latour and Vaillant, but she brought in many others who were not white.

Archbishop reflects the kaleidoscope of American cultures, something which Cather experienced growing up in Nebraska among immigrant farmers, in Pittsburgh and New York City where she lived, and on her many travels to the Southwest. Her hero Bishop Latour has a keen eye for multiculturalism, recognizing that the silver bell in San Miguel Chapel originated with the Moors. "The Spaniards handed on their skill to the Mexicans, and the Mexicans have taught the Navajos to work silver; but it all came from the Moors" (45). When Vaillant prepares onion soup for Christmas, Latour notes approvingly, "A soup like this is not the work of one man. It is the result of a constantly refined tradition. There are nearly a thousand years of history in this soup" (38).

Figure 49. Established around 1610, San Miguel Chapel is a fabulous blend of Hispanic and Native architecture. In the foreground is the church's bell, which Cather's Vaillant taught a Mexican boy to ring the Angelus, and which Latour used to demonstrate the multicultural influences in New Mexico. San Miguel Chapel.

Besides the two French priests, there are only a handful of white American characters in the novel, notably Kit Carson, Doña Isabella, and the murderous Buck Scales. None of them rise to the level of major character. Cather quipped, "I can't see many people in a moving-picture-world caring much about a book with no woman in it but the Virgin Mary," but her novel does include numerous women, though as minor characters. They include Doña Isabella, Magdalena, and Sada. Others are barely mentioned in passing, including Jacinto's wife, Josefa Jaramillo Carson, and Philomène, Father Vaillant's (and Machebeuf's) sister. Cather's focus remains on the two priests and their friendship. *Archbishop* is a male-centered story, not an uncommon thing for Cather.[86]

Legendary frontiersman Kit Carson appears in a handful of scenes. Much of the nation considered Carson a national hero at the time of the novel's publication, and while Cather clearly admired him in her book, she considered him critically. Cather and Lewis had visited Canyon de Chelly and learned of Carson's 1864 military campaign to round up the Navajos and the humanitarian disaster at the Bosque Redondo. She stated, "It was his own misguided friend, Kit Carson, who finally subdued the last unconquered remnant of that people" (291). Cather essentially got it right about Carson: She reduced him from mythical frontier hero to a real person. Carson's heroic status wasn't reconsidered until Americans began reckoning with our own history of colonization and how Manifest Destiny had bulldozed tribes out of the way for white settlers.

Cather's novel romanticized Native Americans, idealizing the fictional characters Eusabio and Jacinto as kind souls. Natives "seemed to have none of the European's desire to 'master' nature, to arrange and re-create," Cather noted. "It was the Indian's way to pass through a country without disturbing anything; to pass and leave no trace, like fish through the water, or birds through the air" (233). "The land and all that it bore they treated with consideration; not attempting to improve upon it, they never desecrated it." (234)

At a time when the official US government policy was to stamp out Native cultures through assimilation and Indian Schools, Cather made a quiet case for respecting the Indigenous people for who they are without turning them into mainstream Americans. Many Americans of the time harbored racist and stereotypical images of Native people as primitives or savages or viewed them romantically through the lens of James Fenimore Cooper's fiction, but Cather portrayed them as kind and peaceful. She grasped the importance of land to Native peoples. Considering that the novel came out just three years after the federal Indian Citizenship Act, this is remarkable. Cather seemed ahead of her time in including sensitive Native portraits.

Through Latour's voice, Cather wrote prophetically, "I do not believe, as I once did, that the Indian will perish. I believe that God will preserve him" (296). This was four decades before President Richard Nixon ended the federal government's assimilationist policies toward Indigenous people.

Hispanics make up the vast bulk of characters in *Archbishop* (she called them Mexicans, which is how the population self-identified in the 1800s), and Cather's treatment of them runs the gamut from villainous to virtuous. While she was mostly sympathetic, she oversimplified their lives and disregarded the racism they had long experienced in the United States. Still, the book has a broad range of Hispanic characters. Some characters like Manuel Chávez and Padre Martínez she portrayed as anti-American and violent, while the Mexican priests (Gallegos, Lucero, Fray Baltazar) were corrupt and worldly. But she portrayed others such as Magdalena as pious, Sada as a sainted victim, and Manuel Lujon as reluctantly bighearted. She pointed out Hispanic generosity in contrast to the behavior of capitalist Americans and reminded the reader how important Catholicism is to Mexican culture.

On my Willa Cather's Santa Fe walking tour, the most frequent comment I hear from *Archbishop* readers is how much they appreciate Cather's sparse but stunning descriptions of New Mexico's landscape, something that she wrote from her own experiences. The desert is austere, minimal, and unfurnished, like Cather's prose. In the first chapter, she introduces her protagonist, Bishop Jean Marie Latour, who is lost in the desert: "Every canonical hill was spotted with smaller cones of juniper, a uniform yellowish green, as the hills were a uniform red. The hills thrust out of the ground so thickly that they seemed to be pushing each other, elbowing each other aside, tipping each other over" (18).

The next most common observation I hear comes from Catholics, who are impressed at how accurately Cather captured church rituals. It is remarkable, especially since she wasn't Catholic. Cather published a mainstream novel that painted Catholicism in a positive light at a time when many Americans were deeply prejudiced against the church and Protestant fundamentalism was seeing a resurgence. When New York Governor Al Smith, a Catholic with a deep accent, ran for the presidency in 1928, his opponents played the anti-Catholic card from the bottom of the deck. Herbert Hoover won the presidency in a landslide. The country was not ready for a Catholic president, waiting until the election of John F. Kennedy in 1960.

Cather was neither Catholic, Hispanic, Indigenous, nor male, nor a priest, and yet she wrote a brilliant and beautiful novel encompassing all these things. Catholics deluged her with fan mail and expressed their gratitude for writing a pro-Catholic novel. No one accused her of cultural appropriation or demanded that she stay in her lane as a white person. Her empathy for the human experience was profound.

Cather often experimented with her writing, and in the case of *Archbishop* she focused the novel on episodes, rather than a solid narrative. It's like the New Testament's Book of Acts, which tells the story of the early Christian church. Although the novel unfolds roughly chronologically and is mostly set in the 1850s, Cather included flashbacks, memories, and parables. Her writing was deeply nuanced, and at this peak in her writing career, she had mastered the art of showing rather than telling. You find places in the novel where you unexpectedly tear up, such as Father Latour giving Vaillant the two mules, or the final scene where Latour envisions waiting for the stagecoach with Vaillant, with the stagecoach serving as a vessel to carry his soul away. Cather wove this story into the novel three times, like a theme that repeats itself in a Navajo rug.

The author held a bias in favor of European culture over Mexican culture, even though the latter was ancient and steeped in tradition. In her perspective, Europeans were superior and more cultivated than the Indigenous people and simple Mexicans that Latour encountered. Throughout the novel, she signaled her approval of the shift from primitivism to civilization. Westerners like Latour brought Christianity, order, and progress, as they saw it. His mission was to establish the church's authority over the frontier, but Cather was more interested in exploring Latour's spiritual experiences in the desert than how Lamy governed his diocese.

The novel's tone rings of nostalgia. This was a common theme in Cather's books, her longing for the past, for the lost frontier, for childhood, for past trips. *Archbishop* is above all a book about friendship. Bishop Latour seldom if ever does anything wrong and lives a life largely without conflict. He lives what Bette Weidman called an "optimistic fatalism." The one open conflict is with Padre Martínez, which Cather's Latour handles passively, and she never provides an ending to this episode. She simply declares victory for Latour and moves on.[87]

Besides unfurnishing a novel, Cather developed a technique in the 1920s that she called juxtaposition. She defined it as a way "to cut out all analysis, observation, description, even the picture-making quality, in order to make things and people tell their own story simply by juxtaposition, without any persuasion or explanation on my part." Cather got her point across by showing rather than explaining ideas in contrast with one another, hence the idea of juxtaposition.[88]

In *Archbishop*, Cather uses juxtaposition through the various tableaus that form the novel, like paintings lined up at an exhibit. A prominent example is her placing Latour and Vaillant's visit to the quarry adjacent to Latour's dispatching Vaillant to serve Colorado gold miners. She contrasts Fray Baltazar's self-serving and death at Acoma Pueblo and the gourmand bishops in Rome in the prologue against Vaillant's service to the people. There is the juxtaposition of the grand architecture of the Vatican compared to the immense landscape of the American Southwest. Or the green carpet of France against the ochre, sagebrush desert of New Mexico, or the Catholic orthodoxy juxtaposed against the mysteries of Native faith.[89]

Cather employs a fair amount of nonlinear writing in *Archbishop*. That is, the plot does not always advance from point A to point B along a chronological line; rather, she uses flashbacks, such as the archbishop experienced in the final chapter as he recounts his life and remembers the stagecoach taking him and Vaillant away in the final moments. The legend of Fray Baltazar takes place one hundred fifty years before the novel's main story.

Fanny Butcher recalled a conversation with Cather: "Once when we talked about *The Archbishop*, she said, 'It's an altogether new kind for me, and how I loved doing it. I was as if you had, after playing only modern composers, taken the time and used the control to practice Bach awhile without any comparison." Cather clearly came to love this novel and her protagonist Latour, leaving behind the dramatic treatment and focusing instead on hagiography set on the American frontier.[90]

We've looked at how Willa Cather's Southwestern travels influenced her writings, in particular *Death Comes for the Archbishop*. In the next chapters, we'll take a deeper dive into the historical record compared to Cather's frontier novel. We'll explore Archbishop Lamy, Padre Martínez, Native faith, the St. Francis Cathedral, and finally, how death came for the archbishop and for Willa Cather.

Chapter 7

The Vicar Apostolic

"Everything showed him to be a man of gentle birth—brave, sensitive, courteous. His manners, even when he was alone in the desert, were distinguished. He had a kind of courtesy toward himself, toward his beasts, toward the juniper tree before which he knelt, and the God whom he was addressing."

—Willa Cather, *Death Comes for the Archbishop* (19)

New Mexico has a surprising and largely hidden French history. Some of the first Frenchmen to live in the territory weren't Catholic priests, but rather French-Canadian fur trappers who settled in Taos, the southernmost beaver pelt market. Willa Cather was a Francophile, and she was probably surprised to learn of New Mexico's French influence. But it's no surprise that she was drawn to the elegant-looking French bishop whose statue stands in front of the St. Francis Cathedral in Santa Fe, which he built.

But we must ask: What was a French bishop doing in New Mexico when there was a small cadre of Mexican priests already working there? The answer lies in the American occupation of the Southwest during the Mexican-American War of 1846–1848. The United States government seized a huge swatch of Mexican territory in the peace treaty, paying Mexico just $15 million, and it needed authority figures to help establish American authority. The existing bishop was in Durango, Mexico, a thousand miles to the south, and that simply would not do. The federal

Figure 50. Bishop Jean-Baptiste Lamy around 1860. He served as the prototype for Jean Marie Latour in Cather's novel. Palace of the Governors Photo Archives (NMHM/DCA), Image 035878.

government asked the Catholic Church to appoint a bishop to Santa Fe. The church chose a French missionary priest who was working in Kentucky and Ohio. His name was Jean-Baptiste Lamy.

Lamy was born on October 11, 1814, in the town of Lempdes, part of the south-central region of Auvergne, France. He was the youngest of eleven children born to a peasant family deeply rooted in the Catholic faith. Three of Lamy's siblings lived to adulthood: His brother Louis became a priest, his sister Marguerite became a nun, while only a brother, Etienne, married and had children. Two of Etienne's children, Antoine and Marie, became a priest and a nun, respectively, and both would serve in New Mexico under their uncle. Etienne named another son after his brother, and this younger Jean-Baptiste would likewise make his way to Santa Fe.

Lamy attended the College of Clermont and then the seminary at Montferrand, which became known as the Nursery of the Missionaries of the New World for the high number of priests who served in America. The future Bishop Lamy would recruit heavily from Montferrand. There he met Joseph Machebeuf, a man who became his lifelong best friend and the model for Cather's Father Vaillant. Machebeuf was two years older than Lamy, and the two men were quite the contrast. Lamy was tall, slim, and Gallic looking, with a head of wavy brown hair that would recede over time. He was serene and quietly confident. He would prove to be a good administrator and leader.[1]

Machebeuf was short and fair-skinned—his friends nicknamed him *Blanchet* (Whitey). They also called him *Trompe-la-Mort*, or Death's Deceiver, as he was constantly getting ill but then would recover. Cather used both these nicknames for Vaillant. "One of the first thing a stranger decided upon meeting Father Joseph was that the Lord had made few uglier men," (37) Cather wrote.

Figure 51. Father Joseph Machebeuf accompanied Lamy to the United States and to New Mexico. He became the first bishop of the Denver diocese. Cather based the character of Father Vaillant on him. Reverend Joseph P. Machebeuf, ca. 1885. History Colorado. Accession #89.451.2552.

Indeed, Machebeuf was not particularly good looking, but he was animated and a charming storyteller who had a way of putting people at ease. He was also a man of outspoken opinions and strong in his convictions. He was seldom intimidated, and his moral courage gave him the ability to act decisively, even alone.[2]

Lamy was ordained in December 1838. The following year, he met the Irish-born bishop of Cincinnati, John Baptist Purcell, who was recruiting missionary priests. Purcell convinced Lamy and Machebeuf to serve in Ohio. The bishop became a lifelong friend to Lamy, as well as a valuable mentor who helped steer him through the Vatican bureaucracy. Lamy and Machebeuf made plans to sail for America, where they would spend their careers.[3]

Knowing that Machebeuf's stern father would object to his son leaving for America, Lamy and Machebeuf took a midnight stagecoach to Paris without telling their parents. It broke Machebeuf's heart to leave his family this way, but he felt it was the only way he could respond to his calling. Father Howlett explained that Machebeuf "lay down on the floor of it [the stagecoach] in order to escape observation" as it drove past his father's house.[4]

Cather included three versions of this story in her novel, carefully inserted as flashbacks. The fictional Vaillant suffers greatly as his heart is torn in two over abandoning his father, while Latour encourages his friend to make the trip. "That parting was not a parting, but an escape—a running away, a betrayal of family trust for the sake of a higher trust," Cather wrote (204).[5]

In Ohio, Lamy and Machebeuf were separated but stayed in touch: Lamy built church communities in northern Kentucky and southern Ohio, while Machebeuf was stationed in Sandusky on Lake Erie. As missionary priests, both had to establish congregations, raise funds, and build churches.

After Lamy spent ten years working in the Ohio diocese, and after the United States had captured the vast territories in the Southwest from Mexico, Pope Pius IX named Lamy the vicar apostolic (a precursor to bishop) for the New Mexico Territory on November 24, 1850. Lamy then faced the arduous journey to reach his remote vicariate.

Numerous bishops cautioned Lamy to recruit priests to assist him. He would need allies, as he was a new authority in a territory that had long existed with little church oversight. Lamy did not take their advice. He only recruited only one person to join him: Joseph Machebeuf.[6]

Lamy asked Machebeuf to be his vicar general, his second-in-charge. Machebeuf wrote his siblings about Lamy's written invitation: "They wish that I should be a Vicar Apostolic, and I wish you to be my Vicar General, and from these two vicars we shall try to make one good Pastor." Lamy traveled to Cincinnati to meet his friend "and settle the matter once for all with him. As soon as he saw me he grasped my hand and summoned me to keep my part of the agreement which we made never to separate."[7]

Rather than take the overland route to Santa Fe through Independence, Missouri—the nine-hundred-mile Santa Fe Trail—Lamy opted for the longer route that would bring him to Texas by ship. This meant steaming down the Mississippi River to New Orleans, then boarding a ship to Galveston, then another to Indianola in Matagorda Bay, then going overland to San Antonio, then westward over Texas's vast plains to the Rio Grande, and finally northward to Santa Fe.

Before Lamy could begin the overland journey, his ship, the *Palmetto*, wrecked in a storm at Indianola. He escaped unharmed but lost most of his possessions (he did pay a young slave to retrieve his trunk full of books). Machebeuf joined Lamy in San Antonio, and from there they joined an Army supply train that crossed the Texas plains to El Paso. It was important to have an escort, as there were hostile tribes like the Apache and Comanche who might kill isolated travelers.

In 1849 James Calhoun was appointed as the first Indian agent for the New Mexico Territory. He assessed the challenges facing this vast, dangerous country in early 1850: "This territory is encircled by wild Indians—the Apaches—Comanches—Navajoes, and Utahs, and a large portion of the country within this circle, checkered by Pueblos of Indians, known as the 'Christian Indians', and in close proximity to these, are various Spanish, or Mexican villages." He continued, "Those within the circle and those who form the circle look upon each other as natural enemies, and they are eternally at war, robbing and enslaving each other." Calhoun later became territorial governor.[8]

As Lamy and Machebeuf traveled north toward Santa Fe from El Paso, they met poor Mexicans who were observant but uneducated and with little priestly guidance, wealthy landowners, and a few obstinate priests, who were less than excited about new foreign leadership, even if the two Frenchmen weren't Americans. Machebeuf sensed trouble. He wrote, "But, alas! the great obstacle to the good which the Bishop is disposed to do among them, does not come from the people but from the priests themselves, who do not want the Bishop, for they dread a reform in their morals, or a change in their selfish relations with their parishioners."[9]

Word had preceded the new bishop's arrival in Santa Fe. Padre Juan Felipe Ortiz, the bishop of Durango's *vicario forane* (rural dean), who had served in the position since 1832, traveled south to welcome Lamy at Tomé and accompanied him to the capital. Ortiz was rotund, fair-skinned, and easygoing. He enlisted the civilian and military authorities to provide a warm welcome for the new bishop. At every village, hundreds of Mexicans gathered along the side of the road and built triumphal arches to welcome Lamy, who stopped at numerous parishes and was feted along the way.

On August 9, 1851, Lamy and Machebeuf found an impressive welcome awaiting them as they approached Santa Fe. Territorial Governor James Calhoun and a military escort met the newcomers along the Camino Real six miles south of the city. They rode into the capital like a triumphant parade. Most of the city, whose population numbered only forty-five hundred people, lined the road and cheered the vicar apostolic's arrival. The guns of Fort Marcy fired salutes in his honor. Lamy was thirty-seven when he took up his position. Machebeuf was thirty-nine but looked decades older.

Lamy conducted a Te Deum at the Guadalupe sanctuary just south of the Santa Fe River, then entered the city. The procession halted at La Parroquia, the nickname for San Francisco de Asís, the early eighteenth-century adobe parish church that looked like a small castle with its crenelated roofline, where Lamy and prominent citizens celebrated mass. Padre Ortiz hosted a feast that night. Ortiz generously offered Lamy the use of his large home, which he had turned into a suitable ecclesiastic house.

Despite the warm welcome, Lamy soon learned of political

Figure 52. La Parroquia, or the parish church of Santa Fe, around 1867. Palace of the Governors Photo Archives (NMHM/DCA), Image 010059.

factionalism in the city. The territorial governor, James Calhoun, had enemies who sought to discredit him. They first sought to draw the judiciary against him, but when the judges declared their neutrality, they seized upon an innocuous transfer of property between the judiciary and the church to make it seem like religious freedom was under threat, which in turn would inflame local opinion.

A chapel for the Mexican garrison, Our Lady of the Light, better known to locals as La Castrense, had stood on the south side of the Plaza since 1760. The chapel had fallen into disrepair and the US Army requisitioned it for storage. The military later cleared out the building so territorial judge Grafton Baker could convene his court there. When Lamy arrived in Santa Fe, he sought to have the chapel returned to the Catholic Church.

The Santa Fe Gazette published an irresponsible article alleging that Judge Baker had stated he would rather see Lamy hanged than return the chapel. Local men circulated a petition demanding that the chapel be returned and threatened that the judge might be lynched for his comments. Lamy found himself confronted by angry parishioners. He urged them to remain peaceful and return home without harming the judge.

In fact, there was no dispute between the church and judiciary. Court clerk Caleb Sherman served as the intermediary as they negotiated an agreement to return the church to Lamy on August 25. The bishop would reimburse the costs for building improvements, and Judge Baker agreed to move his court to the Palace of the Governors. The next day, Baker ceremoniously handed the keys to Territorial Governor James Calhoun, who in turn handed them to Lamy.[10]

Lamy considered whether La Castrense could serve as his cathedral; however, the church faced the Plaza, which was far too noisy for quiet contemplation. He moved his cathedral to a quieter location, La Parroquia, a block away. Later that year, wealthy gambling house owner Maria Gertrudis Barceló, known as Doña Tules, died, and her extravagant $1,649 funeral paid for renovations to La Castrense. The chapel reopened for several years. She was buried in La Parroquia.[11]

Besides *The Santa Fe Gazette*, another local newspaper began publishing two years before Lamy's arrival: *The Santa Fe New Mexican*. It was a frontier newspaper for the growing Anglo community, which published four pages: two in English, the other two in Spanish. Many of the merchants were German Jews, such as the Spiegelberg and Staab families, who would become Lamy's friends.

One of the merchants who worked on the Santa Fe Trail for most of the 1830s was Josiah Gregg, who rode across the plains eight times and spent considerable time in New Mexico. He published his observations in the influential book *Commerce of the Prairies* in 1844, two years before the Mexican-American War broke out. The book stirred Anglo feelings (and prejudices) about the Spanish-speaking inhabitants. "The New Mexicans appear to have inherited much of the cruelty and intolerance of their ancestors, and no small portion of their bigotry and fanaticism," he wrote. However, he also observed that "there are to be found among them numerous instances of uncompromising virtue, good faith and religious forbearance."[12]

Carousing, dancing the fandango, gambling, and horse racing were the pastimes in this small town. Prostitution was common, and virtually everyone had turned a blind eye to it for centuries. William Davis, who came to New Mexico in 1853, was scandalized as only a white Protestant could be. "Probably there is no other country in the world, claiming to be civilized, where vice is more prevalent among all classes of the inhabitants," he observed. "The people of New Mexico have inherited all the vices of their ancestors," parroting Josiah Gregg's 1844 book. He was appalled by unmarried (common law) couples living together and raising children, in part because of high fees the church charged for weddings, and shocked at how many married men kept mistresses—and likewise how some married women kept a man on the side.[13]

Conventional wisdom long held that Padre Juan Felipe Ortiz refused to recognize Lamy's authority, despite Lamy's papers from the Vatican. Ortiz supposedly only recognized the Bishop of Durango, José Antonio Laureano de Zubiría, since New Mexico had long been under his domain. What followed was the widely told story of how Lamy traveled to Durango, taking Ortiz with him, to ask Zubiría to recognize Lamy's authority. Cather included this in *Archbishop*. But the story wasn't true.

Historian Fray Angélico Chávez challenged this myth in the 1980s. Ortiz never disputed Lamy's authority. After all, he organized the welcoming party for the new vicar apostolic, and even cleared out his home for Lamy. These were not the actions of one who was challenging the authority of his new boss. Lamy and Ortiz did in fact set out for Durango in September 1851, traveling the thousand miles to the Mexican city. This was not to seek recognition, but rather for Lamy to discuss jurisdictional boundaries with Bishop Zubiría. The Mexican bishop was indeed surprised by Lamy's visit, as he had no word from the Vatican on the appointment. Ortiz was close to Zubiría and had other business to conduct with him.[14]

Neither Lamy nor Machebeuf were impressed with the Mexican clergy and may have been stunned at how few there were: just seventeen working priests for this vast territory, and several of them beyond retirement age. American Protestants gossiped about the Catholic clergy, and this may have influenced Lamy and Machebeuf even before they arrived in Santa Fe to believe that the clergy were corrupt, dissolute, and inept. What followed was a culture clash between a heterodox French Catholic bishop and the few Mexican priests, who had largely been on their own, and who had struggled for years since Mexican independence to serve their congregations with the meager resources at hand.[15]

When Lamy arrived in 1851, there were only twenty-five churches and forty chapels in the territory. Many villages hadn't seen a priest in years.[16] Machebeuf maintained a bias against the Mexican priests, as he described in a letter: "In a population of 70,000, including the converted Indians, there are but fifteen priests [actually seventeen], and six of these are worn out by age and have no energy. The others have not a spark of zeal, and their lives are scandalous beyond description."[17]

Lamy's decision to bring only one ally with him, Machebeuf, came to haunt him. He began suspending priests or forcing them into retirement, but initially he had no one to replace them with besides Machebeuf. Lamy was more conservative than the Mexican priests and authoritative, and the people he trusted most were the clergy trained at Montferrand, who shared a similar cultural and theological background. Simply put: he had a manpower shortage, and thus he recruited from France, rather than from Mexico.

Fray Angélico Chávez, one of New Mexico's most prominent twentieth-century historians, defended the Mexican priests, believing the accusations of corruption were overstated. He particularly took aim at Machebeuf, who he believed "loved to exaggerate like a gossipy hen, and was not averse to deliberate lying when it suited his sexual preoccupation best." Chávez believed Machebeuf to be deeply flawed, while Lamy was blind to Machebeuf's faults. Or worse: Machebeuf had "a sick preoccupation with sexual matters which in its headlong blind fanaticism took a grim delight in sniffing out immorality everywhere he turned."[18]

New Mexican Catholicism is deeply rooted in ritual and tradition, with special veneration for Our Lady of Guadalupe, the 1531 apparition of the Virgin Mary in what is now Mexico City. Much of the population was illiterate, so religious art like *bultos* (carved wooden statues) and *retablos* (paintings) were important for interpreting the living faith. It was a distinct church culture that developed through isolation and the absence of strong authority. As the fictional Padre Antonio José Martínez states in Cather's novel, "Our religion grew out of the soil, and has its own roots" (146). A culture clash between Lamy and the local clergy would not be surprising in this context.

The St. Francis Cathedral in Santa Fe added a towering altar screen in 1986 that highlights important Catholics in the Americas. Soon after, artist Diane Quasthoff designed a stunning set of bronze doors that tell the story of the Catholic Church in New Mexico through twenty panels. Lamy appears in five of those panels. He is a big deal here, having instituted many reforms, as well as serving as Cather's prototype for her novel.

Lamy built new churches, heavily recruited French priests to fill the many vacant parishes, and made education a priority. He helped establish health care. He brought his diocese squarely under church authority. Lamy helped lobby for the railroad to come to Santa Fe. He constructed the St. Francis Cathedral, a monument to God, but which we can also view as a contemporary monument to Lamy.

Lamy realized that educational resources were lacking in New Mexico, especially for young women. He appealed to the Sisters of Loretto in Kentucky to send nuns to open a school. Lamy traveled east in 1852 to attend a conference of bishops in Baltimore; on his return he brought six sisters with him. The mother superior died enroute, while another fell ill

Figure 53. Our Lady of Light Academy, better known as the Loretto school, the first parochial school that Lamy established in 1853. Only the neogothic Loretto Chapel (center) still stands. Palace of the Governors Photo Archives, (NMHM/DCA), Image 013262.

and returned. Lamy arrived in Santa Fe in late 1852 with the four sisters, now headed by Sister Mary Magdalen Hayden. They opened the Academy of Our Lady of Light to an initial class of forty-two female students. The Loretto school would eventually occupy an entire city block. More sisters arrived to meet the burgeoning demand for education. At its peak, the Loretto academy supported three hundred students.[19]

In the summer of 1853, the Vicariate of New Mexico became the Diocese of Santa Fe, and Lamy was elevated to bishop, two years after his arrival. That same year, the federal government acquired a strip of land from Mexico in what is now southern Arizona and New Mexico, known as the Gadsden Purchase. This secured a right-of-way for a southern transcontinental railroad. The region, which had been under the ecclesiastical authority of the bishop of Durango, was now Lamy's responsibility.

Lamy departed for Europe in February 1854 and was absent for almost ten months. During his absence, Machebeuf served as acting bishop in Santa Fe. Lamy traveled to Rome, where he met Pope Pius IX and recruited a Spanish priest, Damaso Taladrid, for service in his diocese, and then journeyed to France to recruit more priests.

Lamy now had a growing contingent of French priests to fill the vacant parishes, and he had reinforcement to replace problematic Mexican priests. He assigned Father Antoine Juillard to Belén, Father Jean François Martin to Isleta Pueblo, Father Etienne Avel to Santa Fe to assist the bishop, and Father Peter Eguillon initially to teach theology, then assigned him to Socorro. Father Taladrid was assigned to Santa Clara and San Ildefonso pueblos in 1854, then to Taos in 1856 when Padre Antonio José Martínez announced his retirement. Machebeuf returned to the Albuquerque parish. When a priest was assigned to a parish, it was not just to a single church: He had to cover numerous villages. Priests spent considerable time on horseback or in a wagon, journeying to visit settlements within their parishes. Cather witnessed this firsthand during her visits to the Southwest in the early twentieth century.

Lamy seemed to trust his fellow Frenchmen the most. He recruited so many French missionary priests from Montferrand that his diocese became known as "Little Auvergne."[20] Of the 160 priests who served in the diocese during the Lamy era, 114 were French.[21] The nuns he recruited for the schools and hospital, however, were largely American women. He imported French culture into New Mexico and stamped European architecture (Neo-Gothic, Romanesque, and Second Empire styles) on Santa Fe.

Fray Chávez lamented that the French replaced the indigenous Mexican priests. "Lamy was chosen on the philistine assumption that French priests, for speaking a language derived from the Latin, were ideally suited for a people who spoke a Latin-derived language of their own." But French, Mexican, New Mexican, and Spanish cultures are distinctly different, despite their languages' common origin, and many of the French priests looked down on the Mexicans.[22]

The counterargument to this was that most of New Mexico's population was illiterate. There was almost no education system in the territory, and there wasn't a pipeline of native priests. Lamy had to look elsewhere—and he looked where he knew best, the seminary at Montferrand.

The few Mexican clergy, who were largely from elite families who could afford education for their sons, were often more progressive than the Catholic Church at large. Many of them were educated in Mexico in the exciting era when Mexico broke free of Spain and embraced democracy and liberalism. There were bound to be fault lines between the more authoritative and conservative Lamy and the liberal Mexican priests.

In March 1856, Lamy sent Machebeuf to France to recruit priests and to answer to the Vatican for the significant charges brought against him for gossiping about confessions. Father Howlett, Machebeuf's first biographer, left this embarrassing episode out of his biography. Machebeuf returned to Santa Fe with numerous priests, including Father Gabriel Ussel, who served in Taos for decades.

By 1859 Lamy's recruiting had expanded the number of parishes in the diocese to eighteen. Father Peter Eguillon became Lamy's vicar general when Machebeuf was dispatched to Colorado during the Pike's Peak Gold Rush. Lamy sent his new vicar to France, where he proved to be a considerable recruiter. Eguillon brought back fourteen priests, including Jean-Baptist Salpointe, who would become Lamy's successor, as well as four Christian Brothers to establish a boy's school known as St. Michael's College.[23]

Lamy invited this large group of priests to dinner, where they got to chattering in French at the table. The bishop interrupted them. "Gentlemen, you do not know, it seems, that two languages only are of necessity here, the Spanish, which is spoken generally by the people of this Territory, and the English, which is the language of the Government," he said. "Make your choice between the two, for the present, but leave your French parley for the country you have come from." As almost none of the priests spoke either language, they fell silent at the table.

Father Salpointe, who was one of the silent priests, noted, "This uneasy situation however did not last long. The Bishop himself put an end to it, by bursting into laughter, and by reopening the conversation in French. Still, he explained to use the necessity of applying ourselves, at once, to the study of the languages."[24]

Lamy and Machebeuf worked together in New Mexico for nine years (1851–1860). After Machebeuf's trouble with the Mexican priests and being called to Rome to answer for breaking confession, Lamy may have quietly directed his friend to take longer journeys that removed him from the territory, such as his extensive trips to Mexico (1858) and Arizona (1859). He reassigned him to Colorado in 1860.

In 1859 the Vatican assigned the Arizona missions to Bishop Lamy, and he dispatched Father Machebeuf to visit the sparsely populated region. Its only town of significance was Tucson, with four hundred inhabitants. The Apaches made the territory dangerous to travel in.[25]

Lamy keenly missed his friend during this considerable absence, and he summoned Machebeuf back to Santa Fe. When Machebeuf asked why he was recalled, Lamy responded, "Oh, there was nothing in particular, and you were so long away that I was lonesome for your return. Just stay here with me for now a while and rest. It will be pleasant to talk over old times. We have not had too much consolation of this intimate sort and I feel that we need some now. In a short time you can go again." Cather borrowed this story for her novel.[26]

After the United States annexed Texas in 1845, columnist John O'Sullivan wrote, "Our manifest destiny is to overspread the continent allotted by Providence." The country would build a North American empire composed of white settlers, and California would be next. "Already the advance guard of the irresistible army of Anglo-Saxon emigration has begun to pour down upon it, armed with the plough and the rifle, and marking its trail with schools and colleges, courts and representative halls, mills and meeting-houses."[27]

Thus was voiced the words Manifest Destiny, the nineteenth-century American ideology that it was the country's God-given right to seize the continent from the Atlantic to the Pacific and everything in between. Manifest Destiny meant removing Indigenous peoples so that settlers could take their lands, all in the name of progress.

A year after O'Sullivan's statement, President James Polk made Manifest Destiny a reality when he launched a war against Mexico whose key purpose was to seize California and extend the continental empire to the Pacific Ocean. The Santa Fe Trail became a pathway for Manifest Destiny, as the US Army captured Santa Fe without firing a shot in August

Figure 54. An 1873 print of *American Progress* shows the allegorical figure of progress leading westward expansion while routing the Indigenous population. Prints & Photographs Division, Library of Congress.

1846, then marched on to capture southern California. In the Treaty of Guadalupe Hidalgo that ended the Mexican-American War in 1848, the United States seized a vast amount of territory from Mexico, including California, Nevada, and the Four Corners area, all of which, prior to Mexican independence in 1821, had been part of the Spanish Empire.

As mentioned earlier, the federal government requested that a bishop be assigned to help cement American authority over New Mexico and its Mexican inhabitants. Cather clearly understood this. The fictional Latour states, "I mean to help the officers at their task here. I can assist them more than they realize. The Church can do more than the Fort to make these poor Mexicans 'good Americans'" (35–36). Cather meant this without irony. She was no anti-colonialist.

Biographer Janis Stout called Latour a "benevolent imperialist."[28] Astrid Haas called Latour and Vaillant "missionaries of Manifest Destiny," as they helped cement American authority over the Southwest. She added, Cather's "narrative fails to acknowledge, and more to criticize, the complicity of the Catholic Church in the United States policy of Manifest Destiny." Cather never seemed to question Manifest Destiny, but then again, neither did the country until the twentieth century, when we began examining the costs of our colonial past.[29]

In novel after novel, Cather deftly displayed her ability to write about the Nebraska frontier, the subject that she knew best, having been a pioneer as a child and grown up to see the frontier close. She had a blind spot toward the pioneers, whom she placed on a pedestal. She occasionally mentioned the Indian days in her novels, but rarely addressed that Indigenous peoples living on the Great Plains were removed so white settlers could farm the land. In *Death Comes for the Archbishop*, Cather shifted the frontier to New Mexico, and her heroes were two pioneer priests, which repeated her pattern of writing about pioneers in a new country.

Lamy was responsible for an enormous diocese, and he spent considerable time traveling. The railroad did not reach Santa Fe until 1880; before then, Lamy served his vast diocese in the saddle, which he called "purgatorial work." He explained to Sister Blandina Segale, "I always carried bread, crackers, and a few hard boiled eggs. No greater kindness could be shown than our native population always shows us, but I cannot eat *tortillas* which is the most used edible in all the ranchos. *Chili con carne* gives one strength and it is no common thing to use meat one month old—dried in the sun, of course."[30]

Lamy's early biographer, Louis Warner, called him the "Apostle of the West."[31] The bishop often traveled through his diocese alone, though the countryside was dangerous. He carried a pistol for self-protection and to shoot game. Generally, the seminomadic Apaches and Navajos left priests alone, who were considered holy men, though a lone traveler was apt to be robbed or killed. Cather took note of how the priests traveled, and her opening scene featured Latour traveling alone and lost in the desert.[32]

Lamy's successor, Jean-Baptiste Salpointe, noted that "the Bishop, who could do with one meal a day even at home, provided he had a cup of black coffee and a piece of bread morning and evening, always objected to making ample provisions of victuals for traveling."[33] Years later, Salpointe told Father James DeFouri, "I never shall forget how the Bishop seemed to enjoy those meals consisting only of a rabbit roasted at the end of a stick, eaten without salt or pepper. I thought this mode of life exceedingly hard, because I was still young in the missions, whereas they seemed of familiar occurrence to my Bishop." Lamy had no difficulty sleeping on the frozen ground, wrapped in blankets.[34]

Things were similar for Machebeuf. As a missionary priest, he traveled with a horse to carry him and a mule for his pack and valise full of religious articles. When people asked where he lived, Machebeuf would respond, "In the saddle!" or sometimes, "They call me *El Vicario Andando* (the Traveling Vicar) and I live on the *Camino Real* (the Public Highway!)"[35]

During the Civil War, the Confederacy invaded New Mexico from Texas with the intention of capturing the Colorado gold fields. A brigade-sized army defeated the Union force at the Battle of Valverde, then occupied Albuquerque and Santa Fe for a month. Although the territorial government evacuated the capital, Lamy remained in Santa Fe.

An unusual force of Colorado gold miners, Hispanic volunteers, and Union Army soldiers rallied to defeat the Texans at Glorieta Pass, just north of Pecos Pueblo. The battle was just a skirmish compared to major

Civil War battles, but the battle was decisive in that it prevented the Confederacy from capturing the West. With some hyperbole, but much pride, New Mexicans call the Battle of Glorieta Pass "the Gettysburg of the West."

On June 14, 1863, Machebeuf was thrown from his buggy on a Colorado mountain road and broke his right femur. It was not set properly. He would never ride a horse again, and now he walked with a heavy limp and the assistance of a cane. Lamy rushed to Denver, bringing Father Salpointe with him to check on their friend. The bishop stayed several days, visiting the mining camps where Machebeuf had established missionary churches in places like Central City and Denver.

The federal government split off Arizona from the Territory of New Mexico in 1862. Lamy retained responsibility for the church in both territories. In fall 1863, he began a strenuous trip to California to recruit priests to serve in Arizona. He ventured through wild Arizona and then to the village of Los Angeles. This was while Kit Carson besieged the Navajos in Canyon de Chelly, and Lamy traveled through Arizona with a military escort. He was gone for six months and returned in early 1864.

The Santa Fe New Mexican noted, "The Bishop had found traveling in his ambulance so difficult, that he had parted with it, and taken solely to the saddle." Lamy's diocese was a vast wilderness, roads were primitive, and traveling was hard on the body and time-consuming. Lamy wore himself out physically over thirty-five years managing his flock.[36]

The fictional Bishop Latour is sympathetic to Native Americans, but Bishop Lamy was less so—especially toward those nomadic tribes that were not considered "civilized," like the Apache, Comanche, Navajo, and Utes, who raided farming communities, attacked caravans, and committed atrocities. These he considered savages, as did most New Mexicans, as did, frankly, most Americans at the time.

Lamy traveled to Rome in the fall of 1866. On his return the following spring, he shepherded a group of Sisters of Loretto and Jesuit priests down the Santa Fe Trail to their new home. They were part of a large caravan protected by an army detachment. After the Sand Creek Massacre in Colorado in November 1864, the Santa Fe Trail became far more dangerous, and the tribes along it such as the Comanche and Kiowa turned hostile to travelers. The wagon train was well armed for the prairie crossing.

As the caravan passed along the Arkansas River, ravaged by cholera, a Kiowa war party attacked on July 30. Lamy described the ordeal for *The Catholic Telegraph* (an account that was reproduced in *The New York Times*). "In the second attack the fight lasted nearly three hours; the savages averaged, I suppose, about three hundred warriors, all well mounted, yelling and shooting at us as they passed at full gallop." The one hundred men who protected the wagon train repelled the attack, losing two people: a sister, and a young man.[37] Father Jean Baptiste Brun, who was one of the new recruits in the endangered caravan, wrote in his journal, "The good Bishop was everywhere encouraging the men to fight bravely and defend themselves to death if necessary. He held a gun in his hand, and gave orders with great coolness and deliberation, showing to all an example of courage and calmness."[38]

Toward the end of *Death Comes for the Archbishop*, Latour states, "I have lived to see two great wrongs righted: I have seen the end of black slavery, and I have seen the Navajos restored to their own country." He was referring to the disastrous Navajo roundup, directed by General James Carleton, and the Long Walk to the Bosque Redondo that witnessed thousands of Navajo deaths (290). There was never much Black slavery in New Mexico—the desert climate is unsuitable for the mass production of crops—but Indian slavery was another matter.

For centuries, warring tribes raided communities not just to capture livestock and food but also to seize children and women who could be traded into bondage. The Comanches and Utes were particularly active in the Indian slavery market, and their key target were the Navajos. Hispanics were the recipients, adding Indigenous children to their extended families and raising them as their own in exchange for trade goods. Padre José Manuel Gallegos had three Navajo women in his Santa Fe household, and Padre Antonio José Martínez came from a long line of enslavers.[39]

"In New Mexico, the Civil War led to the greatest Indian slavery boom in the territory's recorded history," wrote historian Andrés Reséndez. The simple reason was the roundup of the Navajos in 1864, which provided a major opportunity for slavers to seize captive Navajos and sell them to New Mexican families.[40] Territorial Chief Justice Kirby Benedict estimated in 1865 that there were at least two thousand enslaved Navajos in the territory. He noted that everyone from Governor Connelly on down seemed to have one or more Navajo children in their household.[41] Historian Hampton Sides estimated that nearly a third of the Navajo population were enslaved in Hispanic or white households in what he called "New Mexico's dirty little secret." Even Kit Carson adopted three Navajo children into his family, all three of them kidnapped by Utes.[42]

In the Doña Isabella chapter, Cather describes a historical Mexican person, Manuel Chavez, as going on numerous raids to hunt Navajos. "A company of Mexicans would ride west to the Navajo country, raid a few sheep camps, and come home bringing flocks and ponies and a bunch of prisoners, for every one of whom they received a large bounty from the Mexican Government," she wrote. He was part of a fifty-man raid that was surrounded and nearly killed to the man near Canyon de Chelly except for the sixteen-year-old Chavez (183–84).

Slavery was officially banned in the United States with the Thirteenth Amendment in 1865, and Congress addressed the Indian slavery question two years later with the Peonage Act. The new law was widely ignored, as New Mexicans were reluctant to give up their Indigenous children. *The Santa Fe New Mexican* defended the practice, calling the Navajos "a savage and barbarous people" and claiming that peonage had civilized them. Returning the children to their rightful parents was "a serious question of humanity," the newspaper opined, expressing the opinion that the children would prefer to remain in the American world than return to their Navajo roots. Oliver LaFarge, the historian of the newspaper, wrote sardonically in 1959 of the paper's stance: "Surely no Southerner ever drew a more touching picture of the benefits of happy, voluntary slavery."[43]

When the Navajos were allowed to return to Dinétah (their homeland) in 1868, peace commissioner William Tecumseh Sherman gave them permission to search for their kidnapped children and reunite their families. Aiding their efforts was a special commissioner, William Griffin, an ardent abolitionist, who convened a grand jury and indicted the system of Indian slavery itself, signaling to New Mexicans that keeping Indigenous children was no longer acceptable. He subpoenaed owners, peons (largely Hispanics indentured to work off their debts), and the enslaved to testify. Griffin's actions freed 291 Indian slaves and sixty peons. Indian slavery continued, but its days were numbered. The raids to kidnap children came to an end. The rule of law had prevailed over an unjust system.[44]

When a priest named Stephen Avel was poisoned to death in Mora in 1858, he left three thousand dollars to establish a hospital in New Mexico. Lamy recruited four Sisters of Charity from Cincinnati to open St. Vincent's Hospital for both orphans and the sick. They arrived in September 1865. The bishop invited the sisters to share his sizable home. As the need for hospital space grew, he eventually moved into a smaller adobe house behind the cathedral. Construction on a new, larger hospital commenced in 1877.[45]

On Christmas Eve 1865, Lamy was asleep when an intruder, a former employee, entered his home. The intruder woke Lamy and, flashing a revolver, demanded that Lamy give him fifty dollars, or he would kill him. The mayordomo was awakened by this and entered the room. Lamy told him to escort the man out and give him the money. The servant took the man outside but refused to pay him. The desperado shifted to a nearby apartment occupied by two priests, where he started a fire in the fireplace. When the priests woke, he demanded something to eat, then shot and wounded both men. The intruder was quickly arrested, and fortunately the two priests recovered from their wounds.[46]

One of the more legendary figures in New Mexico's history was Sister Blandina Segale, born Rosa Maria Segale in Italy in 1850. She emigrated to the United States with her family when she was four years old. She became a Sister of Charity in 1868, and four years later she was assigned to the Southwest—first in Trinidad, Colorado, then Santa Fe in 1876. She spent the next four years working at St. Vincent's Hospital and diligently kept a diary, encountering many legendary people from Santa Fe's history, including Archbishop Lamy, Billy the Kid, and Governor Lew Wallace.

Figure 55. Sister Blandina Segale was a Sister of Charity who helped expand St. Vincent's Hospital in Santa Fe, befriended Billy the Kid, and stole Archbishop Lamy's vegetables. Palace of the Governors Photo Archives (NMHM/DCA), Image 067735.

St. Vincent's had virtually no budget or funds, and yet the hospital's mission was to support anyone in need. Segale was practiced in making do. During the construction of the Santa Fe Railway in 1879, injuries spiked and the hospital wards were soon overcrowded. One day the sister in charge of the kitchen told her, "Sister, we have not a handful of vegetables to prepare for dinner, and seventy-two patients, thirty-five orphans, and sixteen Sisters to feed. Please figure it out, you, who, I have been told, are never daunted!"

Sister Blandina responded, "That problem will be solved in ten minutes." She climbed over the wall that separated the hospital from the archbishop's garden and began picking his vegetables, as she believed that it is better to apologize than ask permission. Her narrative of the vegetable heist exposed both her pluck and the archbishop's generosity.

> Throwing over into our vacant garden at least two dozen cabbage heads, I did the same with each of the other vegetables, only in

greater number, as the sizes were smaller. Then I went to His Grace's door and rapped.

"Come in."

I opened the door and stood, saying: "I have come to make confession out of the confessional." He looked at me with that benevolent expression which once seen can never be forgotten. In that look he also saw that I was covered with dust, and he said, "My little Sister, what have you been doing?"

"Stealing, Your Grace. With never a thought of restitution, I dug up enough vegetables from your garden to last us three days."

"And then?"

"Whatever you say."

"Tell Louis to give you all there are."

"Thank you very much," is all I could say.

Shortly after this, Mr. Frank Manzanares, of the firm Brown and Manzanares sent sacks of coffee and sugar. I think His Grace is guilty.[47]

Cather noted how important gardening is to the fictional Latour. Gardening was indeed a serious hobby for Lamy, and his garden covered six acres behind the cathedral. It included apple, peach, pear trees, grape vines, and English walnut trees. His favorite cherry tree was called the "Belle of Santa Fe." A spring fed a fishpond and an acequia irrigated an extensive kitchen garden to grow herbs and fresh vegetables. Pathways throughout the garden invited the public to stroll beneath the shade trees, and Lamy was an enthusiastic chaperone to visitors. If the bishop gifted an apricot to a visitor, it came with the stipulation that they plant the stone to spread fruit trees around Santa Fe. Lamy's garden was a little piece of France that he imported to the high desert. It is today the parking lot behind the St. Francis Cathedral. But part of his legacy are the many apricot trees that are all over the city and which drop their fruit in July.[48]

Lamy complained about the high cost of maintaining the diocese, given how expensive it was to transport anything over the long and dangerous Santa Fe Trail. "The expense of equipping a caravan is enormous. It is necessary to buy both animals and wagons, to carry the baggage of

Figure 56. An 1880 image of Archbishop Lamy (center) and Machebeuf (to the right, hand on hip) in Lamy's Garden. Palace of the Governors Photo Archives, (NMHM/DCA), Image 049017.

the Missionaries and the effects of the churches and schools; to take also provisions for two months, and camping outfits," he reported to the Society for the Propagation of the Faith. The high cost of transportation left New Mexico poor, with no industry and only subsistence farming and ranching. Without the railroads, New Mexico could not develop economically.[49]

The year 1866 marked Lamy's fifteenth year in office. He had made considerable progress in extending the church's reach, as 135 chapels and churches now operated in the diocese—eighty-five of them new. The church had taken the lead in education, and the Christian Brothers were operating three schools for boys, while the Sisters of Loretto were operating five schools for girls. He noted that his diocese numbered 110,000 Mexican and 15,000 Indigenous Catholics, and he had forty-one priests working in Arizona, Colorado, and New Mexico. Lamy had also opened

St. Vincent's Hospital in Santa Fe.[50] Lamy's diocese continued to grow. By 1872, he counted 180 churches, forty church-run schools, and five convents within his diocese.[51]

The Catholic Church subdivided the Diocese of Santa Fe in 1868 by creating the vicariates of Arizona and Colorado, as the territory was too vast for any one person to manage. Lamy nominated his two close friends, Jean-Baptiste Salpointe and Joseph Machebeuf, and was relieved when the Vatican accepted the appointments. Eventually both vicariates were elevated to diocese—and both men were promoted to bishop.

In 1869 Lamy began the construction of the Cathedral of St. Francis of Assisi in Santa Fe. It was built in fits and starts over the next decades, as funding was always short. The cathedral's twin spires were never built. Soon after breaking ground for the cathedral, Lamy traveled to Rome to participate in the First Vatican Council (1869–1870). There Pope Pius IX pushed the controversial doctrine of papal infallibility.

On February 12, 1875, the Vatican elevated the Diocese of Santa Fe to an archdiocese, and Lamy was promoted to be its first archbishop. The ceremony was held on June 16. The cathedral was too small for the occasion, so the ceremony was moved outdoors to behind St. Michael's College. Machebeuf attended and delivered the sermon in English, while Peter Eguillon preached in Spanish. Salpointe placed the pallium, the traditional woolen adornment for an archbishop, on Lamy's shoulders. The town was lit up with luminaries, an army band played in the Plaza, and fireworks exploded in the sky. Lamy hosted a dinner in his garden that night.[52]

Three dioceses now reported to Archbishop Lamy: Arizona, led by Bishop Jean-Baptiste Salpointe in Tucson; Colorado, headed by Bishop Joseph Machebeuf in Denver; and New Mexico, led by Bishop Peter Bourgade. Lamy became the first of five French archbishops who would serve in the Santa Fe archdiocese. Salpointe and Bourgade were two of his successors.

The railroad finally came to New Mexico in 1879 with huge anticipation, but Santa Feans were in for disappointment: the AT&SF Railway bypassed the town and went directly to Albuquerque, which was now destined to become the territory's commercial center. Community leaders, including Lamy, proposed a bond measure to finance a railroad spur line to Galisteo Junction, eighteen miles to the south. Voters approved the $150,000 bond in October and construction began.[53]

Not everyone was excited about the railroad. Sister Blandina Segale, working at St. Vincent's Hospital, had to deal with the sharp increase in hospitalized workers who were injured during the railroad's construction. She also knew that the railroad would bring land sharks and speculators who would prey on the isolated territory. "Consumptives, men with money looking to become millionaires, land-grabbers, experienced and inexperienced miners, quacks, professional deceivers, publicity men lauding gold mines that do not exist," she tut-tutted in her diary.[54]

Lamy donated a plot of land from the church's holdings at Galisteo Junction, and in thanks for his civic charity, locals renamed the town after him. The railroad spur line from Lamy to Santa Fe opened on February 9, 1880, to great fanfare. Governor Lew Wallace helped drive in the last spike. Railroads now linked the New Mexico Territory to the rest of the continent. The cost of transporting foodstuffs and trade goods to Santa Fe dropped. Bricks began to be hauled in, and Santa Fe quickly transformed its architecture away from adobe. The railroad eventually yielded a bounty of tourism, which became the mainstay of the economy. Aging priests such as Lamy could now travel with far greater speed and comfort.[55]

During summer 1879, Lamy fell ill for five weeks, and many thought he would die. Though he recovered, his old strength never returned. He could no longer fulfill the duties that his younger self had. He found his memory declining. Seeing a portrait of him from this time is startling: Lamy's hair has turned white, and he looks gaunt and noticeably aged. Recognizing that he needed a successor, Lamy asked the Vatican to name Salpointe as coadjutor. Hoping to complete his cathedral before he stepped down or died, Lamy traveled to Mexico by train to raise funds.

To Lamy's relief, the Vatican appointed Salpointe as his coadjutor, and the latter was ceremoniously promoted on May 1, 1885. Bishop Machebeuf traveled from Denver and delivered the sermon. On August 28, Salpointe was formally installed as archbishop.

Lamy's resignation letter was read in all the churches on September 6.

Figure 57. Archbishop Lamy aged considerably in the 1870s and early 1880s, leading to his retirement in 1885. Palace of the Governors Photo Archives (NMHM/DCA), Image 065116.

"What has prompted this determination is our advanced age, that often deprives us of the necessary strength in the fulfillment of our sacred ministry, though our health may apparently look robust," he wrote. "We shall profit by the days left us to prepare ourselves the better to appear before the tribunal of God, in tranquility and solitude." He retired to his country lodge four miles north of town, Villa Pintoresca.[56]

These are the basic facts about Lamy's life. But how do they square with the fictional character of Bishop Latour?

Cather's Latour

Many people see Lamy and Latour as one and the same, but they were not. Cather took historical events and real people and fictionalized them in *Archbishop*. Her book is a novel, not a history.

Cather's Latour is a sophisticate. He admires art and high culture. He is refined. He appreciates good food and wine. He has an insightful perspective on history, which he recognizes in an ancient pueblo dwelling, the Moorish origins of silversmithing, or even a bowl of onion soup. He has difficulty connecting with people: "But Jean, who was at ease in any society and always the flower of courtesy, could not form new ties. It had always been so. He was like that even as a boy; gracious to everyone, but known to a few" (251).

Latour's spirituality is that of a rational modernist. When Father Vaillant praises the apparition of Our Lady of Guadalupe, Latour responds that miracles are everywhere—we just have to open our eyes to them.

> "Where there is great love there are always miracles," he said at length. "One might almost say that an apparition is human vision corrected by divine love. I do not see you as you really are, Joseph; I see you through my affection for you. The Miracles of the Church seem to me to rest not so much upon faces or voices or healing power coming suddenly near to us from afar off, but upon our perceptions being made finer, so that for a moment our eyes can see and our ears can hear what is there about us always." (50)

Cather created a character in Latour who is deeply introverted—that is, someone who is energized by being alone. One of my favorite passages in the book—one that speaks to me as a fellow introvert—contrasts Latour's introversion with Vaillant's gregariousness.

> In his youth, Joseph had wished to lead a life of seclusion and solitary devotion; but the truth was, he could not be happy for long without human intercourse. And he liked almost everyone. In Ohio, when they used to travel together in stage-coaches, Father Latour had noticed that every time a new passenger pushed his way into the already crowded stage, Joseph would look pleased and interested, as if this were an agreeable addition—whereas he himself felt annoyed, even if he concealed it. (227)

This episode could well have been Cather on the train to New Mexico, quietly enjoying the landscape from her window with Edith Lewis, only to have another person sit down and attempt conversation. Cather's friend

Elsie Sergeant wrote that "she never had the least little bit of small talk, not an iota of ease or light friendliness with a stranger who seemed intrusive."[57]

"Latour himself was much cooler and more critical in temper; hard to please, and often a little grey in mood" (225), Cather wrote. A Jesuit priest, Father Thomas Steele, observed that "Latour's personality is for the most part Willa Cather's."[58] The personality of Latour has little in common with the real Lamy, who was extraverted and, like Machebeuf/Vaillant, friendly and gregarious. But that would not suit Cather's purpose of creating characters who were temperamentally opposites.

Father Vaillant

Joseph Vaillant is the fictional rendition of Joseph Machebeuf, Lamy's best friend. Cather nailed Machebeuf's outgoing personality through Vaillant, in part because she relied on Father Howlett's biography. In terms of character, Machebeuf and Vaillant are the same.

There is no doubt that Machebeuf was a gregarious extravert, just like his literary avatar Vaillant. When Vaillant meets Pope Gregory XVI, he brings his enthusiasm and not one but two valises with items for the pope's blessing. He stays beyond his allotted appointment, showering the pope with stories about his missionary experiences. The pope announces at the end, "*Coraggio, Americano*!" He addresses Vaillant as an American, though Vaillant is French.

The meeting with Pope Gregory was real. It was in 1844, when Machebeuf traveled to Rome while a missionary priest in Sandusky, Ohio. This was eight years before he relocated to Santa Fe to support his friend Jean-Baptiste Lamy. The pope did in fact say, "Coraggio, Americano!"[59]

Father Howlett first met Machebeuf in Denver in 1865. "He had not yet completed his fifty-third year, but his hair was turning grey, and his face was as thin and wrinkled as that of a man of eighty," he observed. "The twenty-five years of such missionary life as he had lived seemed to have left him a weather-beaten wreck near the limit of its power to hold longer together." The priest's appearance was deceptive: although limping after his 1863 accident, Machebeuf lived another twenty-six years and was energetic to the end. "In spite of his lameness his movements were rapid, and he never remained long in any one place or position. He seemed to be all energy, activity, and business."[60]

"To remain quiet was to wear out, and *rest in action* was his hope of life," Howlett observed about Machebeuf.[61] Cather adopted this phrase for Vaillant directly from Howlett's biography. Machebeuf (and Vaillant) was a people person and an outstanding missionary, one who easily adapted himself to New Mexico's cultures. Toward the end of the novel, Latour admits to his friend, "You are a better man than I. You have been a great harvester of souls, without pride and without shame—and I am always a little cold—un pédant, as you used to say" (259–60).

Machebeuf came to love his Mexican parishioners. "The Mexicans may have queer ways in the eyes of some people—they are ignorant, they are poor and not very saving, but everybody has his faults, but they have redeeming qualities, and often more of them than their critics," Machebeuf stated.[62] Cather captured this sentiment. In *Archbishop*, Vaillant goes native, though he is French: "I have almost become a Mexican! I have learned to like *chili colorado* and mutton fat. Their foolish ways no longer offend me, their very faults are dear to me. I am *their man!*" (208)

Chapter 8

Native Faith

"No white man knows anything about Indian religion, Padre."

—Willa Cather, *Death Comes for the Archbishop*, 134

"I do not believe, as I once did, that the Indian will perish. I believe that God will preserve him."

—Willa Cather, *Death Comes for the Archbishop*, 296

In *Death Comes for the Archbishop*, Willa Cather penned two chapters that incorporated Pueblo Indian spirituality but were written from the point of view of Bishop Latour—that is to say, from a Western perspective. In the first, Latour celebrates mass at Acoma Pueblo, but he fails to connect with the people, whom he felt are so deeply rooted in ancient traditions as to be unreachable. In the second, Latour encounters a hidden cave that served as a kiva, an underground Pueblo worship space, and he is unnerved by the experience.

In both cases, Cather demonstrated a deeper understanding of the Pueblo world than we might suspect, at a time when few Americans had even heard of Pueblo Indians. She visited numerous Ancestral Pueblo sites during her six visits to the Southwest, including Mesa Verde, Homolovi, and Walnut Canyon, along with most of New Mexico's nineteen pueblos and the Hopi in Arizona. The ancestral sites were undergoing excavation at the time of her visits, and having a curious mind, Cather absorbed much about these ancient cultures. She developed two Native characters, Eusabio and Jacinto, to help project Navajo and Pueblo cultures into her novel.

Author Kali Fajardo-Anstine, a self-described "Colorado Chicana, a mixed person of Filipino, Indigenous, and European ancestry," was surprised by her first reading of *Archbishop*. "I've never seen the history of my ancestors glimpsed this way before in a novel. It's not from our perspective or anything like that, but there we are, alongside those priests in the lands of my ancestors." She added, "I had been startled into attention at seeing my own history on the page."[1]

Over the years, I've met Europeans who naïvely declare that there is nothing old in the United States. My response is always a skeptical, "Oh really . . . have you not heard how long people have lived in the Americas?" In Cather's day, the assumption was that Indigenous people had been here for about three thousand years, but the clock keeps moving back. For decades, the thirteen-thousand-year-old Clovis and Folsom points from the ice age were the benchmarks for human arrival in the region—until footprints were found in White Sands National Park that pushed the timeline back to around twenty-three thousand years ago. People started migrating south from Beringia (a Texas-sized landmass that is now mostly under the Bering Straits) long before. Humans arrived not *after* the last ice age, but rather *during* it, and they may have navigated down the Pacific coast by boat, then migrated inland.

What allowed these hunter-gatherers to settle down was corn, which came up from what is now Mexico around 2000 BCE and provided an excellent source of nutrition in an arid climate. In bountiful years, the people grew surpluses, which they stored first in baskets and later in pottery, that they in turn stored in caves or buildings. Indigenous ancestors established farming-based communities and practiced their religion tied to the seasons, and at the heart of these civilizations was corn.

The Ancestral Puebloans emerged in the Four Corners area and coalesced around a set of common cultural and spiritual practices while maintaining their individual cultures and languages. I like to use the metaphor of the solar system for the Pueblo world, where the sun represents the spiritual practices, while the planets represent the different migratory groups that came into orbit around these ideas. Together they formed a sophisticated and multicultural civilization.[2]

The heart of Ancestral Pueblo culture was Chaco Canyon, which emerged around 850 CE. The Chacoans were outstanding astronomers and engineers. They built massive stone great houses in Chaco and elsewhere, usually aligned with lunar or solar events, and connected by an extensive road network. All roads led back to Chaco Canyon for pilgrimages, trade, and tribute. Pueblo Bonito, the largest of thirteen great houses in Chaco, is the size of the Roman Coliseum, and suggests a hierarchical, strongly organized but also highly unequal civilization.

We don't know why the Chaco world fell apart, whether from drought, famine, political strife, inequality, war, or a combination of these factors, but the centrifugal forces that held it together came apart during the early twelfth century after three hundred years. As Chaco declined, many family groups began migrating eastward toward the Rio Grande or south away from Chaco, while Ancestral Puebloans who remained in the Four Corners area began fortifying their settlements against marauders and perhaps against each other. At Mesa Verde, they moved from the mesas down to the cliffsides, building amazing cliff dwellings that Willa Cather and Edith Lewis experienced during their 1915 visit. But that was temporary: By 1300 CE, Mesa Verde had emptied out, the people having migrated away. The migration out of a troubled land is a key origin story for today's Pueblos. The Pueblo world was never static, but always fluid as the people often migrated to new locations for better farmland and water access. Migration isn't just the physical relocation, but also "the process of becoming," as archaeologist Samuel Duwe described it, the fluid adaptation to the ever-changing world that has enabled Pueblo culture to survive.[3]

Just north of Santa Fe are six Tewa-speaking pueblos that originated in Mesa Verde and the San Juan River basin. They established new mesa-top communities on the Pajarito Plateau on the eastern and northern slopes of the Jemez Mountains, as well as throughout the Chama River valley. These were initially small family settlements, followed by larger villages, essentially replicating what they had in the Four Corners Area.

They constructed multistory settlements for protection. These had no doors, but rather ladders to access the structure. If their enemies raided, the residents pulled up the ladders, creating an instant fortress.

The Ancestral Puebloans relied on rainwater to dry farm, and in rare cases used irrigation. The most intact of these settlements is Puye Cliff Dwellings, the ancestral Santa Clara Pueblo site surrounded by four satellite locations. To their south were the ancestors of San Ildefonso Pueblo, and one of their sites, Tsankawi, is open to the public as part of Bandelier National Monument. Frijoles Canyon in Bandelier, where most visitors go, marked the southern boundary of the Tewa world. Beyond that were the Keres-speaking Pueblo tribes who are now mostly south of Santa Fe. Each of these large settlements was like a city-state, carefully guarding its farmland and resources while also trading with the outside world.

Farming was always difficult on the Pajarito Plateau, which was crowded with farming settlements and field houses. People often relocated as the soil depleted, or they moved closer to the mountains during a drought. Over time large game became scarcer and forests thinned from overharvesting. A severe drought struck the Pueblo world in the mid-1500s and the water courses dried up, while the intensive farming had depleted the soil beyond its ability to feed a large population. The Pueblo Indians took a potentially dangerous step: They migrated from the Pajarito Plateau down to the Rio Grande for a better water supply, leaving them more vulnerable to raids from their enemies. In some ways the move was fortuitous: They claimed the best farmland along the river in the years before the Spanish colony arrived in 1598.[4]

The Spanish found nearly one hundred of these Indigenous farming communities along the Rio Grande, and they gave them the name "pueblo," Spanish for village. The Franciscan missionaries renamed many pueblos after Christian saints, such as San Felipe, Santa Ana, and Santa Clara, but in recent years some have readopted their historical names. In 2005, San Juan Pueblo changed its name to Ohkay Owingeh. In 2010 Santo Domingo reverted to Kewa Pueblo, but that name change didn't seem to stick—most people still call it Santo Domingo. Zuni is in the process of restoring its ancestral name: A:Shiwi, from which the Spanish derived Zuñi and later Zuni.

Westerners look up to the winter night sky and see the Greco-Roman constellation Orion. The Tewas call him Long Sash, a tribal leader who led his people away from a troubled land. The Hopi in Arizona see the constellation not as a human figure but rather as a map of their world and their migration path. The three stars in Orion's belt represent First, Second, and Third Mesas, where the Hopi live, and the other stars are ancestral sites. Around 1696 CE in the wake of the Spanish reconquest of New Mexico, one of the Tewa tribes relocated from the Rio Grande to Hopi First Mesa. They served as reinforcements for the Hopis, who were challenged by an emerging threat: the Athabascans.

Anthropologists have long held that the Athabascans migrated to the Southwest from the Pacific Northwest between 1300 and 1500 CE, but more recent archaeological evidence and oral history may indicate that they were here much earlier, including during the Chaco period. These were seminomadic hunter-gatherers who divided into subgroups, including the Diné (Navajo) and the numerous Indé (Apache) tribes. Though the Apaches and Navajos were long at odds with each other, they are part of the same linguistic group, indicating their common origin.[5]

The Athabascans were hunters, the Chacoans farmers. They traded and exchanged ideas. When Chaco and Mesa Verde emptied out, the Athabascans remained. Small groups of hunter-gatherers could better sustain themselves in the face of drought than large communities dependent on a bounty of corn.[6]

What we think of as contemporary Navajo culture was something that the disparate seminomadic groups evolved into. Historians Klara Kelley and Harris Francis called this "'ethnogenesis,' the process of becoming a distinct people," when different tribes coalesced into a common identity and language. As the people who became the Navajos (Diné, or the People, as they call themselves) interacted with the Chacoans, there was much cross-cultural influence. You see it in the Diné belief that they emerged from several underworlds, something that they may have picked up from the Ancestral Puebloans. The Navajos integrated Pueblo, Ute, and other cultures into the greater Diné narrative and later adopted sheep herding, wool weaving, and silversmithing, things they learned from the Mexicans and Spanish.[7]

The Navajos and the Pueblo Indians diverge in how they consider the dead: The Navajos seldom discuss the deceased, lest you invite in their *chindi* to haunt you, the toxic spirit that remains behind. The Pueblo people view their ancestors as present and beneficial, and they make pilgrimages to ancestral sites to pray and commune with them. The dead are never gone: Their spirit is still with us, and an ancestral site is rarely considered abandoned. While on a tour of the Zuni Halona village, I told my guide about how a large flock of elk had descended on Chaco Canyon before my eyes. "Those are our ancestors, checking up on the place," he remarked.

Even as the Ancestral Puebloans moved toward the Rio Grande, the seminomads continued trading with them, but also raided the pueblos to steal food—and later cattle, horses, and sheep after the Spanish introduced these. This invited retaliatory raids, including kidnapping children. The arrival of the Spanish upset the power dynamics between the tribes, as the Spanish sometimes favored the Navajos, and other times the Comanches and Utes. Thus guerilla warfare worsened in the Southwest, a key reason why many Pueblos allied with the Spanish after the 1692–1693 reconquest: The Spanish had the military might to hold the nomads at bay and protect the farming communities. This was a problem made worse by the Spanish incursion into a complicated and fraught situation.[8]

As we discuss the history of the Navajos and the Pueblo Indians, there is the temptation to label these stone age cultures as primitive. Their technology may have been primitive, but the people were anything but. These were human beings with the same brain and intelligence you and I have, with the same opposable thumbs that give us the ability to use tools. They had architecture and art, astronomy, engineering, music, politics, religion, science, sophisticated agricultural practices, and spoken language. They adapted themselves to the harsh desert climate, and they traded over great distances.

The Pueblo people don't necessarily have gods but believe in spirits (kachinas or katsinas) that can aid humanity. You'll often hear about Mother Earth, who nurtures us, and Father Sky, who brings the rain that grows the crops. A Pueblo guide once told me, "The earth is our Bible." The Pueblo Indians had no written language but carved or pecked petroglyphs into rock panels. You see them at Chaco, at Mesa Verde, and subsequent Ancestral Pueblo sites. A common petroglyph is the spiral, the journey of life that was often used as a calendar to mark important solar events, such as the summer solstice. The spiral concept traveled far: I have seen one at Donner Pass in northern California.

The Pueblo Indians believe they emerged from three underworlds through a hole in the earth called a sipapu. When they conduct private spiritual services, they enter a kiva, a partly underground structure that is either round or square, depending on the pueblo. Many Pueblo spiritual practices originated in what is now Mexico, brought up by migrants such as the Hopis (both kiva and sipapu are derived from Hopi) or along the trade routes. The Hopis are quite independent, having spent centuries resisting the Navajos and the Spanish, and they prefer the word *village* rather than *pueblo*.

The Pueblo Indians have distinctly different languages, indicating their diverse origins as migratory groups. There are three major linguistic families: Keresan, Tanoan, and Zunian. Keres is largely spoken by the southern communities, including Acoma, Laguna, and Santo Domingo. The Tanoan linguistic group is broken into Tewa, Tiwa, and Towa languages, and these are mostly spoken by the northern Pueblo peoples, though the southern communities of Isleta and Sandia that straddle Albuquerque speak Tiwa dialects. Towa is only spoken at Jemez Pueblo, and Zuni is only spoken at Zuni.[9]

The Franciscans so oppressed the Pueblo Indians from practicing their native faith that the latter finally had enough. They organized under a spiritual leader named Po'Pay—no easy task, given that the communities spoke many languages and were often at odds with each other—and they rose up on August 10, 1680. The Pueblo Revolt killed twenty-one Franciscans and about four hundred Spaniards. The Spanish fled south to El Paso, abandoning the colony for twelve years. These Indigenous farmers kicked out the Spanish Empire, ninety-six years before the American Declaration of Independence from the British Empire.

Pueblo culture survives because the communities stood up for themselves. When a new Spanish governor, Diego de Vargas, reestablished the colony in 1692–1693, he granted the Pueblo Indians considerable concessions. They could practice their native faith alongside Catholicism. He ended the feudal practices and enabled self-governance; the communities elect governors to this day. And he recognized pueblo lands as their own, documenting it via land grants. The Pueblo Indians are on their lands to this day, a sharp contrast to Oklahoma, which is full of displaced tribes. There has long been a myth among New Mexican Hispanics that de Vargas was a peaceful reconqueror; in fact, not all the pueblos wanted to go back under the Spanish Crown, and de Vargas waged military campaigns to bring them back under the fold.

The ancient spiritual traditions are alive and well, and they are deeply meaningful to the Pueblo Indians. On the holiest days, a pueblo may close its gates to visitors. Other spiritual days, such as around Christmas, feast days are open to the public. Dancing, which is central to Pueblo faith, is prayer in motion. They ask that guests refrain from taking photographs, as the dance is a spiritual service, not a performance. You don't applaud or cheer but keep a respectful silence. A feast day is dedicated to a patron (Christian) saint, and the pueblos roll out the welcome mat to visitors. Don't be surprised if you get invited into someone's home for a feast of southwestern delights.

Willa Cather's close friend, Elsie Sergeant, had a strong conscience and an eye for social reform. At Cather's behest, Sergeant first visited New Mexico in 1920, and the following year purchased an adobe house in Tesuque with a friend. During the Great Depression, she worked for the Bureau of Indian Affairs in New Mexico, advocating for the Pueblo Indians. She noted critically that Cather seemed less concerned with tribal life. Sergeant observed:

> Primitive man, in New Mexico, a state three fifths the size of France, is living in a stratified society. The few whites—"Anglos"—on top, the native Mexicans, on the next layer, and the Indians at the bottom of the heap. The classes and the masses, as in Europe or in a French or British colony. What is the Pueblo Indians relation to American democracy?
>
> Willa did not ask herself such questions.[10]

Both Cather and Sergeant were friends with Mabel Dodge Luhan and stayed at her Taos home. Sergeant noted how Mabel pushed her views of Indigenous communitarianism onto her guests. She wrote, however, "But she made no headway with Willa Cather. The tribal side of the Indian meant little to her." Sergeant knew Cather for decades, and she knew that Cather was no activist. However, Sergeant overlooked the subtle humanitarian portraits that Cather developed in her two major Indigenous characters in *Archbishop*, Eusabio and Jacinto, and her accurate portrayal of Pueblo culture.[11]

Mabel was partnered with Tony Lujan of Taos Pueblo for forty-four years, but she never came close to understanding the Pueblo's religion, in part because they kept it secret from outsiders. She once asked him, "Well, what is the religion of the Indians?"

"Life," he responded, dodging the question.[12]

She noted how he would stare at Pueblo Peak, the mountain that towers over Taos, as if he were communing with its spiritual force. He would ask, "Can you feel the power coming out of the mountain?" Another time he stated, "Taos is the beating heart of the world. Do you know that this world *lives*?"

"When he spoke so I felt a strange vibration pass over from him through me, and I almost understood something hidden from me," Mabel observed. "But I gradually realized he never told me anything definite about the Indian religion." Another time she woke to find Tony preparing for a ceremony, which he would not discuss. When she pressed him, he responded, "Secret."[13]

Pueblo Indians do not discuss specifics of their spiritual practices. It is deeply private, in part because only some are trusted with the sacred knowledge, and what happens inside of a kiva is not shared with outsiders. The communities also had to evade the Franciscans, who actively sought to stamp out Pueblo faith, a key reason for the Pueblo Revolt. Later, when American anthropologists published books about the Pueblos, revealing their oral history and spiritual practices to the world, the Pueblo Indians felt they had lost control of their own narratives.

Today the Pueblo Indians are more forthcoming about their

traditions, certainly more so than in Cather's day. I have found Natives to be open to sharing their culture, in part so that visitors can better understand them. And with understanding comes empathy, respect, and a recognition that our country has not always treated our Indigenous population fairly. One difference between Cather's time and today is that many tribes have developed tourism and offer tour guides to tell their history. I suggest that if you visit tribal lands, hire a local guide. It's well worth it. There are countless layers of culture and history to explore, and a guide can help you gain a deeper understanding.

The Mass at Ácoma

Acoma Pueblo is a spectacular place, well earning its nickname: Sky City. The name always reminds me of Cloud City and dashing Lando Calrissian in *The Empire Strikes Back*, but this is something far more ancient. Acoma is a pueblo dramatically set atop a mesa 365 feet above the surrounding plain. It was first occupied around 1150 CE, making it the oldest continuously inhabited settlement in North America. The pueblo is sixty miles west of Albuquerque on Interstate 40, about a two-hour drive from Santa Fe. Most Acoma people no longer live atop Sky City, but in three modern towns nearby. Modern conveniences such as electricity and running water are not allowed in the historic pueblo.

Willa Cather dedicated a chapter to Acoma Pueblo in *Death Comes for the Archbishop*. She called it "The Mass at Ácoma." Her descriptions of the pueblo are accurate and stem from her 1925 visit with Edith Lewis. She transposed her own experiences into that of the fictional Bishop Latour.

The summer of 1925 witnessed a busy monsoon season that left Cather and Lewis stranded in Lamy for three days, then another three days at Laguna Pueblo, as the roads were washed out. But the sudden, drenching monsoons were seared in Cather's memory, an episode that she recounted in *Archbishop* as a thunderstorm hit during Latour's approach to Acoma. She described the cloud formations that hovered over the mesas:

> One thing which struck him at once was that every mesa was duplicated by a cloud mesa, like a reflection, which lay motionless above it

Figure 58. An overhead shot of Acoma Pueblo from 1928 showing the village high atop the mesa. In the center is San Estévan del Rey Mission Church. Prints & Photogaphs Division, Library of Congress.

> or moved slowly up from behind it. . . . The great tables of granite set down in an empty plain were inconceivable without their attendant clouds, which were a part of them, as the smoke is part of the censer, or the foam of the wave. (95)

The approach to Acoma is striking: On the mostly flat plain are dozens of massive boulders and stone formations that seem primordial, and above them towers the mesa, home to the pueblo. "The mesa plain had an appearance of great antiquity, and of incompleteness; as if, with all the materials for world-making assembled, the Creator had desisted, gone away and left everything on the point of being brought together, on the eve of being arranged into mountain, plain, plateau," Cather wrote. "The country was still waiting to be made into a landscape" (94–95). You may have noticed Cather's parallel description of Nebraska in *My Ántonia*: "There was nothing but land: not a country at all, but the material out of which countries are made."[14]

Enchanted Mesa looms three miles northeast of the pueblo. Cather wrote about the mesa in her 1909 short story "The Enchanted Bluff," and now she got to see it for the first time. She revisited the story of the Acoma people who were trapped on the mesa in *Archbishop*. Latour's guide, a Pecos Pueblo Indian named Jacinto, points out "that on this, too, there had once been a village, but the stairway which had been the only access to it was broken off by a great storm many centuries ago, and its people had perished up there from hunger" (96).

Cather noted two routes up to Sky City: a narrow pathway wide enough for a donkey, and a steep sandstone staircase straight up the cliff. A paved road has replaced the pathway, and the tour buses that start at the Sky City Cultural Center and Haak'u Museum drive visitors to the mesa top via this route. The tour lasts about an hour, and afterward you can return on the bus, or better yet, climb down the historic staircase. If you can put aside any fear of heights, the staircase is well worth it. It has smooth handholds embedded into the cliff from centuries of use. "Wherever the footing was treacherous, it was helped out by little hand-holds, ground into the stone like smooth mittens" (98), Cather accurately observed. Clearly Cather and Lewis took this route during their visit, as Cather described the small tunnel-like overhang where Latour and his guide Jacinto take shelter during a thunderstorm. I can well imagine that Cather and Lewis took refuge there too.

Latour and Jacinto reach the village atop the mesa. "The white dwellings, two and three storeyed, were not scattered, but huddled together in a close cluster" of three rows. "Both the rock and the plastered houses threw off the sun glare blindingly" (100). At the far end of the mesa stands San Estévan del Rey Mission Church. Using forced labor, the Franciscan friar Juan Ramirez built the massive church starting in 1629. The trees were cut from forests on Mount Taylor, some twenty-five miles to the north, then hauled on the shoulders of Acoma men back to the mesa. This was the only church to survive the Pueblo Revolt of 1680. Cather described it as "the old warlike church of Ácoma, with its two stone towers" (100).

Figure 59. A 1934 image of San Estévan del Rey Mission Church at Acoma Pueblo, the only church to survive the Pueblo Revolt. Cather set Latour's mass at Acoma here. To the left is the loggia, where the fictional Fray Baltazar held his fateful dinner party. Prints & Photographs Division, Library of Congress.

The Acoma mesa is virtually barren, and there are several pools for collecting rainwater. There is a single tree about which the guides make a joke that I won't spoil for you. No photography is allowed in the mission church or in the adjacent cemetery; you may be surprised at how many of the tombstones are for Acoma people who served in the US military, denoted by Veterans Administration headstones.

The reason why the Acoma people lived atop the mesa was safety. Acoma is like a citadel. "A man can do whole lot when they hunt him day and night like an animal," Jacinto explains. "Navajos on the north, Apaches on the South; the Ácoma run up a rock to be safe" (96–97). Latour views the safety of the mesa through his Christian perspective:

> The rock, when one came to think of it, was the utmost expression of human need; even more feeling yearned for it; it was the highest comparison of loyalty in love and friendship. Christ Himself had used

> that comparison for the disciple to whom He gave the keys to His Church [St. Peter, whose name derived from the Greek pétros, or rock]. And the Hebrews of the Old Testament, always being carried captive into foreign lands,—their rock was an idea of God, the only thing their conquerors could not take from them. (97)

This brings us to Latour's mass that he delivers at Acoma's mission church, one of the more unsettling passages in the book. Latour has difficulty getting through the service, as he doesn't connect with or understand the people. "He felt as if he were celebrating Mass at the bottom of the sea, for antediluvian creatures; for types of life so old, so hardened, so shut within their shells, that the sacrifice on Calvary could hardly reach back so far," Cather wrote. Acoma was ancient and primordial, and its people seemed to exist since before time began. At the end of the mass, "When he blessed them and sent them away, it was with a sense of inadequacy and spiritual defeat" (100).

Seeing them wrapped in their blankets and stone-faced, Latour thinks of the Acoma people as reptiles, never changing but as timeless and unreachable as the rock that Acoma was built upon, in contrast to Western culture which continued to evolve. "Through all the centuries that his own part of the world had been changing like the sky at daybreak, this people had been fixed, increasing neither in number nor desires, rock-turtles on their rock," Cather wrote. "Something reptilian he felt here, something that had endured by immobility, a kind of life out of reach, like the crustaceans in their armour" (103).

One might interpret Cather's writing about the Acoma people as dehumanizing. But perhaps she had learned of the Pueblo origin stories and of the underworlds from which they came. My guide at Zuni noted that humans were once lizards in the underworld until one of their spirits severed the webbing in their feet so they could rise to the next world. Many Native people refer to North America as Turtle Island.

The Acoma people were fine. The problem was with Latour and his European perspective, and here Cather was perhaps offering a subtle criticism. Latour encounters a Native faith that he cannot explain, let alone reconcile with his own perspective. Acoma lived on, with or without him, despite the Catholic Church's (and the US government's) best effort to silence Native traditions and convert them to Western ways.

The Legend of Fray Baltazar

At the end of the Acoma chapter, Cather did something unusual: She added an event set one hundred fifty years before the novel, and seemingly unrelated to it, other than that it occurred at Acoma Pueblo. She called it "The Legend of Fray Baltazar."

Fray Baltazar Montoya is a Spanish-born man "of a tyrannical and overbearing disposition" (103–4), a man who "lived more after the flesh than after the spirit" (105). He demands labor from the pueblo to grow his garden atop the mesa, port water to his home, and to cook for him. He is a gourmand. One day he throws a dinner party for his fellow priests, who travel from distant pueblos to reach Acoma. They drink too much brandy, and a servant boy accidentally spills gravy on one of the men. Fray Baltazar throws a pewter mug at the boy in anger, striking him in the head and killing him. The priests flee, leaving Baltazar to face the consequences.

Baltazar retires to his loggia and waits. "The moon was the clock which began things in the pueblo," (112) Cather observed, and as the moon rises, the Acoma people come to the loggia, tie him up, and bring him to the cliffside. "The four executioners took him up again from the brink where they had laid him, and, after a few feints, dropped him in mid-air." (113) The pueblo takes no revenge against the church, nor against Fray Baltazar's successor, a modest man. They act out of justice for killing one of their own, though the women, who literally had to carry his water, took joy in watching his garden wither.

Cather explained in her November 1927 *Commonweal* article, "I had all my life wanted to do something in the style of legend, which is absolutely the reverse of dramatic treatment."[15] There are two inherent contradictions in the Fray Baltazar episode: It is myth, rather than legend (though based on legendary events, as we'll discuss), and it is dramatic, probably the most dramatic moment in the book.

The context for the Fray Baltazar episode was the Pueblo Revolt of 1680, where either one or three priests were killed at Acoma Pueblo—and none of them named Baltazar Montoya. Cather decontextualized the story, setting it several decades later, making it about an individual priest who serves himself rather than his flock. There are many variations of this legendary story, most but not all set during the revolt.

In his 1893 history *The Land of Poco Tiempo*, Charles Lummis described how Fray Juan Ramirez came to Acoma Pueblo in 1629, but the pueblo objected and threw him off a cliff. "His priestly robes upheld him miraculously and saved his life; but this is a myth without foundation or fact," Lummis wrote. A later missionary, Lucas Maldonado, was not so lucky: He was killed in the Pueblo Revolt. Lummis acknowledged that no one really knew how Maldonado died, whether he was thrown from a cliff, beaten, or stabbed to death.[16] Historians George James and Ralph Emerson Twitchell repeated that Maldonado was martyred in the 1680 revolt.[17]

Jean-Baptiste Salpointe, citing William Davis's *The Spanish Conquest of New Mexico* (1869), mentioned three priests killed at Acoma during the Pueblo Revolt: Cristobal Figueroa, Albino (not Lucas) Maldonado, and Juan Mora. The three men were clubbed and stoned to death, and their bodies were thrown into a cave, according to this variation.[18]

George Anderson provided two different versions of the story in his 1907 *History of New Mexico*. In one account, he repeated the story of Davis and Salpointe that the three priests—Figueroa, Maldonado, and Mora—were beaten to death at Acoma. In the other, combining several variations of the legend, the three men were compelled to jump to their deaths. Two of them were killed instantly, but the third's billowy attire slowed his fall like a parachute, and he survived. "The Indians, believing his escape from death to have been due to divine intervention, gave him his liberty," Anderson recorded. According to the story, the priest renounced Catholicism and was adopted into the tribe and married a Pueblo woman.[19]

As you can see, there is a great deal of myth surrounding the death of the priest or priests at Acoma Pueblo during the Pueblo Revolt. None of the stories mentioned Fray Baltazar Montoya. He was Cather's invention. Rather, all the legends include Fray Maldonado (rather than Montoya), though his first name varies (Albino or Lucas). Cather made personal corruption the reason for Baltazar's death, rather than the systemic oppression of the Franciscans, a key reason why she shifted the timeline away from the revolt.

These variations of the Acoma legend were written by white men, some of whom recorded what they heard from the Acoma people, while others were repeating hearsay. During my first visit to Acoma, the guide offered a variation of the story with Fray Baltazar being thrown off the cliff for abusing the youth but surviving the fall.

It took me years to figure out why Cather included the fictional episode of Fray Baltazar. It dawned on me after I moved to Santa Fe that Cather used one of her favorite literary tools, juxtaposition, to highlight the self-serving priest. Her style wasn't didactic; rather, she simply presented the facts and the demise of the man, who stood in contrast to Bishop Latour and Father Vaillant, who serve the people, rather than themselves.

Snake Root

Bishop Latour's second encounter with Pueblo religion occurs in the following book, "Snake Root." This is the shortest chapter in *Archbishop*, except for the prologue, and is entirely dedicated to Pecos Pueblo and the myths surrounding a site that is now a national historical park. The chapter raises questions of Pueblo spiritual beliefs but without explaining them. Latour confronts a faith so alien to his perspective that he finds it unnerving. Cather's point was that Native faith remains a mystery, as neither she, Lamy, Latour, nor any Westerner can really understand it.

Pecos Pueblo (also called Cicuye) is in a broad canyon between two arms of the Sangre de Cristo Mountains. The pueblo stands on a ridgeline between two year-round water sources that fed its agriculture: Glorieta Creek and the Pecos River. As the easternmost of the pueblos, Pecos was a powerful tribe that lay along the trade routes between the Rio Grande and the Great Plains. It could field a strong military force and was a buffer that protected the smaller pueblos to the west. Cather described the pueblo accurately, as "lying low on its red rock ledges, half-surrounded by a crown of fir-clad mountains, and facing a sea of juniper and cedars" (118).

Coronado visited Pecos Pueblo in 1540 during his fruitless two-year expedition to find the Seven Cities of Gold. The Spanish found Pecos a thriving community, but one that soon began a swift decline. European diseases killed many. Pecos participated in the Pueblo Revolt of 1680 and destroyed the massive mission church the Franciscans had forced them to build; however, after Governor de Vargas returned in 1692 to reestablish the Spanish colony, Pecos sided with him against the rebellious Pueblos. Pecos rebuilt a smaller-scale mission church whose remains date to 1717.

By the late eighteenth century, Pecos's population had severely declined from disease and the wars against the Comanches, and now there were just a handful of people still living there. Cather included a footnote that in fact some years before the remaining inhabitants of Pecos had moved away. (123) They joined their fellow Towa speakers at Jemez Pueblo in 1838, two decades before Cather set her scene at Pecos.

The historical context for this episode was in fall 1861, when Father Machebeuf fell ill from typhoid in Denver, and Bishop Lamy dispatched Father Gabriel Ussel to look after him. Once Machebeuf had sufficiently recovered, the two priests traveled to New Mexico so Machebeuf could recover in a better climate. In the chapter "Snake Root," Cather shifted the timeframe to the 1850s when Machebeuf (and the fictional Vaillant) was still doing missionary work in New Mexico.[20]

In the novel, Vaillant falls ill from black measles in Las Vegas, New Mexico, a small city on the eastern slopes of the Sangre de Cristo Mountains. Latour races to aid him. As sundown approaches, Latour halts at Pecos Pueblo, where he meets his friend and guide Jacinto. Jacinto and the Pueblo elders insist that he stay the night, as a winter storm is approaching.

Frustrated with the delay, Latour paces "up and down the crust of bare rock between the village and the ruin of the old mission church." He sleeps in the sacristy of the crumbling mission church, whose remains still stands. "The great red earth walls of the mission, red as brick-dust, yawned gloomily before him,—part of the roof had fallen in, and the rest would soon go." (119) Cather, who had visited Pecos in 1925 with Edith Lewis, described the pueblo as "empty houses ruined by weather and now scarcely more than piles of earth and stone." (123)

Figure 60. Pecos was once a powerhouse pueblo. Shown here is a round kiva, where the pueblo practiced their native faith, and behind it the 1717 mission church. The pueblo is now the heart of Pecos National Historical Park. Cather visited in 1925 and included the pueblo in *Archbishop*. Photograph by Garrett Peck.

Figure 61. The remains of Pecos Pueblo's mission church, which Cather and Lewis explored in 1925. Palace of the Governors Photo Archives, (NMHM/DCA), Image 006506.

The next morning Latour and Jacinto ride through the wilderness to find Father Vaillant. As the Pecos elders had warned, a great blizzard breaks upon them. Desperate for shelter, Jacinto leads the bishop to a cliffside cave, one whose mouthlike opening looked like "two great stone lips" (126) The cave is a hidden kiva. Jacinto reluctantly takes the Catholic priest to this sacred site—the Franciscans had done everything they could to destroy the kivas, as they were the centerpiece of pueblo faith. Kivas like the stone lips cave were in the wilderness, where the Pueblo could conduct ceremonies in secret and away from prying Spanish eyes.

After climbing through the stone lips and down a twenty-foot ladder, "like that used in kivas," Latour "found himself in a lofty cavern, shaped somewhat like a Gothic chapel." He interprets it along European lines without realizing the limits of his perspective. Despite the need for shelter in the storm, Latour has "an extreme distaste for the place. The air in the cave was glacial, penetrated to the very bones, and he detected at once a fetid odour, not very strong but highly disagreeable" (127). Latour encounters a faith that was beyond his own, and it makes him deeply uncomfortable. This is his first time in a kiva.

The cave-kiva can be interpreted literally but also in psychosexual and symbolic terms. There are the stone lips, which seem vaginal. A cave is a feminine symbol, a womb. It is part of Mother Earth, and the Pueblo Indians believe that they emerged from the three underworlds. The cave-kiva thus resembles an earth-womb. As Catholic priests are celibate, Cather may have hinted toward Latour's repressed sexuality.

Inside the cave, Jacinto finds a pile of wood stacked neatly; however, he hesitates to disturb it. Latour thinks that Jacinto should start building a fire right away, but instead Jacinto slowly inspects every piece. Cather wrote her niece Virginia, "There are many opinions about what was in the cave—but I think it was a rattlesnake den. Jacinto thought there might be some around loose under the faggots. He was afraid the heat would warm the dry fellows up and bring them out. An Indian always knows the rattlesnake smell, but this Bishop hadn't enough experience."[21]

Once Jacinto gets a fire burning, "Latour perceived an extraordinary vibration in this cavern; it hummed like a hive of bees, like a heavy roll of distant drums" (129). The young man leads Latour deeper into the mountain through a tunnel and dug out a clay-filled crack, which is clearly a sipapu. Latour puts his ear to the mountain and hears "the sound of a great underground river, flowing through a resounding cavern. The water was far, far below, perhaps as deep as the foot of the mountain, a flood moving in utter blackness under ribs of antediluvian rock. It was not a rushing noise, but the sound of a great flood moving with majesty and power" (130).

Latour wakes in the middle of the night. He witnesses Jacinto "standing on some invisible foothold, his arms outstretched against the rock, his body flattened against it, his ear over that patch of fresh mud, listening; listening with supersensual ear, it seemed, and he looked to be supported against the rock by the intensity of his solicitude" (131). Jacinto appears to be convening with Mother Nature, or perhaps with the spirits of his ancestors, through the sipapu. It is a deeply spiritual experience for the young man. Latour closes his eyes and keeps secret what he has witnessed.

Latour's experience with native faith is that of an outsider looking in. He is sympathetic to a point, but "He was already convinced that neither the white men nor the Mexicans in Santa Fé understood anything about Indian beliefs or the workings of the Indian mind" (133). Latour (and Cather) viewed the divide between Natives and whites as unbridgeable, but he was also respectful and accepting of the Native perspective.

> The Bishop seldom questioned Jacinto about his thoughts or beliefs. He didn't think it polite, and he believed it to be useless. There was no way in which he could transfer his own memories of European civilization into the Indian mind, and he was quite willing to believe that behind Jacinto there was a long tradition, a story of experience, which no language could translate to him. (92)

The next day Jacinto and Latour emerge from the cave-kiva to a world covered in snow. Giving up on finding their mules, they trudge out of the mountains and soon find Father Vaillant, already recovering. Kit Carson had reached him first. Carson and Latour bring him back to Santa Fe.

There is in fact a sacred cavern called Terrero Cave that the descendants of Pecos Pueblo still use for pilgrimages. It is deep in the Pecos River canyon, about fifteen miles north of the pueblo, and it is fenced off and closed to the public. Cather and Lewis visited Pecos Pueblo with Mary Austin and her niece in July 1925. They made no record if they visited that cave, but I am skeptical that they did, given its isolation, though Cather may have heard about it.

Cather took her inspiration for the stone lips cave-kiva from a real place, but it is in an unexpected location. It is nowhere near Pecos Pueblo, but rather a few miles outside the village of Arroyo Seco north of Taos. During Cather and Lewis's visit to Taos in July 1925, Tony Lujan drove them to the cave, known as El Salto del Agua (the "jumping water") for the waterfall that falls over the cave's entrance. The road can be a challenge, as Lewis recorded in her Blue Jay notebook: "Rode in car to Ceremonial Cave. Car fell in ditch above Arroyo Seco." The sound of the water must have struck a chord with Cather, along with the cave's obvious use in ceremonies.[22]

Mabel Dodge Luhan had first visited the El Salto cave in 1918 with Tony Lujan and was enchanted by it, such that she wrote about it in three separate books (*Lorenzo in Taos*, *Winter in Taos*, and *Edge of Taos Desert*). Against Tony's objections they hiked up the mountain through the snow to the cave, as she wrote in *Winter in Taos*.

> Tony led the way in behind the water to the shadowy cave. The light came in green and subdued and we found a large, dry chamber of rock with a high, domed ceiling, and with the sides sloping upwards to meet it. He showed me where there were steps, apparently roughly hewn out at the back wall, leading up to a ledge; and above the ledge and far above us, impossible to reach without a long ladder, there was the faint painting of a sun.
>
> "Rising in the east," Tony said; and true enough, it was at the point where the sun comes over the mountains in the middle of winter.[23]

Mabel took D. H. Lawrence and his wife Frieda to the cave when they visited Taos in 1922. Here is how Mabel described it in *Lorenzo in Taos*:

> The vast, pelvic-shaped aperture faces the west and yawns upward to the sky; and over it descends the mountain water, falling thirty feet across the face of the entrance to form an icy pool below. We skirted the waterfall and entered the cavern; chill and damp and dark it was, too! Here there are holes hollowed out in the rock walls where Tony says the bears sleep in the winter; and at the right-hand side of the back wall of the place there are a number of rude climbing steps that lead up to a shelving ledge. Above this altar-like ledge there is a faint sun painted high up to the east of it. One by one we climbed to the high altar, and, looking before us, we saw the clear fall of water across the opening, green and transparent.[24]

Mabel called it "the ceremonial cave of long forgotten days, where sacrifices were made behind the waterfall that veils its recessed altar." D. H. Lawrence included the cave in his 1924 short story, "The Woman Who

Figure 62. El Salto del Agua Waterfall near Arroyo Seco, a village near Taos, was the inspiration for the stone lips cave-kiva in Cather's *Death Comes for the Archbishop*. D. H. Lawrence's 1924 short story "The Woman Who Rode Away" included the cave, and Mabel Dodge Luhan wrote about the cave in three of her four memoirs. Photograph by Garrett Peck.

Rode Away." In the story, an American woman (obviously modeled on Mabel) travels to a remote part of Mexico, where an Indigenous tribe sacrificed her as the last rays of the setting sun penetrated the icy cave during the winter solstice.[25]

Taos Pueblo had misgivings about the cave, and Tony was reluctant to take Mabel to it. "The cave had a bad name among these Indians who believed it was still used by witches, and that it had been used for terrible things in the faraway past before the memory of this tribe," she wrote in *Edge of Taos Desert*.[26]

Anthropologist Adolph Bandelier explored the remains of Pecos Pueblo in 1880 and met Mariano Ruiz. Ruiz had been adopted into Pecos in its last years and maintained the pueblo's deed for safekeeping after it relocated to Jemez Pueblo. He mentioned that they kept holy embers, and that one member was elected each year to keep the embers burning. Ruiz also mentioned that they worshipped a giant snake, which they kept hidden, and that they may have taken it with them to Jemez along with the holy embers.[27]

A US Army lieutenant, James William Abert, visited Pecos in 1846 and wrote afterward:

> The village of Pecos is famed for the residence of a singular race of Indians, about whom many curious legends are told. In their temples they were said to keep an immense serpent, to which they sacrificed human victims. Others say that they worshipped a perpetual fire, that they believed to have been kindled by Montezuma, and that one of the race was yearly appointed to watch this fire. As the severity of their vigils always caused the death of the watchers, in time this tribe became extinct.[28]

What Abert recounted was mythology. Montezuma II, the last leader of the Aztec Empire, was falsely said to be born at Pecos, and it was believed he would one day return. Pecos had dwindled not because of dedication to its faith, but because of disease and warfare. And the pueblo never went extinct but rather relocated to Jemez.

Josiah Gregg observed the last years of Pecos Pueblo in the 1830s, and he too relayed the stories about the holy fire and the huge snake. The latter he believed to be fiction, a story "so firmly believed in by many ignorant people." He scoffed at tales that the Pueblo fed infants to the serpent.[29] Historian John Kessell noted that the holy embers and rattlesnake myths derive from "a blend of Pueblo mythology up from Mexico and rampant 19th century Anglo-American romanticism."[30]

In Pueblo religion, the plumed serpent Avanyu, also known as the Horned Water Serpent, is equated with lightning and rain. Snakes live in two worlds: above and below ground, thus uniting the Pueblo cosmos and the immortal Mother Earth and Father Sky. Avanyu is often seen on ancestral petroglyphs as a zigzag line and may represent an appeal for rain, which watered crops and in turn fed the people. He is echoed in the sky in lightning that proceeds a monsoon (a thunderstorm), as we call it in the Southwest.[31]

Cather addressed both legends when Latour asks a trader named Zeb Orchard about the holy embers and the snake. He (and by extension Cather) is skeptical but level-setting: They could be true. The embers might be a flame held in a small oven meant to continuously burn. Regarding the snake, Orchard isn't certain. Late one night, he saw the Pecos people carrying a large chest but admitted it could be rocks or something else spiritually important, not necessarily a large serpent. "No white man knows anything about Indian religion, Padre," Orchard confides to Latour (134).

Native peoples are much more open today to sharing aspects of their culture to outsiders, in part so we can better understand each other. But there is also much that isn't shared, particularly sacred knowledge, and that's okay. When you are a guest at a tribe's dance or feast day, you may not comprehend its deeper meaning or the subtleties of the message, but you are a witness to something ancient and essential, to a culture that continues to thrive despite the pressures of the modern age. We may not fully understand each other, but more important is to live in community and to have mutual respect for our fellow human beings.

CHAPTER 9

Padre Martínez and the Mexican Priests

"He was rather terrifying, that old priest, with his big head, violent Spanish face, and shoulders like a buffalo; but the day of his tyranny was almost over."

—WILLA CATHER, *Death Comes for the Archbishop*, 32

RIDING UP THE CHAIRLIFT one day at Ski Santa Fe, I got to talking with an attorney from Albuquerque whose last name is the same as my street. He stated his objection to *Death Comes for the Archbishop* on the grounds of how Cather treated Padre Antonio José Martínez. I've heard this complaint many times. This is the most controversial aspect of her novel, especially among northern New Mexican Hispanics (*norteños*), who tend to revere the priest.

While Cather's treatment of Martínez and the other Mexican priests is controversial to many, Cather did not see it as such. In researching *Archbishop*, she used historical material (albeit flawed) that was available to her, and she was influenced by other peoples' bias. I don't necessarily fault her for this. The received wisdom among many people of Cather's day was that Martínez was a villain, and the record wasn't set straight until decades later.

Cather wrote a novel, not a history, though her book is based on real people. Her fictional Latour had to do what the real Lamy did: to establish the Catholic Church's orthodoxy in the territory and discipline the Mexican priests, who were independent and had had little oversight for decades. This was bound to cause discord. In this conflict, Cather took the side of the French over the Mexican priests, showing her bias toward Europeans over Mexicans.

John Murphy observed humorously that "Latour's confrontations with the wayward native clergy make him a kind of frontier lawman. . . . Martinez, Gallegos and Lucero, a trio of clergymen as lawless as any company of cattle rustlers, challenge the new bishop's authority by practices as varied as political intrigue, gambling, hoarding money and siring children." There is an element of truth to this, but it is mostly myth.[1]

Martínez was a historical person, but also a legendary figure, a hero, and a villain, all wrapped in one. How do we unpack such a complicated and real person? In this chapter, we'll look at how Cather treated the Mexican priests, and how this compared to the historical record.

The Firing of Padre Gallegos

In book 3, "The Mass at Ácoma," Bishop Latour sets out on a missionary journey to the Indian pueblos. He first visits Albuquerque, where Padre José Manuel Gallegos is the pastor at San Felipe de Neri Church, and then on to Isleta, Laguna, and finally Acoma. Cather describes Padre Gallegos as being far too worldly, and that was not far off the mark from the actual historical figure. He enjoys dancing the fandango, playing poker, and hunting and keeps a well-stocked cellar. Gallegos fakes an injury so that he won't have to accompany Latour to Acoma. "As a priest, he was impossible; he was too self-satisfied and popular ever to change his ways," Cather wrote. "There was but one course: to suspend the man from the exercise of all priestly functions, and bid the smaller native priests take warning" (83–84).

The real Gallegos did in fact live with a woman, María de Jesús Trujillo, his business partner in a dry-goods store in Albuquerque. They often rode together in the same carriage, and she lived in the rectory with her children. Gallegos had taken the family in, and Trujillo wasn't his lover—but that's not the way Father Machebeuf read the situation. Besides living

Figure 63. José Manuel Gallegos, a Catholic priest who Lamy suspended in 1852 and then went into territorial politics. Palace of the Governors Photo Archives (NMHM/DCA), Image 009882.

with a woman, which raised questions of his commitment to celibacy, Gallegos was also an active participant in New Mexico politics.

Cather overlooked the real reason why Bishop Lamy defrocked Padre Gallegos: negligence. While Lamy traveled to Baltimore for a bishop's conference in 1852, Gallegos went to Durango, Mexico, to meet Bishop Zubiría, traveling with a large wagon train and possibly conducting business for his dry-goods store. He arranged for a substitute priest in his absence.

When Lamy returned from Baltimore, Machebeuf informed him of Gallegos's unauthorized trip to Mexico. Lamy suspended Gallegos in September 1852, replacing him with Machebeuf, as Albuquerque was a significant parish. Gallegos had not yet returned from Mexico, and his congregation did not know what was about to hit them until Machebeuf read the suspension order on December 5.

Gallegos was the fifth priest that Lamy suspended, all of them based on Machebeuf's recommendation, as the vicar apostolic weeded out alleged corruption, concubinage, and retired older priests who could no longer serve. This was all in Lamy's first year, a year in which he spent most of his time traveling to Durango and Baltimore. Machebeuf was left in charge of the vicariate (it was not elevated into a diocese until 1853, two years after Lamy's arrival).

When Gallegos returned from Mexico in March 1853 after his lengthy absence, he incited his congregation to protest. Within a few days, 950 prominent citizens of Albuquerque signed a letter protesting Gallegos's suspension, Machebeuf's incessant demands for tithes, and for the French priest's alleged breaking of the confessional seal. There was much outcry in Albuquerque over this, as Gallegos was popular.

Machebeuf penned a letter to his sister Marie Philomène of how he found himself locked out of the church one day, and once he gained entrance, he found Gallegos preaching from the pulpit. He wrote that he strolled up to the altar and publicly refuted Gallegos, then repeated the news to the congregation that the priest had been suspended. This was the only eyewitness account of Gallegos's suspension, and it must be taken with some skepticism.

According to Machebeuf, who made himself the hero of the moment, the episode revealed him as both fearless and stubborn. He had the force of law on his side and was not to be swayed by a hostile crowd. He claimed to be a popular priest in Albuquerque, winning over the opposition that had previously supported Padre Gallegos. He continued the Christmas novenas that the Mexicans had long enjoyed and began lively preaching from the pulpit, something that had long been absent. When he was reassigned to Santa Fe, there was a large protest, including from many of his former opponents. That is what Machebeuf wanted people to believe for posterity. The truth is more complicated. He traveled a great deal, visiting many parishes, and his Albuquerque parishioners complained to Lamy that Machebeuf was often absent, playing missionary priest rather than tending to his congregation.[2]

A Franciscan priest and Korean War veteran, Fray Angélico Chávez, became one of New Mexico's most important twentieth-century historians. In 1985 he published *Très Macho*, a biography and apology for Padre

Gallegos. Chávez placed Gallegos's ouster squarely on Machebeuf, whom he called Gallegos's "arch-foe." He also called Machebeuf a "sex-troubled fanatic, and a chauvinist as well." I don't particularly buy Chávez's argument that Machebeuf's ambition was to take over the Albuquerque parish: The French priest had indeed witnessed Gallegos engage in conduct that was not befitting of a priest.[3]

"For Padre Gallegos and his people, there was nothing wrong if he could afford and enjoy good liquors, or liked to shuffle cards with his cronies, or even took part in harmless folk-dances," Chávez wrote in his defense. "There was no denying that Gallegos was a worldly man beyond the canonical sense of 'secular' priest."[4] Yet Chávez didn't completely let Gallegos off the hook: "Don José Manuel Gallegos appears to have been both vain and pretentious as well as indiscreet, and therefore not entirely guiltless" in the showdown with the French priests.[5]

After Gallegos was fired, he and Machebeuf quarreled over who owned the church rectory, which Gallegos claimed was his private residence. The dispute landed in court, and Lamy bought Gallegos out of the property. The former priest returned to Durango to complain to Bishop Zubiría, hoping he would relay Machebeuf's sins to the Vatican, which the Mexican bishop declined to do, as this was now Lamy's problem. Gallegos traveled back to Santa Fe to participate in the territorial legislature, in part to get even with Lamy and Machebeuf. In 1853 Gallegos was elected New Mexico's territorial representative to Congress.

Another problem that Lamy had to resolve was rooted in New Mexico's poverty. The Mexican priests charged high fees for their services, and they kept most of the money. This meant that Lamy's diocese was starved for cash, and Lamy unsurprisingly sought to reform this system. At Christmas 1852 he published a pastoral letter establishing tithing to fund the church's operations and reduced the fee schedule by two-thirds. The priests were allowed to keep one-fourth of the income for their parishes, while the rest of the money or in-kind contributions would go to the diocese. The Mexican priests were not pleased with this arrangement, nor was the public. Lamy likewise tripled the penalties for church members who refused to comply. When some parishioners refused to pay, Lamy challenged them in court and won.[6]

On January 5, 1853—exactly a month after Gallegos's suspension—Padre Antonio José Martínez dispatched a letter to Bishop Lamy. He complained of Father Machebeuf's abuses and that Gallegos was suspended without cause, that Machebeuf preached incessantly for money, and worst of all, that Machebeuf had broken the confessional seal by gossiping. The French priest had publicly repeated what he had heard in confession from a notable person in Peña Blanca. In his defense, Machebeuf responded that what he discussed was common knowledge. Other priests and civilians joined the complaint. Gallegos was one of their own, and his suspension drove a wedge between Lamy and the Mexican clergy.[7]

On January 1, 1856, Gallegos's allies in the New Mexico territorial legislature approved a Gallegos-drafted letter to the pope censoring Lamy for protecting Machebeuf after the latter knowingly broke the confessional seal. This spelled trouble, and Lamy dispatched Machebeuf to the Vatican to defend himself against the charges. Machebeuf spent an anxious nine weeks in Rome. He exaggerated Gallegos's faults, calling him "very vain and pretentious," and accused him of scandalously living with a prostitute, Jesusita Trujillo, suggesting that the nature of their relationship was sexual. (To recall, Trujillo was an honest businesswoman, not a sex worker). After this screed against Gallegos, the Vatican acquitted Machebeuf.[8]

By now Lamy had established his own political allies in New Mexico, and they came to his defense. When Gallegos won reelection to Congress in 1856, Miguel Antonio Otero, an American-educated Hispanic and Lamy ally, claimed fraud and took the case to Congress. Congress unseated Gallegos and seated Otero instead.

Gallegos moved to Santa Fe in 1857, where he rejoined the territorial legislature. He built a large home north of the Plaza and served as speaker of the house from 1860 to 1862. The Confederates arrested Gallegos in 1862 when they briefly occupied the city during the Civil War. In 1868 Gallegos married his housekeeper of many years, Candelaria Montoya. He returned to Congress to serve a second term from 1871 to 1873, then died of a stroke two years later at the age of sixty.

Lamy and his former vicar, Juan Felipe Ortiz, likewise fell into dispute. Lamy had installed Machebeuf as his vicar, as was his right, which left

Ortiz with diminished authority over the Santa Fe parishes. Lamy then split the Parroquia into two jurisdictions, as he wanted to make the adobe church his cathedral. Ortiz was the *cura propio*, or permanent pastor, a lifelong appointment in the Mexican church but which the American Catholic Church did not recognize. Ortiz protested by resigning and invited Lamy to move out of his stately house, which the priest owned. Lamy moved into another dwelling. Ortiz appealed to Rome, and Lamy responded by suspending him. The priest soon decamped to southern New Mexico, thoroughly disenchanted with Lamy's regime. Ortiz died in January 1858, removing a considerable source of ire for the bishop. This came just months before the showdown with Padre Antonio José Martínez.

Padre Martínez: Hero or Villain?

Father Thomas Steele, a Jesuit teacher and prolific writer, recalled an actor friend who created a one-man show about Padre Martínez. The play began with him exclaiming, "¡Esa mujer!—That woman!" Cather had "stolen all the greatness" from a man many norteños hold in high regard.[9]

Cather briefly introduces Padre Martínez early in her novel in rather startling terms, though she does not refer to him again until the midpoint of the book. This is a foreshadowing of the novel's main conflict, a conflict that she never resolves.

> He [Latour] was not troubled about the revolt in Santa Fé, or the powerful old native priest who led it—Father Martínez, of Taos, who had ridden over from his parish expressly to receive the new Vicar and to drive him away. He was rather terrifying, that old priest, with his big head, violent Spanish face, and shoulders like a buffalo; but the day of his tyranny was almost over. (32)

In book 5, "Padre Martínez," Cather devotes an entire chapter to the priest. She turns the man into the novel's villain, though her protagonist Latour deals with him passively, waiting for the old man's time to come.

Latour travels to Taos to visit the congregations and to meet with

Martínez. Cather writes, “Martínez had been dictator to all the parishes in northern New Mexico, and the native priests at Santa Fé were all of them under his thumb” (139). She then describes how Martínez instigated the Taos Revolt of 1847 against the American government, which led to the death of Governor Charles Bent and eleven Americans. The US Army under Colonel Sterling Price (later a Confederate general) put down the revolt by besieging the rebels at Taos Pueblo’s San Geronimo Church. Some 154 people were killed inside the church, and Price ordered a dozen ringleaders hanged, including seven from Taos Pueblo.

According to Cather, Martínez escaped being charged and profited from the revolt. The seven Taos Indians who were condemned asked Martínez for help, and he agreed to assist them only after they signed over the deed to their lands. Having accomplished this, Martínez took no further action but left town while the men were hung. “Martínez now cultivated their fertile farms, which made him quite the richest man in the parish,” Cather noted dryly (140).

Cather’s description of Padre Martínez paints him in ugly, even racist terms. “His broad high shoulders were like a bull buffalo’s, his big head was set defiantly on a thick neck, and the full-cheeked, richly coloured, egg-shaped Spanish face—how vividly the Bishop remembered that face! . . . His mouth was the very assertion of violence, uncurbed passions and tyrannical self-will; the full lips thrust out and taut, like the flesh of animals distended by fear or desire” (140–41).

Latour’s response to Martínez is passive: “Father Latour judged that the day of the lawless personal power was almost over, even on the frontier, and this figure was to him already like something picturesque and impressive, but really impotent, left over from the past” (141).

The fictional Martínez escorts Latour to Ranchos de Taos, where the women throw down their shawls for Latour to walk on as he enters the famed San Francisco de Asís Church, and congregants throng to kiss his ring. Afterward Latour and Martínez ride to his home in Taos, where a great crowd gathers to see the new bishop. A boy keeps his hat on, and Martínez cuffs his ears for the offense. When Latour quietly protests, Martínez declares, “He is my own son, Bishop, and it is time I taught him manners” (142).

Figure 64. Padre Antonio José Martínez, highly regarded by northern New Mexicans but who served as the antagonist in Cather's *Death Comes for the Archbishop*. Palace of the Governors Photo Archives (NMHM/DCA), Image 011262.

Over supper, Martínez asks Latour "if he considered celibacy an essential condition of the priest's vocation." Latour responds that this had been settled centuries ago. "Nothing is decided once for all," Martínez protests. "Celibacy may be all very well for the French clergy, but not for ours" (145). He further explains that "celibate priests lose their perceptions. No priest can experience repentance and forgiveness of sin unless he himself falls into sin," and thus "it is better for him to know something about it" (146).

When Latour states that he would challenge these practices and require his priests to obey their vow of celibacy, Martínez laughs.

> It will keep you busy, Bishop. Nature has got the start of you here. But for all that, our native priests are more devout than your French

> Jesuits. We have a living Church here, not a dead arm of the European Church. Our religion grew out of the soil and has its own roots. We pay a filial respect to the person of the Holy Father, but Rome has no authority here. We do not require aid from the Propaganda, and we resent its interference. The Church the Franciscan Fathers planted here was cut off; this is the second growth, and it is indigenous. Our people are the most devout left in the world. If you blast their faith by European formalities, they will become infidels and profligates (146).

When Latour states that he would relieve priests if they don't reform their practices, Martínez counters, "You cannot deprive me of mine, Bishop. Try it! I will organize my own church. You can have your French priest of Taos, and I will have the people!" He threatens that if Latour abolishes "the bloody rites of the Penitentes, I foretell an early death for you" (147). Later he hints that the revolts of 1680 and 1847 could be repeated, which led to the expulsion of the Spanish in the first, and the death of the American governor in the second. "He boasted that there had never been trouble afoot in New Mexico that wasn't started in Taos" (150).

Latour stops by Kit Carson's house east of the Taos Plaza. He asks Josefa, the frontiersman's Mexican wife, if he should act against the Penitential Brotherhood. Josefa advises him to leave the brotherhood alone: "It would only set the people against you. The old people have need of their old customs; and the young ones will go with the times" (154–55).

Back in Santa Fe, Latour meets with Vaillant and resolves, "I shall do nothing to change the curious situation at Taos." The congregation is strong there and the people devout, but the people are very devoted to Martínez. "For the present I shall be blind to what I do not like there" (156). When Vaillant protests, Latour responds, "I do not wish to lose the parish of Taos in order to punish its priest, my friend" (157).

Cather writes that Latour bided his time, sensing that Martínez's time was coming to an end: "He was a man of the old order, a son of Abiquiu, and his day was over" (153). The author never provides a clear ending to the conflict with Padre Martínez, a valid criticism of the novel. But it was clear that there was little about Bishop Lamy that was passive.

Who Were Los Penitentes?

In *Death Comes for the Archbishop*, Padre Martínez warns Bishop Latour not to interfere with Los Penitentes. Cather offered little explanation of the brotherhood, why they mattered, or how they fit into New Mexico's history.

La Fraternidad Piadosa de Nuestra Padre Jésus Nazareno, also known as Los Hermanos Penitentes—the Penitent Brothers—was a confraternity created in the context of New Mexico's isolation. Since the Middle Ages, the Franciscan Third Order had allowed lay people to participate in St. Francis's peaceful mission, fasting, making penance, and displaying the sacraments during Lent. These traditions made their way to New Mexico.

The king of Spain withdrew the Franciscans after Mexico won its independence in 1821. The young republic "secularized" the Catholic Church, meaning it would not subsidize the church. Priests would not come from established religious orders, but rather from families who sent their sons to seminary. The problem was, New Mexico had virtually no education system, and thus there were far too few secular priests to attend to the people's spiritual needs.

Devout lay people of Rio Arriba (northern New Mexico) stepped in, organizing the first Penitentes in Santa Cruz, which also served as a mutual aid society. The brotherhood spread to Mexican mountain villages and into southern Colorado. A parallel women's movement known as the Carmelitas likewise sprang up.

The Penitentes included flagellation as part of their rituals. They scourged themselves during Holy Week in the runup to Easter, retraced the suffering that Jesus experienced on his way to execution at Golgotha. Meanwhile, one man was tied to a cross in commemoration of Jesus's crucifixion.

When Bishop Zubiría ordered the Penitentes suppressed in 1833, they continued their rituals in windowless adobe buildings known as "moradas," giving them privacy from prying eyes. Archbishop Lamy largely left the brotherhood alone. His successor, Jean-Baptiste Salpointe, suppressed them more than the two previous bishops had.[10]

Charles Lummis observed and photographed a Penitente ritual in 1891, which left him dismayed. "They flay their backs with plaited scourges, wallow naked in beds of cactus, bear crushing crosses, and on Good Friday actually crucify one of their order, chosen to that supreme honor by lot," he wrote.[11]

When New Mexican historian Angélico Chávez misbehaved as a child, his father would threaten, "One of these days I'm going to turn this *bribón* [rascal] over to the Sangre de Cristo!," meaning to the brotherhood for punishment. His mother would scold her husband for saying such things, but it wasn't until much later that Chávez realized "it was all part of a running game of sharp teasing between my parents . . . she said that the menfolk on her side were too high a type of Catholics to be Penitentes, while none on my father's were good enough Christians to deserve being one of them." Chávez became a Franciscan who wasn't keen on scourging, but he did recognize that "religious flagellation is an act of loving empathy with what once happened upon a cross, not any particular interest in the bleeding itself."[12]

Mabel Dodge Luhan observed Penitente rituals, as La Morada de Nuestra Señora de Guadalupe stood on Taos Pueblo land right behind her house. She observed, "Their Catholicism is violent and their violence is catholicized; and since the preponderance of the population in this part of the state is Mexican, the vote is a Penitente vote." The Penitentes continue their practices, though they are a diminished force in New Mexico with the declining population in mountain farming and ranching towns.[13]

The Making of a Myth

In 1987 Father Thomas Steele and Ronald Brockway published a scholarly edition of William Howlett's biography of Machebeuf. They wrote in an afterward that *Death Comes for the Archbishop* "has done more than any other book (perhaps more than all other books combined) to create the popular American view of the Roman Catholic Church in the Southwest. It has compelled readers with its unfair—its savagely libelous—portraits of Fathers Gallegos, Martínez, and Lucero, each of them presented under his own real name; but a morality play needs a devil or two or three."

Figure 65. The Morada del Alto, just up the hill from Georgia O'Keeffe's house in Abiquiú. Photograph by Garrett Peck.

Cather might have avoided the controversy if she had simply given these historical figures fictional names.[14]

Cather's Padre Martínez comes across as a reactionary, when in fact the old priest was anything but. He was a progressive advocate for education and Indigenous rights and is revered by many norteños. Oliver LaFarge noted, "It has become usual for popular writers to describe this notable priest as a villain of the deepest dye, a characterization definitely not warranted by the record."[15]

In her defense, Cather repeated the conventional story about Martínez that had been retold for decades, a story of an unprincipled tyrant who bore only small resemblance to the more complicated truth. Rather, the blame lies in the partisan invective against Martínez from his many opponents, which date back to the 1830s. We must fault the sources that Cather had access to at the time, and which had a strong anti-Martínez bias. In essence, Martínez was smeared—but he was also no innocent. He took an active part in his own undoing.

William Davis, a contemporary of Padre Martínez and the New Mexico territorial secretary, was the first to put in print that Martínez had helped lead the Taos Revolt. In his 1857 book *El Gringo*, Davis wrote, "A large body of the rebels, composed mainly of Pueblo Indians, and incited to the act by Priest Martinez and others, attacked his [Governor Bent's] residence, and murdered him and several others in cold blood."[16]

American historians built upon the rumors that Martínez's enemies had started until he had become a fully-fledged villain. Fathers Howlett and Salpointe were circumspect about the priest (and they in turn relied upon earlier biased sources, such as Davis's *El Gringo*), though they believed he helped instigate the Taos Revolt. Cather relied on these historical sources to research her novel—and nothing was more damning than George Anderson's 1907 book *History of New Mexico.*

Anderson acknowledged that Martínez was "one of the most remarkable men ever identified with the history of New Mexico."[17] He assumed, as did many historians of his day, that the priest instigated the Taos Revolt, but also admitted, "It is difficult to state just what part this priest bore in the uprising of 1847. His crafty methods rendered it impossible for the American authorities to prove his actual participation and leadership in the revolt."[18]

"The home of Fr. Jose Antonio Martinez was generally regarded as the headquarters for the insurrectionists prior to the uprising and until after the attack upon Taos," Anderson stated, though this was categorically false. "His power over his parishioners was absolute and his hatred of Americans and American institutions was recognized by all." He continued, "Father Martinez was notorious for his great immorality," though Anderson never spelled out how exactly Martínez was immoral.[19]

"He was, to all intents and purposes, not only an arbitrary spiritual guide, but a monarch," Anderson opined. "He ruled with a tyrannical hand and was obeyed. The pueblo Indians at Taos frequently manifested their extreme dislike of him and his methods," an aversion that continues to this day. Martínez was allied with Padre Mariano de Jesús Lucero of Arroyo Hondo, and Anderson had little good to say about the latter.

"Though notorious for his selfishness and miserly disposition, the Indians reverenced him, while hating Father Martinez."[20]

And there we have it. We see in George Anderson's 1907 history the key source that influenced Cather to paint Martínez as a tyrant and Lucero as a miser.

In addition to Anderson's history, Cather was likely influenced by Mabel Dodge Luhan during Cather and Edith Lewis's stay in Taos in 1925. Mabel repeated rumors of Padre Martínez as if they were fact. "He did not believe in celibacy and a great many women loved him and apparently they all called their offspring Martinez; so his descendants of that name are to be found at all the cardinal points of the valley," Luhan wrote in her memoir, *Edge of Taos Desert*. She added, "I have a charcoal drawing of him, made by an admirer from Ranchos de Taos, showing a fierce, bullet-shaped head, intense eyes, and a lower lip that pushes the upper lip up like an iron brace."[21]

Mabel's bias against Martínez may have come from her husband, Tony Lujan. Martínez remains controversial at Taos Pueblo, in part because of the allegations that he kept Pueblo lands after the Taos Revolt. Taos erected a statue to the priest on its Plaza in 2006, a statue that many at the pueblo frown upon.

As it turns out, much of this received wisdom about Padre Martínez is wrong.

It was not until the 1970s and Paul Horgan's *Lamy of Santa Fe* that scholars began reexamining the legendary priest. Some call these historians revisionists, but that's a complicated word, evoking alternative facts and fake news. In this case, they challenged the received wisdom passed down through earlier, mostly white historians, that in turn influenced Cather and the public mythology about Martínez. Their research showed the documented facts about the controversial priest differed from the mythology that Cather repeated.

Foremost of these new historians was Fray Angélico Chávez, who investigated Martínez's historical record through the church's extensive archives. He published a biography of the man, *But Time and Chance: The Story of Padre Martínez of Taos*, in 1981, launching a long overdue and necessary reexamination of the priest's life. His biography is a reminder

Figure 66. The statue of Padre Antonio José Martínez in Taos Plaza erected in 2006. Photograph by Garrett Peck.

that history is not a static science, but one that is in continuous discussion as new documents, facts, and perspectives emerge.

Chávez's own views on Martínez evolved. In his 1974 book *My Penitente Land*, he declared that Martínez was "Hispanic New Mexico's greatest son."[22] After examining the facts while researching his 1981 biography of the man, he tempered this assessment: "While one has to retract for this very reason, and with sore regret, a statement made in a previous book that Padre Martínez was New Mexico's greatest son, one can still say that he was her major genius in his own century as well as those before and after his time."[23]

While Chávez did not let Martínez off the hook for his behavior, he made clear that much of the invective directed toward Martínez was from his enemies, in part because the priest was so politically outspoken and prone to criticizing others in the press. Martínez was a pragmatist who quickly adjusted to and even welcomed the American occupation of New

Mexico, knowing that the United States was more democratic than Mexico, upheld religious toleration, and had a stronger rule of law. But Martínez was also a man with an inflated ego and an oversized sense of self whose mental faculties may have diminished as he aged.

Chávez noted that, rather than support the Taos Revolt, Martínez berated the insurrectionists and warned them of military reprisal. He took numerous refugees into his home, saving lives from the mob, and advocated for leniency for the prisoners. Chávez called the rumors of Martínez's leadership in the revolt "false accusations."[24] Historian E. A. Mares went even further: "There has never been a shred of historical evidence to support the contention of certain enemies of Padre Martínez that he had organized the Taos uprising."[25]

I don't agree with Chávez on every point in his groundbreaking Martínez biography. He too often turned Father Machebeuf into the villain while giving Bishop Lamy a pass, and he was overly defensive about the Mexican priests. He called Machebeuf an "indefatigable scandalmonger." Both he and Ray John de Aragón, who examined the Lamy/Martínez question in 1978, overlooked the rumored 1857 Taos uprising, an event that likely triggered Martínez's break with Lamy. And Chávez comes across as homophobic. He describes one priest as a "limp-wrist fop," and in his 1985 biography of José Manuel Gallegos, he accused Machebeuf of having a "latent homosexual inclination" from which rose "a tense fanaticism against any impurity detected or even suspected in others." This was during the HIV/AIDS crisis, and Chávez's attitude very much reflected the blind prejudice directed towards gay people in his time.[26]

In his biography, Chávez acknowledged Cather's fictional portrayal of Padre Martínez, but he neither blamed nor condemned her for this. She was simply repeating the conventional story of the priest as a villain. It was this sentiment that he sought to overturn.

Antonio José Martín was born in Abiquiú in 1793 on the northern frontier of the Spanish Empire. The town, best known today for artist Georgia O'Keeffe, was founded in 1754 as a *genízaro* settlement. Genízaros, who comprise much of New Mexico's Hispanic population today, originated as Spanish-acculturated Indians who were kidnapped as children and sold into slavery, then emancipated at age eighteen. Neither the Hispanic nor Indigenous communities wanted these people around, so the Spanish government settled them in buffer zones to protect the colony. Abiquiú was one of those settlements, blocking the Chama River from Apache raids.

When Antonio José was eleven, his father, Antonio Severino Martín, moved the family to Taos and began building the Martínez Hacienda, a walled farming compound along the Rio Pueblo. Two central courtyards and no outside windows protected it from the Apaches, though the hacienda was never attacked. Taos Pueblo was friendly, and the Martín family traded with them, as well with Mexican and the American traders. The Martíns were one of the most wealthy and powerful in New Mexico, and their ranch measuring five square miles was the largest in Taos. Young Antonio José grew up as a rancher, the oldest of six children.

Antonio José Martín married at eighteen, and when his wife died in childbirth a year later, he considered becoming a Catholic priest. He began his studies in Durango, Mexico, in 1817, a center of liberal theology. He was ordained in 1822, the year after Mexico won its independence, and returned to Taos to serve his community. The young priest adopted the more distinguished last name Martínez. We see early on a bright, ambitious young man brimming with self-worth. He intended to use his position and his family name and wealth to improve the lives of his parishioners.

And indeed, Martínez became a progressive champion in northern New Mexico. He opened a school for both boys and girls in Taos in 1826 and began training promising boys for seminary, as he wanted to build up the native clergy. His students included José Manuel Gallegos and Mariano de Jesús Lucero. Martínez sponsored the latter for seminary, and they were lifelong friends and allies, though Cather would portray them as frenemies.

Noting how illiteracy contributed to the poverty of the region, Martínez acquired a printing press in 1835. Contrary to popular belief, this was neither the first printing press in New Mexico, nor did it publish the first newspaper; however, it did publish the first book in the territory, *Cuaderno de ortografía*. From his press flowed numerous publications such as the primer *La Cartilla de primeras letras*, the speller *La Ortografía castellana*, *Aritmética y retórica*, *El Catecismo de la doctrina cristiana*, and others. This tells us much about Martínez's advocacy for literacy.[27]

Recognizing that many people could not afford to tithe (handing over 10 percent of their income to the church), Martínez lobbied the Mexican government to shift to a fee-for-service system in 1833. The government approved this reform, though the fees were expensive, and many couples consequently skipped church weddings. The fee for Christian burial for the dead could leave the surviving family destitute. As already mentioned, Bishop Lamy reimposed tithing at Christmas in 1852 to much protest from the Mexican clergy.

Martínez was spread thin, supporting congregations in Taos, Taos Pueblo, Ranchos de Taos, Picuris Pueblo, and later Mora. He also oversaw the church at Arroyo Hondo. Additionally, he belonged to the Third Order of Franciscans and was sympathetic to Los Penitentes, who considered him their chaplain. Martínez was ecumenical, welcoming people of other denominations, and he cared as deeply for Catholic Hispanics as he did for the Indigenous.

Martínez was also a political being, and this got him into trouble. When a local rebellion started against the Mexican government in Santa Fe in 1837, Martínez sided with strongman Manuel Armijo, who crushed the rebels and became governor. Rumors circulated that Martínez had backed the insurrectionists, which he had not. This would not be the last time that people accused the outspoken priest of rebellion.

Contributing to this was the Martínez's habit of insubordination, especially regarding his superior, the vicar Juan Felipe Ortiz, whom the Taos priest felt superior to. The Ortizes were a wealthy and influential family, so Mexican Bishop José Antonio Laureano de Zubiría had naturally chosen one of them as vicar, which irked Martínez. Martínez also supported the Penitent Brothers, even when Zubiría denounced them along with the Mexican habit of filling churches and homes with primitive *bultos* and *retablos* (hand-carved statues and paintings). And as Martínez stood with his people, his insubordination and outspokenness caused some to assume the worst of him.

Unsurprisingly, Martínez gained many enemies who sought to defame him. For example Taoseño Cornelio Vigil and trapper Ceran St. Vrain were speculators who took advantage of Mexico's liberalized land grant system to gain ever more lands. In 1843 they petitioned Governor Armijo for a four-million-acre parcel in southern Colorado, known as the Las Animas Grant. The governor approved. Ceran and Vigil then conveyed a one-sixth portion of the grant as a kickback to the governor, as well as to silent partners Charles Bent, Donaciano Vigil, and Eugene Leitensdorfer.

Martínez vocally opposed this corrupt land grab, which helped frame the enmity that these land speculators had for him. It also helps explain why the insurrectionists of the 1847 Taos Revolt sought to murder them and their families. Though he had opposed the insurrection, his outspokenness in part had fueled the community's grievance.

Martínez was no promoter of free love, as Mabel Dodge Luhan accused him; however, he may not have taken the vow of celibacy literally. Fray Chávez argued that Martínez may have fathered three, and possibly up to five, children with his next-door neighbor, Teodora Romero.[28] Other historians dispute this claim. Ray John Aragón noted that "physical evidence, other than malicious rumor, . . . has never come to light." There are people who claim they descend from the priest—but the only way to know for certain is DNA testing.[29]

There are plausible reasons why Martínez's neighbor ended up with these children, besides the possibility that the priest was their father. They may have been children of unmarried teenaged girls who got pregnant, and Martínez sequestered the babies to save the girls' reputation. Perhaps they were Native children who were kidnapped and sold into slavery, an all-too-common practice at the time.

Martínez and his younger brother Juan Pascual Bailón were active in politics, and both served in the New Mexico Territorial assembly. Shortly after the American occupation of the Southwest, Martínez took the oath of citizenship to the United States. This was not surprising, as Mexico was in political turmoil and had done little to support New Mexico, while the Americans were religiously tolerant, actively bringing in trade, and had a more muscular policy to contain the nomadic tribes that threatened the territory.

Martínez became president of the assembly that drafted the territorial constitution in 1850. He was aboard with New Mexico becoming part of the United States, actions that belie his reputation as someone who was anti-American, let alone conspired to kill Americans. Chávez wondered, "When one looks back to the Taos rebellion of 1847 and everything which followed up to this point, one begins to wonder why, in spite of the facts to the contrary, subsequent writers could so blandly assert that Padre Martínez had been rabidly anti-American and against all American institutions."[30]

Martínez's enemies smeared his reputation by accusing him of being a land robber, ironically the same accusation he had lobbed against them. They claimed that the priest took advantage of the Natives when the Taos Revolt failed and stole Taos Pueblo land. Unfortunately, Fray Chávez, who did so much to correct the record about Padre Martínez, didn't address these specific allegations.

The received wisdom holds that Martínez resented the arrival of the new vicar apostolic Lamy in 1851, which supplanted his friend, Bishop Zubiría, and that Lamy and Martínez soon came into conflict. The facts don't bear this out. Martínez was a realist, and the two men got along for years before any conflict arose. Lamy represented hierarchical authority, while Martínez was a liberal who fought for social advancement. The two men were bound to clash, but not for the reasons that Cather or earlier historians gave.

Martínez's Downfall

In early 1856, Padre Martínez notified Bishop Lamy that he was considering retiring because of his declining health. Martínez suggested his replacement, a native priest whom he had groomed. Lamy responded that the young priest was too far behind in his studies, and instead assigned Damaso Taladrid, a Spaniard whom Lamy had recruited in Rome two years earlier. Taladrid took up office in May. That is when the trouble began.[31]

The three leading Hispanic settlements in northern New Mexico were Albuquerque, Santa Fe, and Santa Cruz (near today's Española). Taos was likewise an important center but whose population was more mixed.

Lamy understood the political nature of appointments, especially in these more prestigious towns, and that some looked askance at his replacing the Mexican Gallegos with the Frenchman Machebeuf in 1852. He likely wanted to avoid repeating this scenario, and thus appointed a Spaniard to replace Martínez. Being Spanish, Taladrid would hopefully better understand the culture.

With an eye toward public opinion, Martínez announced his retirement in *The Santa Fe Gazette* as Taladrid came aboard. Martínez was clearly unhappy that he had not gotten his handpicked successor, and he considered his retirement conditioned upon that requirement. He later claimed he had not retired. He was trying to have it both ways: stepping down from office while still retaining authority. Meanwhile, Lamy, who was Martínez's superior, viewed the resignation as an accomplished fact.[32]

Martínez and his key ally, Padre Mariano de Jesús Lucero of Arroyo Hondo, resented the arrogant Taladrid, who looked down on the Mexicans. It was here that the real trouble between Lamy and Martínez began. Taladrid aligned himself with the Anglo and French-Canadian faction that was attempting to gain more lands around Taos.

Martínez and Taladrid quarreled over everything, including access to the sacraments for Mass and tithing. Martínez wanted to operate a private chapel for his followers, which Taladrid refused to permit. The Spaniard argued with members of Martínez's family and challenged Martínez's brother José Maria de Jesus to a duel, who declined. Angered at the Martínez family, Taladrid forbade the priest from conducting the marriage ceremony for his niece.

Martínez complained to Bishop Lamy, but not getting satisfaction he submitted a series of opinion pieces in *The Santa Fe Gazette* under the pseudonym Jose Santistevan (this was his mother's maiden name). He lamented the suspension of Mexican priests and criticized how foreign priests coerced tithing on congregations.[33] Lamy suspended Martínez from priestly duties for insubordination. Taladrid counterattacked with his own articles under the pen name Religiose Observante.[34]

Fray Chávez, who was a historian, not a psychologist, diagnosed in Martínez "a latent schizophrenia [that] had finally and almost of a sudden reached its climax." Martínez wrote respectful letters to the bishop, then under his pseudonym penned scurrilous opinion pieces for the *Gazette*. This wasn't necessarily mental illness. His attempts to both curry favor with Lamy while pseudonymously criticizing him came home to roost when the *Gazette* outed him as Jose Santistevan in 1858. Chávez noted that Martínez was "oblivious to the fact that he was tilting at windmills" like Don Quixote.[35]

Lamy and Martínez exchanged letters that fall, with the bishop attempting to soothe the priest's anger. Lamy wrote his mentor Bishop John Baptist Purcell in March 1857 that "the opposition we met at our first coming here, and which manifested itself on several occasions, is far from being crushed down. Their number, we hope, are diminishing, but unfortunately, the less they seem to be, the more head strong they are getting. The few native clergy that are out of their office"—Gallegos, Martínez, and Ortiz—"keep up a bad spirit against us."[36]

Meanwhile, Machebeuf returned from Europe in early 1857 after being absolved of breaking the seal of confession. The vicar brought with him six seminarians, European reinforcements in the conflict with the Mexican priests, who were slowly but surely being pushed aside. In the wake of Machebeuf's return, a writer under the pseudonym Un Observador (An Observer), possibly Martínez, again criticized Lamy in the *Gazette* for replacing native priests with foreigners.[37]

In April 1857, Martínez penned another complaint to Lamy. Lamy did not write back. There was no point fanning the flames. He dispatched Machebeuf to Taos that month to meet with the old priest, with whom he was on good terms. As a result of the visit, Machebeuf recognized that the situation between Martínez and Taladrid was irreparable.

In late May, Taladrid sparked a rumor, telling his ally Kit Carson that Martínez was fomenting another outbreak, ten years after the Taos Revolt. Carson quickly called for the US Army to dispatch troops, and thirty-two mounted soldiers rode to Taos from nearby Cantonment Burgwin. The troopers arrived just after midnight at Martínez's house. The acting governor, territorial secretary William Davis, noted that the priest, "a quiet and peaceable citizen," was asleep, as was everyone in his household. Finding no evidence of an uprising, the soldiers retired, and Davis was left with a public relations nightmare. There was simply no rebellious plot. He had to soothe tensions in a town where people were outraged that they were considered disloyal. Some 212 Taoseños signed a complaint directed at Carson and the army, but the real culprit was Padre Taladrid. Davis responded with an apologetic letter to the Martínez family.[38]

The Santa Fe Gazette in turn excoriated Davis for his letters to the governor and the Martínez family for impugning the reputation of the sainted Kit Carson. It noted a counter petition from leading Taoseños declaring that Carson had done nothing wrong, and that the army had never entered Martínez's house. It pointed out the irony that Davis himself had named Martínez as a ringleader of the Taos Revolt in his book *El Gringo* but was now apologizing to the retired priest.[39] The *Gazette* didn't mince words: the following month, it called Martínez "the main agent in getting up that rebellion."[40]

Bishop Lamy quickly acted. After just thirteen months, he removed Taladrid, sending him to Isleta Pueblo, far from Taos. The Spanish priest would eventually be transferred to Mora, which he also left in chaos. When Jean-Baptiste Salpointe, his successor, arrived in 1860, he found the Mora church "in an almost ruinous condition."[41]

Astutely recognizing that foreign priests piqued Martínez, Lamy assigned a young Mexican to Taos: José Eulogio Ortiz, half-brother of the former vicar. Ortiz tried to smooth things over with Martínez, but quickly found the old priest to be demanding and intransigent. Martínez insisted that he was still the senior priest in Taos, and that Ortiz was his assistant. Martínez realized that Ortiz would enforce Lamy's mandate for tithing, which caused a blow up between the two men.[42]

The false accusation of an uprising pushed Martínez further over the edge. Rather than helping, replacing Taladrid with Ortiz had only fanned the flames. Martínez was now angry at Bishop Lamy. The Martínez family was old and distinguished, and some from the Taos community sided with them as Martínez split off to form his own congregation. He had an ally in Padre Lucero of Arroyo Hondo. Martínez maintained a small chapel at his residence where he served his followers. The Taos church community fractured.

As the seeds of distrust between Lamy and Martínez took root,

Martínez became more recalcitrant and vilifying of the situation in the press. He continued to publish opinion pieces in the *Gazette*.

There was another small uproar over the assignment of a foreign priest, possibly fueled by Martínez, when Lamy replaced Padre Lucero at nearby Arroyo Hondo with Antoine Juillard and later Gabriel Ussel, both French clergymen. When Martínez continued to complain, Lamy decided he had had enough. He would excommunicate Martínez and his leading confederate, Mariano Lucero.

Lamy dispatched Machebeuf to Taos and Arroyo Hondo with the unpleasant task, just as he had done for Padre Gallegos earlier. Father Ussel accompanied Machebeuf on the rounds announcing the excommunications. Decades later, as Father Howlett assembled his Machebeuf biography, he asked Ussel to write an account of the excommunications and the Anglo panic in Taos. Howlett included this in his biography, though the original document from Ussel has disappeared. No newspaper articles have surfaced that reported the excommunications. Nor did Father Machebeuf pen a letter to document an event that he probably found tragic.[43]

On three successive Sundays, Machebeuf informed the Arroyo Hondo and Taos congregations that Lucero and Martínez were to be excommunicated. There was high tension in Taos: The fear of violence, as had happened a decade earlier during the Taos Revolt, was real. Many Anglos still assumed Martínez had a hand in it.

As the tensions grew, Kit Carson sought to prevent a repeat of the 1847 uprising. He and other Anglos in Taos assembled men in preparation. "We shall not let them do as they did in 1847, when they murdered and pillaged," Carson declared. "I am a man of peace, and my motto is: Good will to all; I hate disturbances among the people, but I can fight a little yet, and I know of no better cause to fight for than my family, my church, and my friend the Señor Vicario," referring to Machebeuf. (Edith Lewis copied this quote about the Señor Vicario from Howlett into her Blue Jay notebook, one of two such instances, the second being the "whip the cats" quote, which will come up again shortly.) Crucially, Father Ussel recorded this dialogue decades after the event, raising questions about its veracity.[44]

George Anderson, whose interpretation of Martínez as a villain Cather relied upon, wrote that Kit Carson stated that he would be happy "to put a bullet into the scoundrel," a statement that is questionably credible, since Anderson wrote this in 1907.[45]

Father Steele asserted that Machebeuf announced the excommunications at mass on March 21, 1858, in Taos, and March 28 in Arroyo Hondo, and that Padre José Eulogio Ortiz read the charges in Taos on the next two subsequent Sundays, while Father Ussel did the same in Arroyo Hondo.[46] "It is always this way," the vicar told Ussel, who penned the statement in his memoir that Howlett in turn quoted. "Bishop Lamy is sure to send me when there is a bad case to be settled; I am always the one to whip the cats." Edith Lewis copied this sentence in her Blue Jay notebook; Cather included the French expression, *à fouetter les chats* in her novel, but without translating it into English (162).[47]

Enraged at what he regarded as an illegal act, Martínez lashed out at Lamy on March 29, the day after the second excommunication reading, claiming that Padre Ortiz had "committed several sacrilegious acts within the church, had desecrated the holy images, and used profane words which he directed at the Virgin of Guadalupe." These accusations came across as unhinged or even deranged. Martínez topped this with a showstopper, that he "had been compelled to assume total administration of the parish and that Ortiz was subject to automatic excommunication according to Canon law on sacrilegious acts."[48]

This really was the last straw. If anything, it confirmed Lamy's justification in excommunicating Martínez. He had to protect his authority as bishop and to protect his priests, notably Ortiz and Ussel. Still, many have questioned whether Lamy had the authority to excommunicate Lucero and Martínez. Thomas Steele and Ronald Brockway, in their scholarly annotated edition of Howlett's book, wrote that the excommunication "probably wasn't valid."[49] Ray John de Aragón called it an "illegal pseudo-excommunication."[50]

No violence resulted from the excommunications, neither in Arroyo Hondo nor in Taos, but the community was split. An estimated third of the Taos congregation went with Martínez. The excommunication had little impact on how locals viewed the man: They still revered him, and now he was a martyr. There were now two congregations in Taos: the recognized church under Bishop Lamy's authority, and Martínez's followers who met in his home.[51]

Even after the excommunication, Martínez continued to criticize Lamy in newspaper editorials. He was not one to be silenced. He continued his written campaign against tithing, which he viewed as unfair to the poor. He also baptized Taoseño children and held mass in his private chapel. Lamy ignored him.

In June 1862 Martínez published a manifesto declaring that, in so many words, the Catholic Church was not the sole church of Christ. He pointed out that early church was not organized around the hierarchy of cardinals, archbishops, and bishops, but rather around all believers: "They were all equal, and none was greater than the other." Protestants split off from the Catholic Church because of abuses, and yet they are still considered part of the universal church, "as they preserve unity with Christ in faith and practice." This was the universal church to which Martínez claimed he and his followers belonged.[52]

Lamy's biographer, Paul Horgan, noted that the liberal Martínez was offended by outsiders who condescended to Mexicans and Natives. Martínez represented the libertarian streak that New Mexicans had developed in the absence of authority, which clashed with Lamy's more authoritative and conservative approach. Horgan observed that "his intemperate behavior might have been a result of his increasingly bad health in the malaise of premature old age." He took Lamy's side, calling Martínez a "provincial" and a "supreme egotist, a master in a little house who could never be a servant."[53]

Martínez lived nearly a decade after his removal from office, a thorn in Bishop Lamy's side to the end. Martínez died in July 1867, unreconciled with the church and still very much a hero to New Mexicans. *The Santa Fe New Mexican* wrote that Martínez "was universally beloved by all who knew him. Taos county has lost one of her most worthy citizens and will sadly lament his loss." Lamy wisely dispatched a group of charismatic Italian Jesuits to Taos to reconcile the two church communities.[54]

After turning Martínez into a tyrant, Cather next turned her sights on Padre Lucero, the priest in Arroyo Hondo who was Martínez's ally, in the section called "The Miser." Here we see a parallel to Fray Baltazar of Acoma, who lived for himself. Cather's Lucero is grotesque, a man who has lost his moral compass. He loves money, yet he lives a gratuitously destitute life as he pursues his miserly ways. Lucero and Martínez have a love-hate relationship and enjoy gossiping about each other.

Death Comes for the Archbishop is a chaste novel, other than when Lucero brings up the subject of sex in gossiping about Martínez, suggesting that his friend is impotent. "His nose and chin are getting to be close neighbours now, and a petticoat is not much good to him any more. But I can still rise upright at the sight of a dollar. With a new piece of money in my hand I am happier than ever; and what can he do with a pretty girl but regret?" (161) A thief hears about the wealth that Lucero had hidden under his house and attempts to steal it, but the priest stabs him to death. (162)

Lucero soon falls sick from cancer, and Vaillant rides over from Taos to deliver the last rites. Cather was impressed by the setting of Arroyo Hondo, which she and Edith Lewis visited with Tony Lujan in July 1925. The village is in a wide agricultural valley set against the steep mountains, the Rio Hondo providing a steady supply of water. The Mexicans had built a wooden sluice high on the mountain to divert some of the creek, and Vaillant enjoys watching "the imprisoned water leaping out into the light like a thing alive" (165).

Arriving at Lucero's home, Vaillant finds the man emaciated and in great pain. Lucero tells where he had buried his and Martínez's money, explaining that it is to be used for masses in Abiquiú, San Miguel Chapel in Santa Fe, and that his nephew Trinidad Lucero (the slothful priest) is to get the remaining third. "Father Lucero made his confession, renouncing his heresy and expressing contrition, after which he received the Sacrament" from Vaillant, Cather writes (169). In historical terms, this was impossible, as Padre Lucero died in 1870, three years after Martínez, while Machebeuf was serving as the bishop of Denver.

The many watchers wait for Lucero's death, hoping for his final words as he is transported from one existence to another, and he does not disappoint. As Lucero dies, he gazes into the abyss, where he sees Martínez. His last words are a Spanish insult: "*Comete tu cola, Martínez, comete tu cola!* (Eat your tail, Martínez, eat your tail!)" (171)

Cather ends this chapter with a denouement: When Lucero's money is dug up, it comes to nearly twenty thousand dollars, "A great sum for one old priest to have scraped together in a country parish down at the bottom of a ditch," Cather observes (171). That was her understated moral about the miser. George Anderson noted that the historical Padre Lucero had hidden his life savings under his floor, which relatives found after the priest died. Anderson noted that the money weighed 110 pounds.[55]

Despite Cather's creation of a feud between Lucero and Martínez, the two priests were allies to the end. When Martínez died in 1867, Lucero conducted the service in Taos. The Penitent Brothers gave Martínez a big funeral, as he had always supported them. The demonic afterlife for Martínez was a product of Cather's imagination. Fray Angélico Chávez concluded that "Cather's version reflects the cynical view which had come down from the padre's foes."[56]

Martínez remains one of the most legendary figures in New Mexico's history. He did much good for the territory at a time when resources were scarce, but his outspoken activism earned him enemies. It was partly his own fault for playing in politics while in a public service position. His enemies, in their attempts to discredit the man, unfairly blamed him for disloyalty, fomenting uprisings, and even treason. What Martínez was guilty of was ambition, an outsized ego, and insubordination. He had an active hand in his own downfall.

Chapter 10

The Cathedral and the Quarry

"Bishop Latour had one very keen worldly ambition; to build in Santa Fé a cathedral which would be worthy of a setting naturally beautiful."

—Willa Cather, *Death Comes for the Archbishop* (175)

Archbishop Lamy began the construction of the St. Francis Cathedral in 1869. Willa Cather included this in book 8, "Gold Under Pikes Peak," a sad chapter in which Latour sends his best friend Vaillant away for a higher purpose and replaces him with a monument to God. It is *Archbishop*'s penultimate chapter, and the reader feels the profound sense of loss of their friendship.

But Cather didn't just drop this on her readers. She hints toward the cathedral's construction two chapters earlier in "Doña Isabella," the purpose of which is to secure funds for the cathedral's construction. That chapter is the second shortest in *Archbishop*. It lacks the deeper spirituality of the book's shortest chapter, "Snake Root," but it offers a moral about a woman's vanity and ends with a punchline. Cather rarely used humor in her writing, and she was no satirist. The "Doña Isabella" chapter is a rare exception.

Isabella is an American beauty, born in Kentucky and raised in New Orleans. She is well-educated and cultured. She is married to Don Antonio Olivares, a wealthy rancher who is committed to Latour's vision to build a cathedral. Isabella is in her fifties but pretends to be a decade younger. And therein lies the trap.

Don Olivares is based on José Sena, a leading Santa Fe citizen, and his wife, Isabella Cabeza de Baca, who built the downtown hacienda known as La Casa Sena after the Civil War. Sena, who died in 1892, provided significant funds for the construction of Lamy's cathedral.[1]

When the fictional Don Olivares dies, his will creates a trust to support his wife and daughter Inez, and then the money is to go to the Catholic Church. His brothers challenge the will, claiming the inheritance for themselves, and doubting whether Isabella is old enough to be Inez's mother. They take the case to court.

Isabella would rather be poor than confess her age. She is concerned that people will gossip if they know her real age. Cather captures the insecurity among women that was common in the nineteenth century. *The Santa Fe New Mexican* quipped in 1880, "That awful census-taker has begun his rounds in Santa Fe, and the ladies are beginning to decide how old they are going to be this year. The young man just budding into the voting age is nervously trying to decide whether he shall lie and get his name into the book, or tell the truth and remain in virtuous obscurity."[2]

As already mentioned, Cather lied about her own age, subtracting three years from her actual age. Her tombstone in Jaffrey, New Hampshire, lists her birth year as 1876, when in fact she was born in 1873. Cather carried this lie literally to her grave.

Father Vaillant is concerned for Isabella. "'You understand, my child,' he began briskly, 'that your husband's brothers are determined to disregard his wishes, to defraud you and your daughter, and eventually, the Church'" (189). Throughout the novel, Vaillant seems fixated with raising money for the church, though he lives as a poor man. "The Bishop had often been embarrassed by his Vicar's persistence in begging for the parish, for the Cathedral fund and the distant missions. Yet for himself, Father Joseph was scarcely acquisitive to the point of decency" (226).

This contrasts with Latour, who owns property and is far from poor. "The Bishop had a large and valuable library, at least, and many comforts for his house," (226) Cather notes. In fact, Lamy owned considerable property around Santa Fe.

Latour is gentler toward Isabella. "I believe, my daughter, you will come to realize that this sacrifice of your vanity would be for your soul's peace." If she does not confess her age, she will become destitute. Latour flatters her: "I have a selfish interest; I wish you to be always your charming self and to make a little *poésie* in life for us here. We have not much of that" (191). Latour and Vaillant convince Isabella to confess her real age in court. She states that she is fifty-two. She wins the case and retains the family trust.

The chapter ends with a punchline. Isabella holds a reception the evening after winning the legal battle. She tells the priests, "I never shall forgive you, Father Joseph, nor you either, Bishop Latour, for that awful lie you made me tell in court about my age!" (195). The party erupts in laughter. Isabella has sacrificed her vanity but secured her right to be financially independent.

The outline for the Doña Isabella story appears in Cather's handwriting in the Blue Jay notebook that Cather and Lewis used to document their 1925 trip to Taos. Over this entry Cather underlined the title Party at Oteros. She later changed the name to Olivares.[3]

The Doña Isabella chapter has a three-page discourse about Manuel Antonio Cháves (Cather spelled him "Chavez"). Known as *El Lioncito* (The Little Lion), Cháves was part of New Mexico's Hispanic elite and was a real person. He was a wealthy landowner and rancher. Cháves had opposed the American takeover in 1846, but like many Hispanics he made peace with it. He volunteered to fight for the Union during the Civil War and served a critical role in the Texans' defeat at the Battle of Glorieta Pass.

Cather's Chavez likes neither Americans nor Latour. "He distrusted the new Bishop because of his friendliness toward Indians and Yankees. Besides, Chavez was a Martínez man" (185). The fictional Chavez personifies the macho Mexican male as archetype, one who likes to gamble, hunt, and target practice.

In *Archbishop*, Chavez appears at the Olivares's party, though he is never seen in the novel again. It has long struck me as odd that Cather introduced a character who is interesting but nonetheless irrelevant for the plot. But as I transcribed the Blue Jay notebook, the story of Manuel Chavez gradually unfolded from Cather's nearly indecipherable scribbling. These may have been the first words of the novel set to paper, much

Figure 67. Manuel Antonio Cháves came from a storied New Mexican family. Cather portrayed the man as an archetypal Mexican, and her description of him was the first part of *Death Comes for the Archbishop* that she set to paper. Palace of the Governors Photo Archives (NMHM/DCA), Image 009833.

of which she copied into the manuscript. There we see Chavez dressed "very elegant in velvet and broadcloth;" we learn that he was the only survivor of a raiding party on the Navajos, that he was of Castilian ancestry, that he was a crack shot with a weapon and "was jealous of [Kit] Carson's fame as an Indian fighter." The details of Manuel Cháves came directly from Ralph Emerson Twitchell's *History of the Military Occupation of the Territory of New Mexico*, which caught Cather's eye.[4]

Book 8, "Gold Under Pikes Peak," is my favorite chapter of Cather's book. It is a chapter about loss and acceptance. And it prominently includes the quarry that provided the ochre sandstone blocks for the St. Francis Cathedral.

Cather placed the chapter near the end of her novel. One gets the impression that it occurs late in Latour's life, when in fact Cather played with the timeline considerably, linking events that occurred over twenty-one years into a single scene. I remind you: that's okay. It's a novel, not a history.

Gold was discovered in Colorado in 1859, prompting the Pike's Peak gold rush like the one in California a decade earlier. As Lamy's diocese was closest to Denver, he picked up responsibility for Colorado and in 1860 assigned Machebeuf to minister to the mining communities. Machebeuf was once again a missionary priest, literally building the faith in the wilderness and out of almost nothing.[5]

Machebeuf journeyed to his new assignment in September 1860. He prepared an unusual buggy that could not only transport him to the Colorado gold fields but also serve as a bed for the night. "It was also a movable church for him, and many a time, for want of any other roof, he set up his little altar on the rack at the rear of his buggy and offered the Holy Sacrifice under the dome of heaven," Father Howlett wrote. Cather included the unusual wagon in *Archbishop*.[6]

Cather roughly modeled Machebeuf's mission on the historic record. He was doing missionary work in Arizona when Lamy summoned him back to Santa Fe, as he missed his friend. Cather invented a day trip where Latour and Vaillant ride out into the desert on their white mules, Angelica and Contento. The bishop has kept their destination secret until they reach it: a solitary hill that the afternoon sunlight turned golden.

> This hill stood up high and quite alone, boldly facing the declining sun and the blue Sandias. As they drew close to it, Father Vaillant noticed that on the western face the earth had been scooped away, exposing a rugged wall of rock—not green like the surrounding hills, but yellow, a strong golden ochre, very much like the gold of the sunlight that was now beating upon it. Picks and crowbars lay about, and fragments of stone, freshly broken off.
>
> "It is curious, is it not, to find one yellow hill among all these green ones?" remarked the Bishop, stooping to pick up a piece of the stone. "I have ridden over these hills in every direction, but this is the only one of its kind." He stood regarding the chip of yellow rock that

> lay in his palm. As he had a very special way of handling objects that were sacred, he extended that manner to things which he considered beautiful. After a moment of silence he looked up at the rugged wall, gleaming gold above them. "That hill, Blanchet, is my Cathedral." (238–39)

The quarry and the solitary yellow sandstone hill, known as Cerro Colorado, towers over the railroad town of Lamy, where an eighteen-mile spur line connects Santa Fe to the Santa Fe Railway. You can easily see where quarry workers took out a chunk of the mountain, a flat divot crowned by a yellow slag heap. Cather could have readily seen it, given that she and Lewis were stranded at the town's El Ortiz hotel for three days in 1925. They had plenty of time and little to do, so they may well have explored the quarry.

Getting up to the quarry, however, is another matter. Years ago, I hiked up Cerro Colorado. It is a short but steep and very rocky hill, and I was on the lookout for rattlesnakes, which like to sun themselves on rocks. Reaching the quarry at the top was remarkable: there I found neatly piled rows of yellow sandstone rubble, numerous blocks of partially carved ashlar, and graffiti carved into rocks, presumably from quarry workers.

Latour tells Vaillant of his plan to build a church that would become the Cathedral Basilica of St. Francis of Assisi. "Our own Midi Romanesque is the right style for this country," Latour claims (240).

> Every time I come here, I like this stone better. I could hardly have hoped that God would gratify my personal taste, my vanity, if you will, in this way. I tell you, *Blanchet*, I would rather have found that hill of yellow rock than have come into a fortune to spend in charity. The Cathedral is near my heart, for many reasons. I hope you do not think me very worldly. (242–43)

Vaillant is too practical to care about the architectural style: "He himself was eager to have the Cathedral built; but whether it was Midi Romanesque or Ohio German in style, seemed to him of little consequence" (243).

Figure 68. The Lamy quarry on Cerro Colorado was a key source of yellow sandstone for the Santa Fe cathedral. Stonecutters carved out a divot from the mountain and left neatly piled rows of rubble atop the quarry. Photograph by Garrett Peck.

Figure 69. The Lamy quarry stands at the southern end of Cerro Colorado, an ochre-colored sandstone mountain that was the source for the St. Francis Cathedral. There you find rows of rubble neatly piled up, along with quarry-era graffiti. Photograph by Garrett Peck.

Back in Santa Fe, Latour reveals to Vaillant that he is sending him away to serve the Colorado gold miners. "He seemed to know, as if it had been revealed to him, that this was a final break; that their lives would part here, and that they would never work together again" (250). Cather adds, "It was a very hard thing for Father Latour to let him go; the loneliness of his position had begun to weigh upon him" (251). Latour insists that Vaillant take both mules, as they are inseparable, an act that moves Vaillant to tears (252–53).

Cather linked the Pike's Peak Gold Rush with the construction of the St. Francis Cathedral, when in fact they were a decade apart. The gold rush began in 1859, while the construction for the cathedral broke ground in 1869. The sandstone from the Lamy quarry couldn't be retrieved until 1880 when the railroad arrived (do the math: that's twenty-one years). This is one of Cather's finest examples of nonlinear writing. She placed three unrelated events together to raise the emotional tension in the book, creating the profound sense of loss as Latour gives up his best friend for a higher purpose: "The Cathedral had taken Father Vaillant's place in his life after that remarkable man went away" (269).

Bishop Lamy had long desired to replace the old Parroquia with a grander church, one with European rather than native elements. During a trip to France in 1869, he recruited architects Antoine Mouly (Cather called him "Molny") and his teenaged son Projectus to design the church. French and Italian craftsmen and stonemasons followed who created the many artistic works for the cathedral.

Lamy's cathedral might be a case of "superimpositioning," a Christian tradition of building churches atop pagan temples, a practice intended to supplant and erase the memory of the earlier religion. In the case of the St. Francis Cathedral, the intention was to replace the shabby adobe church with a modern cathedral in neo-Romanesque style. The Parroquia was far too small, and it required constant maintenance on its adobe walls. It also leaked and showered dust on parishioners.[7]

The cornerstone for the new cathedral was laid in a public ceremony on October 10, 1869, and was promptly stolen. It contained a time capsule, filled with various treasures that made it a tempting target,

Figure 70. The Cathedral Basilica of Saint Francis of Assisi under construction around the old parish church, La Parroquia. Prints & Photographs Division, Library of Congress.

including gold and silver coins and documents from the day. The cornerstone was never seen again.[8]

The cathedral was built around the Parroquia so that services would not be interrupted. Once the new church was sufficiently built, the parish church was dismantled from the inside out in 1884. Only one part of the old parish would remain: the chapel for Our Lady of Peace, which houses the oldest Marian statue in the Americas.

"That old mud church has stood for years looming up dingy, gloomy and awkward, like an adobe brick-kiln—an eyesore to every man of taste and a disgrace to the city," opined *The Santa Fe Daily New Mexican* in 1873. Its editors hoped that the Catholic Church's new cathedral would "prove the antidote for the mud epidemic which, transmitted from generation to generation, has become hereditary."[9]

The national economic crisis of 1873 put a halt to construction for the next five years. The architect, Antoine Mouly, went blind and returned to France the following year. His son remained behind, as he had been commissioned to build a neo-Gothic chapel for the Sisters of Loretto. Projectus Mouly modeled the Loretto Chapel on Sainte-Chapelle in Paris. Facing criticism for his architecture, the young man resigned from the project and retreated into isolation. The chapel was dedicated in 1878. Sister Blandina Segale was fond of the devout young man, whom she admired for "his sensitive artistic nature" and mourned his unexpected death the following year from typhoid.[10]

In 1877 Lamy journeyed to France to raise money for his cathedral. The following year, a French builder, François Mallet, took over the construction, which recommenced as the economy improved. Sister Blandina wrote in her diary, "The new architect whom the Most Rev. Archbishop Lamy has engaged to continue the building of the Cathedral came to see us this morning. He does not impress me favorably."[11]

Perhaps Sister Blandina's suspicions about Mallet's character were correct. The architect was allegedly having an affair with Mercedes Cháves, the estranged wife of John B. Lamy, who was named after his uncle and had moved to Santa Fe in 1870. The younger Lamy lived on the block between the Exchange Hotel and the cathedral (his home is now the site of La Fonda's parking garage). On September 1, 1879, John Lamy walked up behind Mallet near the hotel entrance, put a gun to the back of his head, and pulled the trigger. Mallet died instantly. Lamy was tried for murder, but the jury found him not guilty by reason of temporary insanity. He and his wife later reconciled.[12]

The cathedral's initial stone came from a quarry just north of Santa Fe, but once the railroad arrived in 1880, the Lamy quarry could now be utilized for the building's edifice. That quarry became a key source, but certainly not the only one. Other stone, lightweight volcanic tufa for the interior, came from Cerro Mogino, twelve miles away. The red sandstone blocks on the facade came from a quarry in town.[13]

After Mallet's murder, construction continued under Michael Machebeuf, Bishop Machebeuf's nephew. Sections of the Parroquia still stood, including the north and south transepts. Lamy's successor, Jean-Baptiste

Figure 71. The St. Francis Cathedral took nearly two decades to build and was the culmination of Archbishop Lamy's career. Cather included the cathedral's construction in *Death Comes for the Archbishop*. Photograph by Garrett Peck, with permission of the Archdiocese of Santa Fe.

Salpointe, established a church museum in the cathedral's south transept to house the church's art collection. Tourists paid an admission fee to help fund the completion of the cathedral.

The St. Francis Cathedral was dedicated in 1886, a year after Lamy's retirement. It had taken nearly two decades to construct, an arduous process that involved constant appeals for funds, and still the building was far from complete. The two spires were never added, and construction wasn't completed until the 1960s, nearly a century after it commenced. By then Lamy had long since passed on.

CHAPTER 11

Death Comes for the Archbishop

"Something soft and wild and free, something that whispered to the ear on the pillow, lightened the heart, softly, softly picked the lock, slid the bolts, and released the prisoned spirit of man into the wind, into the blue and gold, into the morning, into the morning!"

—WILLA CATHER, *Death Comes for the Archbishop*, 273

CATHER'S FINAL CHAPTER BEARS the same name as the title of the book. She created a picture of an ideal death—one that comes in old age, with plenty of time for reflection. It is the most nostalgic chapter in *Death Comes for the Archbishop*. The chapter recounts the thoughts of Archbishop Latour, often wandering into flashbacks of events from his life. Cather captured how our minds wander from topic to topic. Much of the chapter takes place inside Latour's head, who had retired to a small adobe house on a farm four miles north of Santa Fe.

Two years after arriving in New Mexico, Lamy acquired the farm to serve as his country retreat. He built a house and chapel on a hillside and gave the humble dwelling the name Villa Pintoresca for its picturesque views. It has a stunning view of the Tesuque River Valley and the Jemez Mountains beyond and is particularly lovely at sunset. It is today the most historic property at Bishop's Lodge resort.

As Lamy prepared for a nearly yearlong trip to Europe in early 1854, he

Figure 72. Archbishop Lamy built a small adobe home on his farm north of Santa Fe in 1853, which he called Villa Pintoresca. He retired there in 1885, and Cather included the house in her novel. The Lamy chapel is the most historic property at the Bishop's Lodge resort. Photograph by Garrett Peck.

summoned Machebeuf to his country abode. The priest was stunned by the view, as he wrote his sister: "When I talk about a house, don't imagine that it's a palace—I'm talking about the land, the features of the terrain, the high mountains, hills, mounds, and a thousand more of which I do not know the name in French—the richest land that is possible to find, as we have in Santa Fé."[1]

Although Lamy had purchased the farm from the Romero family in 1853, they didn't record the deed until twenty-one years later. Lamy purchased the property for eighty dollars.[2] *The Weekly New Mexican* observed in 1874, "Good work has been done on the Bishop's ranch road. It forms one of the best rides out of the city. This is the work, we presume, of Bishop Lamy."[3]

Lamy's country retreat lay along Little Tesuque Creek, which provided

Figure 73. Artist Gustave Baumann's exquisite woodcut of the Bishop's Apricot, an ancient tree that stood near the entrance of Bishop's Lodge, and which Cather included in *Archbishop*. Gustave Baumann, The Bishop's Apricot, 1924, color woodcut, 6 1/16 × 7 5/8 in. Collection of the New Mexico Museum of Art. Museum purchase with funds raised by the School of American Research, 1952 (891.23G). New Mexico Museum of Art. Photograph by Blair Clark.

water for his garden and orchard. He planted apple, apricot, cherry, peach, and pear trees, which grow well in New Mexico's high desert climate. The remains of the Old Apricot—an ancient tree that died long ago—once stood near the resort entrance, which Cather saw during her visit to Bishop's Lodge in 1926. She described it in *Archbishop* as "an apricot tree of such great size as he [Latour] had never seen before. It had two trunks, each of them thicker than a man's body, and though evidently very old, it was full of fruit" (263).

Figure 74. A broad view of Lamy's farm surrounding Villa Pintoresca. In the foreground, four priests pose for the camera. Palace of the Governors Photo Archives (NMHM/DCA), Image 010647.

In the novel, Cather likewise describes Latour's residence: "Some years afterward he built a little adobe house, with a chapel, high up on the hillside overlooking the orchard" (264). Villa Pintoresca is a small building measuring about a thousand square feet with just four rooms: an entryway, a bedroom, a sitting room, and a tiny chapel where he could pray and hold mass.

Fanny Butcher wrote a rave review for Cather's novel, and years later she visited Bishop's Lodge. "When I was in Santa Fe I saw the setting for *Death Comes for the Archbishop*. I sat inside the tiny chapel where the Archbishop celebrated the mass. It is hardly large enough for six people. I shut my eyes and became again a part of the historical Archbishop Lamy's time and thought, as I had felt I was when I first read the book."[4]

Marion Sloan, a young girl enrolled at the Loretto school, often saw Bishop Lamy. "When we missed him from chapel the sister would tell us that Father had gone to his farm that he might pray for us. They said that everything of consequence that is ever done in the world must first be thought out in solitude, and that every great person must have his forty days alone in the wilderness. . . . And I remember how we learned to expect showers of blessings from Father Lamy's retreat to his farm. I also remember how rested and refreshed he looked when he returned."[5]

Lamy had a second, lesser-known lodge sixteen miles southeast of Santa Fe in what became known as the John Lamy Grant. In September 1857, the church inherited a 16,500-acre ranch that the bishop put into trust. The ranch stretched between Apache Canyon in the north to Cerro Colorado in the south. The Santa Fe Trail passed along the northern edge of the land grant. The Atchison, Topeka and Santa Fe Railway was built through the grant lands in 1879, and as mentioned earlier, Lamy donated land for the railroad spur line interconnection to Santa Fe.

In 1885, Archbishop Lamy announced he was retiring after thirty-five years of leading the Santa Fe diocese and archdiocese. His health was declining, and he could no longer endure the rigors the office demanded. He officially retired on August 26, handing over the archdiocese to his friend Jean-Baptiste Salpointe. In *Archbishop*, Cather repeatedly refers to the new archbishop as "S--------" without giving his full name. Lamy lived at Villa Pintoresca for the remaining two-and-a-half years of his life.[6]

Cather relied upon Salpointe's *Soldiers of the Cross* for the details of Lamy's retirement, sickness, and death. Salpointe wrote:

> After his resignation, July, 1885, the Most Rev. J. B. Lamy retired to a small country place that he had purchased in 1853 in the vicinity of the Tesuque River. This place, which the Prelate designated by the name "Villa Pintoresca," was commonly called "El Cañoncito de Tesuque." Early after the purchase of the premises, the Archbishop had a modest house and a small chapel built on it, and when he felt the weight of years added to that of the administration of his vast diocese, it was there that he was wont to go at times, for some days of rest.[7]

Lamy enjoyed reading and owned a library of well-worn books. He kept busy gardening on his small farm. He insisted that visitors walk the four miles from downtown to visit him. Some did, while others tied up their horses just over the hill then walked the last distance. I love that Lamy kept a telescope at his country lodge, and from the lawn in front of his house I teach stargazing. It's a magnificent place to watch the cosmos, and I imagine him being there with me. The Pueblo Indians teach that the spirit remains after the body dies, and that the ancestors are always with us.[8]

As he aged, Lamy grew thinner, gaunter, his facial features starker and revealing. Lamy's last public appearance came two months before his death, when he helped dedicate the chapel of Our Lady of Light at the Loretto school in December 1887. The Loretto chapel is famous for its masterfully engineered double corkscrew staircase and is one of Santa Fe's top visitor attractions.

In January 1888 Lamy fell ill with a cold, which turned to pneumonia. He asked Salpointe if he could return to his former home in Santa Fe, a request the new archbishop immediately granted. Doctors and the Sisters of Charity attended to the retired archbishop, and many friends came to visit. He seemed to rebound, then fell ill with pneumonia again. Lamy stayed in the city for the last four weeks of his life, his former home serving as his hospice.[9] Learning of Lamy's declining health, Bishop Machebeuf of Denver came to Santa Fe to visit shortly before his friend's death.[10]

In *Archbishop*, the fictional Latour catches a bad cold and coughs for days. He asks his young priest assistant Bernard Ducrot to request the archbishop if he can reoccupy his study at the residence for a short period. "*Je voudrais mourir à Santa Fé.*" I would like to die in Santa Fe.

> "I will go at once, Father. But you should not be discouraged; one does not die of a cold."
>
> "The old man smiled. 'I shall not die of a cold, my son. I shall die of having lived.'" (267)

The archbishop gives Latour permission to move back to his former home. "The next morning Father Latour wakened with a grateful sense of nearness to his Cathedral—which would also be his tomb," Cather writes. From then on, Latour only speaks French. (271). He considers the significant changes that had occurred on the New Mexico frontier during his time of service: "Yes, he had come with the buffalo, and he had lived to see railway trains running into Santa Fé" (271).

During his last visit to Europe, Latour had considered the idea of retiring to Auvergne, the French region where he was born. "But in the Old World he found himself homesick for the New. It was a feeling he could not explain; a feeling that old age did not weigh so heavily upon a man in New Mexico as in the Puy-de-Dôme" (272). Latour would stay in Santa Fe.

Latour's retirement is one of deep circumspection, in which he recalls the episodes of his life. He doesn't experience a tragic death; he knows it is coming. The archbishop faces a quiet, contemplative end. "The Bishop was living over his life," writes Cather. "There were many passages in their missionary life that he loved to recall; and how often and how fondly he recalled the beginning of it!" (281) Cather then tells, for the second of three times, and this time the most detailed, the story of Vaillant's waffling before the stagecoach arrived as they escaped for America, and how Latour gave courage to his doubting friend (281–84).

Cather created an archetypal "good death" for Latour. It was a Victorian ideal, one that allowed the sufferer to reflect upon their life and to have family and loved ones at the bedside in the final hours. She took the facts of Lamy's death from Salpointe's history and wrote the most beautiful passage of the book, intuiting how Latour felt in his final days. If there is a single page in the Cather pantheon that is the most beautiful and most meaningful, it is this.

> In New Mexico he always awoke a young man; not until he rose and began to shave did he realize that he was growing older. His first consciousness was a sense of the light dry wind blowing in through the windows, with the fragrance of hot sun and sage-brush and sweet clover; a wind that made one's body feel light and one's heart cry "To-day, to-day," like a child's.
>
> Beautiful surroundings, the society of learned men, the charm of noble women, the graces of art, could not make up to him for the loss of those light-hearted mornings of the desert, for that wind that made one a boy again. He had noticed that this peculiar quality in the air of new countries vanished after they were tamed by man and made to bear harvests. Parts of Texas and Kansas that he had first known as open range had since been made into rich farming districts, and the air had quite lost that lightness, that dry aromatic odour. The moisture of

> plowed land, the heaviness of labour and growth and grain-bearing, utterly destroyed it; one could breathe that only on the bright edges of the world, on the great grass plains or the sage-brush desert.
>
> That air would disappear from the whole earth in time, perhaps; but long after his day. He did not know just when it had become so necessary to him, but he had come back to die in exile for the sake of it. Something soft and wild and free, something that whispered to the ear on the pillow, lightened the heart, softly, softly picked the lock, slid the bolts, and released the prisoned spirit of man into the wind, into the blue and gold, into the morning, into the morning! (272–73)

Cather's prose is achingly, exquisitely beautiful, combining the innocence of an untamed world with the scent of the air, a breeze that in turn freed Latour's soul for the hereafter. This is the best-known passage from *Death Comes for the Archbishop*.

Yet there is a contradiction. Cather positions Latour as a European who helped elevate Santa Fe's culture—yet he is nostalgic for the frontier before white settlers tore up the prairie grass to plant corn. He yearns for the world that has yet to be settled, but he is part of the wave that ploughed it under. Janis Stout puts it succinctly: "He liked the place better before the changes that he himself has helped to bring."[11]

The "bright edges of the world" were many things: the boundaries of nature, not yet exploited and harnessed by civilization; the edge of the American frontier; and the narrow path between death and life. Cather's oft-quoted statement further reinforces *Archbishop* as a frontier novel. It is also Cather's critique of how materialism devours our environment in the name of progress. Western artist Frederic Remington wrote, "Americans have gashed this country up so horribly with their axes, hammers, scrapers, and plows that I always like to see a place which they have overlooked; some place before they arrive with their heavy-handed God of Progress."[12]

Cather was not an eco-warrior, but rather a conservative who bemoaned the loss of what once was, who saw capitalism and the technological advancements of her time as undermining communities. She never owned a car and preferred to take the train. "I never used the automobile very much because I got more pleasure out of closeness than speed," she wrote in 1946.[13]

Edith Lewis interpreted the "bright edges" as Cather's feelings about her hometown, where she had come of age on the frontier. "When she wrote those often-quoted passages in the last part of the *Archbishop*—of how, in New Mexico, he always awoke a young man—I think she was transferring to him something of her own feelings about waking in the morning in Red Cloud."[14] E. K. Brown noted Cather's own internal divisions: "Torn herself, during so many decades, between the appeal of the Divide and her home in Red Cloud and the appeal of the cities of the east coast, with their opera, concerts, and galleries, she experienced an intense if somewhat sad pleasure in contemplating a life that was not torn but was a seamless unity." Cather, like Latour, had to choose how and where to live. She chose New York. Latour chose New Mexico.[15]

In Latour's final days, he recalls a story of Junípero Serra, the Franciscan who inspired the California missions in the 1770s, and how he and a companion traveled across a parched desert to find a Mexican house. There they met the father, mother, and child and his pet lamb, who were obviously the Holy Family. Latour likes this story: "But how much more endearing was the belief that They, after so many centuries of history and glory, should return to play Their first parts, in the persons of a humble Mexican family, the lowliest of the lowly, the poorest of the poor,— in a wilderness at the end of the world, where the angels could scarcely find Them!" (277–81).

Cather retrieved the Serra story from Fray Francisco Palóu's 1787 *Life and Apostolic Labors of the Venerable Junípero Serra*. Palóu wrote, "The Missionaries therefore considered that it was due to the Divine Providence that they had been favored with that night's lodging and that, without doubt, those who lived there must have been Jesus, Mary and Joseph."[16] The story of Serra echoes Latour's experience early in the novel in the Hidden Water chapter, when he is lost in the desert for two days before he finds the miraculous Agua Secreta and a devout family at the desert oasis. John Murphy observed, "The two legendary miracles not only transfigure the surrounding text but help establish Christianity as indigenous."[17]

Serra was canonized as a saint in 2015. He has long been a

controversial historical figure for his leading the Franciscans to convert California's Indigenous people to Christianity and forcing them into farming. The missions that he built along the California coastline brought the Native population into their orbit, where they were effectively enslaved and exposed to European diseases, which resulted in mass die-offs of people. But Serra also has his defenders, including many Indigenous Catholics.

A key fact Cather changed in her novel was for Vaillant to die before Latour, even though Lamy died before Machebeuf. This heightened the sense of loss, as Latour had sent Valliant to minister to the Colorado gold miners and now lost him to death. This was probably why Cather shifted Latour's death to 1889, a year after Lamy died. Cather acknowledged this in her November 1927 *Commonweal* article: "In actual fact, of course, Bishop Lamy died first of the two friends, and it was Bishop Machebeuf who went to his funeral."[18]

"During those last weeks of the Bishop's life he thought very little about death; it was the Past that he was leaving. The future would take care of itself," Cather wrote. (287) Latour has no rage at the dying of his light, but rather an acceptance that death will end one perspective and begin another. His memories return to him as if they had just happened. "He observed also that there was no longer any perspective in his memories. . . . He sat in the middle of his own consciousness; none of his former states of mind were lost or outgrown. They were all within reach of his hand, and all comprehensible" (288).

Latour's Navajo friend Eusabio visits him, the last of his friends. Father Vaillant, Kit Carson, and the Olivareses have all passed on. Latour is glad to see Eusabio, and it gives him a chance to recall his happiness at the restoration of the Navajos to their ancestral lands. Eusabio comes by railroad from Gallup and notes, "Men travel faster now, but I do not know if they go to better things" (289). This echoed Cather's 1924 interview with *The New York Times*, where she criticized how fast society was moving with the advent of the automobile: "Quick transportation is the death of art. We can't keep still because it is so easy to move about."[19]

Latour's idyllic death does not necessarily comport with reality, of course. Ann Neumann, who published *The Good Death: An Exploration of*

Dying in America, watched her father die from non-Hodgkin's lymphoma, then volunteered for years at hospices, the final stop for those who are terminally ill. The experience caused her to question the romantic notion of death:

> There is no good death, I now know. It always hurts, both the dying and the left behind. But there is a good enough death. It is possible to look it in the face, to know how it will come, to accept its inevitability. Knowing death makes facing it bearable. There are many kinds of good enough death, each specific to the person dying. As they wish, as best they can. And there is really one kind of bad death, characterized by the same bad facts: pain, denial, prolongation, loneliness.[20]

Today the leading causes of death are heart disease and cancer, but pneumonia is also prevalent, especially among the elderly. Sir William Osler famously said, "Pneumonia may well be called the friend of the aged," as it is a relatively pain-free way to die. There were no antibiotics to stave off pneumonia in Lamy's time. Lamy died from the lung disease.

Cather's description of Latour's death is consistent with what happened to Lamy, though none of us can know what Lamy felt or thought as he lay dying. That is the advantage of a novel—we can get inside a character's head and explore their state of mind. Lying on his deathbed and unconscious, Latour has one last vision of his friend Vaillant, a flashback to when they left France for America. Death comes for the archbishop in the guise of his best friend and a stagecoach:

> He continued to murmur, to move his hands a little, and Magdalena thought he was trying to ask for something, or to tell them something. But in reality the Bishop was not there at all; he was standing in a tip-tilted green field among his native mountains, and he was trying to give consolation to a young man who was being torn in two before his eyes by the desire to go and the necessity to stay. He was trying to forge a new Will in that devout and exhausted priest; and the time was short, for the *diligence* for Paris was already rumbling down the mountain gorge (297).

Cather doesn't state explicitly that Latour has died—the reader intuits that—but in the final paragraph she shifts to the moments after Latour's death. The last words of *Death Comes for the Archbishop* read:

> When the Cathedral bell tolled just after dark, the Mexican population of Santa Fé fell upon their knees, and all American Catholics as well. Many others who did not kneel prayed in their hearts. Eusabio and the Tesuque boys went quietly away to tell their people; and the next morning the old Archbishop lay before the high altar in the church he had built. (297)

Archbishop Lamy died the morning of February 13, 1888, surrounded by his Santa Fe family. He was seventy-three. "He passed away as he had lived, calmly and beautifully, a smile of Christian contentment encircling his noble face like a halo of glory," reported *The Santa Fe New Mexican*.[21]

As the cathedral bells tolled to inform the citizens that their first archbishop had died, Lamy's body was taken to Loretto Chapel. A procession was organized to carry his remains around the Plaza to the St. Francis Cathedral. Just as Cather described, Lamy's body lay in state in the cathedral, where an estimated six thousand people paid their respects, which was most of Santa Fe's population at the time.[22]

Lamy's funeral was held at the cathedral on February 16, three days after his death. Machebeuf arrived from Denver and helped Salpointe celebrate Mass. Machebeuf was overwhelmed with grief at the death of his best friend, whom he had known for five decades since their days at seminary. "At the funeral he spoke, if speaking it could be called, through tears and sobs, as only he could speak of the dear dead friend," wrote Father Howlett. They interred their friend's remains in the crypt below the altar. Machebeuf died seventeen months later in Denver.[23]

Two hundred former students from St. Michael's College published a resolution. "We heartily lament the irreparable loss that the Catholic church, the territory in general, and the city of Santa Fe in particular, have been called up on to bear in the death of he who to the church was a second St. Paul," they wrote, deeply appreciative of Lamy's work in the field of advancing their education. They praised him for the work he did to

Figure 75. Archbishop Lamy lay in state in Loretto Chapel, shortly before he was moved to St. Francis Cathedral. LHC21 Images, Schools, New Mexico, Folder 5, Sister of Loretto Heritage Center and Archives (Nerinx, KY).

elevate Santa Fe as a city and for his monument, the St. Francis Cathedral.[24]

Death Comes for Willa Cather

After five years of living out of their suitcases since they lost their Bank Street apartment, Willa Cather and Edith Lewis found a new apartment at 570 Park Avenue in New York City in November 1932. This would be the last home for both women.

As Cather grew older, she published less frequently. After *Archbishop* was published, she had twenty years left to live, and during that time she produced her last three novels: *Shadows on the Rock* (1931), *Lucy Gayhart* (1935), and *Sapphira and the Slave Girl* (1940). She returned to the themes of the Great Plains in her 1932 book *Obscure Destinies*, a collection of three short stories. Her books became more spread out and took longer to write. "The fact that I have not been writing much lately is largely due to the fact that I rather lost enthusiasm," she explained in 1946. Cather was probably clinically depressed.[25]

The 1930s brought Cather a growing pessimism about the world. She was distraught by the rise of Adolf Hitler in Germany, but she also disliked President Franklin Roosevelt's New Deal programs that helped the nation recover from the Great Depression. Her mood darkened and she felt the country was on the wrong track. After years of extolling immigrants and pioneers, Cather blasted them in a 1938 letter to Sinclair Lewis: "(For a hundred years we have been begging all the crooks and incompetents in the world to come over to us and be happy. Well, we've got them). What is worse is that we've got their grandsons, and with the right kind of political manipulation they'll do us all in very nicely." Those same grandchildren would go on to defeat Fascism and Nazism, and we call them the Greatest Generation.[26]

Late in life, Cather befriended Jewish violinist Yehudi Menuhin, his two musically gifted sisters, and their mother, who often visited and called her Aunt Willa. Menuhin was fourteen when they met in 1930, introduced by Isabelle and Jan Hambourg, and he remained Cather's friend until her death. They took many walks around Central Park reservoir and read Shakespeare, everyone taking a dramatic part.[27]

Cather herself had been a tourist numerous times in New Mexico, yet in a 1937 letter to E. K. Brown she decried the impact of tourism: "I am not speaking of the tourists and cheap artists and dude ranches which have infested that country and overwhelmed it since I first knew it." This was, in part, because of the success of *Death Comes for the Archbishop*.[28] "I seem fated to send people on journeys," she wrote in 1943. She disapproved of "the number of people who have gone a-journeying in New Mexico on the trail of the Archbishop."[29]

The year 1938 was a doubly tragic year for Cather. Her brother Douglass, with whom she had traipsed around the Southwest during her first visit in 1912, died of a heart attack. Four months later, her former girlfriend Isabelle McClung Hambourg died. Cather was devastated. She wrote her brother Roscoe, "No other living person cared as much about my work, through thirty-eight years, as she did."[30] Three days later, she explained to Roscoe's daughter Margaret how well the two friends had complemented one another: "I knew something about books. Isabelle knew very little about books, but everything about gracious and graceful living. We brought each other up. We kept on doing that all our lives." She concluded, "One can never form such a friendship twice."[31]

Cather published her final novel, *Sapphira and the Slave Girl*, in 1940. Her health declined in the last six years of her life while World War II raged, and she was distraught at seeing most of Europe conquered by the Nazis. An inflamed tendon in her right hand made it painful for her to write, so she wore a brace. However, she continued to correspond with her many fans, assisted by her longtime secretary, Sarah Bloom. Cather worked intermittently on a novel about Avignon called *Hard Punishments*, but she never completed it.

Cather never visited New Mexico again after her 1926 trip to research *Death Comes for the Archbishop*. However, she and Edith Lewis traveled through the state by train in the spring of 1941 on their way to San Francisco to meet up with Roscoe Cather. "The country had never been more beautiful," Lewis noted with nostalgia. "There had been plentiful rains, and everything was fresh and green. She saw it all with tears. She knew it was for the last time." The two women only saw the view from the train window.[32]

The Fred Harvey company that had hosted Cather on so many of her southwestern travels was declining. Ford Harvey died in 1928, and his brother Byron took over the company just in time for the Great Depression. Byron sold off the Indian Detour business in 1931 to cut costs. With the Depression and the automobile came declining passenger rail service, and as railways added dining cars and converted their locomotives from coal to diesel, they no longer needed to stop as frequently. The company began closing its Harvey Houses and the railroad demolished Cather's beloved El Ortiz hotel in Lamy during World War II.

Fred Harvey had a last burst of energy during the war, when it fed troops moving by rail, but after the war it was over. Most of the Harvey Houses closed for good, save for a handful preserved as museums such as the one in Belén, south of Albuquerque. In 1946 Judy Garland starred in the movie *The Harvey Girls*, which made famous the Johnny Mercer song

"On the Atchison, Topeka, and the Santa Fe" (he won an Oscar for it). The movie may as well have been the eulogy for the Fred Harvey company, though the hotel side of the business operated into the 1970s.

The Catholic Church sold Lamy's former farm, Villa Pintoresca, in 1905, and it went through a series of owners before the Pulitzer sisters purchased it in 1913. After five years, they sold the property to James R. Thorpe, a Colorado businessman, who developed it into a dude ranch and renamed it Bishop's Lodge in 1918. The Thorpe family ran the resort for the next eighty years. Of all the houses that Lamy lived in Santa Fe, the Lamy chapel at Bishop's Lodge is the only one that survives.

Erna Fergusson, the woman who helped set up the Indian Detour program, briefly worked for Bishop's Lodge in 1928, overseeing the restoration of the Lamy chapel while serving as host and director of tours. She wrote Cather, asking her to visit and provide inspiration for the building's restoration. "If you should come, please come to the Lodge as a guest," Fergusson asked. "That you would be a seventh day wonder here goes without saying." She had read *Archbishop*, published the previous summer, and she concluded, "As a New Mexican I feel deeply indebted to you for your beautiful picture of my country."[33]

Cather wrote in a 1943 letter, "The managers of the Harvey House system have repeatedly invited me to come back and stay at the Bishop'[s] Lodge indefinitely, as their guest!" Cather was mistaken here, as the Thorpe family operated the resort, rather than the Fred Harvey company. In any case, Cather didn't take them up on the offer. Like Archbishop Lamy, she was nearing the end of her life.[34]

Edith Lewis romanticized Cather's final years, sidestepping her partner's declining health and depression. Not only did Cather's braced hand interfere with her writing, but managing her health took ever more time. Her energy waned. She experienced stomach issues that led to gall bladder surgery in spring 1942. Recovering at home in their Park Avenue apartment, Cather wrote her brother Roscoe on April 15, five years before her death, of her experience in the hospital.

> But I have no sharp memories of discomfort—just of a soft, warm, lazy stupor and a sense of being awfully grateful for not having to

> care about anything—a kind of release from all likes and dislikes, from sunshine and shadows, which makes me feel quite sure that dying, when one comes to it, must be a rather pleasant affair. If one has lived a pretty full and pretty hard life, I think one will have had a plenty [*sic*] and will feel a kind of satisfaction in slipping out of it. Enough is enough of anything. But, of course, one mustn't tell these things to the young, and I expect that within a few weeks I shall be quite delighted with life again.[35]

In the summer of 1945, Roscoe Cather died of a heart attack, just as Douglass and their father had. Shortly after Roscoe's death, Willa was diagnosed with breast cancer. She had a mastectomy in January 1946, but the cancer continued to metastasize.

Cather and Lewis were together in their Park Avenue apartment on Cather's last day, April 24, 1947. "Her spirit was high, her grasp of reality as firm as always. And she had kept that warmth of heart, that youthful, fiery generosity which life so often burns out," Lewis observed through the patina of romanticism. "She was a little tired that morning; full of winning courtesy to those around her; fearless, serene—with the childlike simplicity which had always accompanied her greatness; giving and receiving happiness," as if Cather effortlessly stepped into the great beyond like her fictional Jean Marie Latour. Lewis didn't relay how Cather suffered in her final hours.[36]

That morning a doctor decided to admit Cather to hospital, as she was not doing well. While they waited for an ambulance, Cather and Lewis had lunch, then napped in their apartment. Cather woke, complaining of a horribly upset stomach. Soon the pain worsened to her head and spine, and at 4:30 p.m. she died of a cerebral hemorrhage. This was not an easy or painless death.[37]

Three decades early, Cather had described the childlike wonder of happiness and death in *My Ántonia*: "I was entirely happy. Perhaps we feel like that when we die and become a part of something entire, whether it is sun and air, or goodness and knowledge. At any rate, that is happiness, to be dissolved into something complete and great. When it comes to one, it comes as naturally as sleep."[38]

Figure 76. Willa Cather in 1936 with a retablo of Jesus entering Jerusalem. Carl Van Vechten Collection, LC-USZ62-42538, Prints & Photographs Division, Library of Congress.

Cather was seventy-three when she died. Lewis had her remains buried in Jaffrey, New Hampshire, where Cather so often came to write at the Shattuck Inn, and where she finished composing *Death Comes for the Archbishop* in 1926. Lewis became Cather's literary executor, posthumous spokesperson, and defender. She died in their Park Avenue apartment twenty-five years later and is buried beside her partner.

In October 1946, six months before she died, Cather wrote E. K. Brown as she looked back on her long literary career. She stated, "I know that 'Death Comes for the Archbishop' is my best book."[39]

Willa Cather eschewed politics and social reform but pursued artistic ideas that inspired her. Her focus on the past might have relegated her to the dustbin of forgotten authors—but that wasn't the case. Cather wrote about universal themes that continue to resonate: the hardship of immigrant life on the frontier, the questions of friendship, love, marriage, happiness, jealousy, midlife crisis, and the role of art. Inspired by her travels to the Southwest and elsewhere, she explored America's past and what it means to us today. Cather is still widely read and remembered, and scholars continue debating the meaning of her many writings. *Death Comes for the Archbishop*, Willa Cather's best book, remains a timeless book of friendship on the American frontier.

Notes

Introduction

1. Willa Cather, "#1741: Willa Cather to E. K. Brown, October 7, 1946," *The Complete Letters of Willa Cather*, ed. the Willa Cather Archive team, The Willa Cather Archive, 2018, cather.unl.edu (hereafter *Complete Letters*).
2. "The Great American Novels," The Atlantic, March 14, 2024.
3. Mark Twain, *The Innocents Abroad, or The New Pilgrim's Progress* (American Publishing Company, 1869), 660.
4. Flannery Burke, *A Land Apart: The Southwest and the Nation in the Twentieth Century* (University of Arizona Press, 2017), 22.
5. Willa Cather, "A Letter from Willa Cather," *Commonweal*, November 23, 1927, 714.
6. Joan Acocella, *Willa Cather and the Politics of Criticism* (University of Nebraska Press, 2000), 67.
7. Willa Cather, "#1622: Willa Cather to Miss Masterson, March 15, 1943," *Complete Letters*.
8. Andrew Jewell and Janis Stout, eds., *The Selected Letters of Willa Cather* (Knopf, 2013), x.
9. Fanny Butcher, *Many Lives—One Love* (Harper & Row, 1972), 356.

Chapter 1

1. Hermione Lee, *Willa Cather: Double Lives* (Pantheon, 1989), 42.
2. Willa Cather, *My Ántonia* (Houghton Mifflin, 1918), 28.
3. Willa Cather, "#0010: Willa Cather to Louise Pound, [June 16, 1892]," *Complete Letters*.
4. Willa Cather, "#0015: Willa Cather to Mariel C. Gere, August 1, 1893," *Complete Letters*.
5. Willa Cather, "#0046: Willa Cather to Louise Pound, October 13, 1897," *Complete Letters*.
6. Edith Lewis, Willa Cather Living: A Personal Record (Knopf, 1953), xi.
7. Joanna Russ, "'To Write Like a Woman:' Transformations of Identity in the World of Willa Cather," in *To Write Like a Woman: Essays in Feminism and Science Fiction* (Indiana University Press, 1995), 152, 156.
8. Annie Fields, ed., *Letters of Sarah Orne Jewett* (Houghton Mifflin, 1911), 250.
9. Fields, *Letters of Sarah Orne Jewett*, 246; "Willa Cather Talks of Work," *Philadelphia Record*, August 10, 1913; Elizabeth Shepley Sergeant, *Willa Cather: A Memoir* (J. B. Lippincott, 1953), 72.
10. Sergeant, *Willa Cather*, 33.

11. Melissa J. Homestead, "Willa Cather, Edith Lewis, and Collaboration: The Southwestern Novels of the 1920s and Beyond," *Studies in the Novel* 45, no. 3 (2013): 410.
12. Lewis, *Willa Cather Living*, xvii–xviii.
13. Alfred A. Knopf, "Miss Cather," in ed. Bernice Slote and Virginia Faulkner, *The Art of Willa Cather* (University of Nebraska Press, 1974), 211.
14. Willa Cather, "#1328: Willa Cather to Edith Lewis, [October 4, 1936]," *Complete Letters*.
15. Willa Cather, "#2155: Willa Cather to Roscoe Cather, October 23, 1939," *Complete Letters*.
16. Sergeant, *Willa Cather*, 10; Yehudi Menuhin, *Unfinished Journey* (Alfred A. Knopf, 1976), 128.
17. Lewis, *Willa Cather Living*, 74; Sergeant, *Willa Cather*, 46–48.
18. Willa Cather, "A Wagner Matinée," in *Willa Cather Collected Stories* (Vintage Books, 1992), 196.
19. Willa Cather, "#1954: Willa Cather to Mary Virginia Boak Cather, February 2, 1917," *Complete Letters*.
20. Willa Cather, "#0498: Willa Cather to Mary Virginia Auld, February 21 [1921]," *Complete Letters*.
21. David McKay Powell, *Cather and Opera* (Louisiana State University Press, 2022), 145.

Chapter 2

1. Charles Cather 1872 diary; Charles Cather's 1927 copy of *Death Comes for the Archbishop*. Both documents in the National Willa Cather Center archives, Red Cloud, NE.
2. Willa Cather, "#0221: Willa Cather to Elizabeth Shepley Sergeant, April 20 [1912]," *Complete Letters*.
3. "Willa Cather to Elizabeth Shepley Sergeant, April 20 [1912]."
4. "Willa Cather to Elizabeth Shepley Sergeant, April 20 [1912]."
5. The hotel she mentioned was not La Posada, which did not open until 1930. "Willa Cather to Elizabeth Shepley Sergeant, April 20 [1912]."
6. Willa Cather, "#0224: Willa Cather to Elizabeth Shepley Sergeant, April 26, 1912," *Complete Letters*.
7. Willa Cather, "#0229: Willa Cather to Elizabeth Shepley Sergeant, May 21 [1912]," *Complete Letters*.
8. "Willa Cather to Elizabeth Shepley Sergeant, May 21 [1912]."
9. Willa Cather, "#0228: Willa Cather to Elizabeth Shepley Sergeant, May 12 [1912]," *Complete Letters*.
10. Janis P. Stout, *Cather Among the Moderns* (University of Alabama Press, 2019), 13.
11. "Willa Cather to Elizabeth Shepley Sergeant, May 21 [1912]."
12. Willa Cather, "#0236: Willa Cather to Elizabeth Shepley Sergeant, June 15 [1912]," *Complete Letters*.
13. Willa Cather, "#2069: Willa Cather to Roscoe Cather, May 29 [1912]," *Complete Letters*.

14. Willa Cather, "#0232: Willa Cather to Elizabeth Shepley Sergeant, June 2 [1912]," *Complete Letters*.
15. Willa Cather, "A Letter from Willa Cather," *Commonweal*, November 23, 1927, 713.
16. Willa Cather, "#0235: Willa Cather to S. S. McClure, June 12 [1912]," *Complete Letters*.
17. Willa Cather, "#0241: Willa Cather to Elizabeth Shepley Sergeant, August 14 [1912]," *Complete Letters*.
18. Willa Cather, "My First Novels (There Were Two)," originally published in *The Colophon*, 1931, reprinted in *On Writing: Critical Studies on Writing as an Art* (University of Nebraska Press, 1988), 92.
19. Willa Cather, "#0242: Willa Cather to Elizabeth Shepley Sergeant, September 12 [1912]," *Complete Letters*.
20. Elizabeth Shepley Sergeant, *Willa Cather: A Memoir* (J. B. Lippincott, 1953), 53.
21. Alice Booth, "Willa Cather Who Believes There Is Nothing in the World Finer to Write About Than Life, Just as It Is, and People, Just as They Are," *Good Housekeeping* (September 1931), 34, 196–98.
22. Willa Cather, "#0244: Willa Cather to Elizabeth Shepley Sergeant, October 6 [1912]," *Complete Letters*
23. Alex Ross, "Cather People," *New Yorker*, October 2, 2017, 32.
24. Sergeant, *Willa Cather*, 107.
25. Hermione Lee, *Willa Cather: Double Lives* (Pantheon, 1989), 60–61.
26. Willa Cather, "#0270: Willa Cather to Elizabeth Shepley Sergeant, November 19 [1913]," *Complete Letters*.
27. Cather, *On Writing*, 94.
28. Latrobe Carroll, "Willa Sibert Cather," *Bookman*, May 3, 1921, 212–16.
29. Edith Lewis, *Willa Cather Living: A Personal Record* (Knopf, 1953), 125–27.
30. Flora Merrill, "A Short Story Course Can Only Delay, It Cannot Kill an Artist, Says Willa Cather," *New York World*, April 19, 1925.
31. Willa Cather, "#0286: Willa Cather to Elizabeth Shepley Sergeant, September 11 [1914]," and "#0287, Willa Cather to Elizabeth Shepley Sergeant, [September 28, 1914]," *Complete Letters*.
32. Lewis, Willa Cather Living, 94; Willa Sibert Cather, "Mesa Verde Wonderland Is Easy to Reach," *Denver Times*, January 31, 1916.
33. David Harrell, "Willa Cather's Mesa Verde Myth," *Cather Studies*, vol. 1, available at Willa Cather Archive, www.cather.unl.edu.
34. Lewis, *Willa Cather Living*, 101.
35. Margaret Harvey, "Willa Sibert Cather Thanks the West for Her Success as a Writer of Stories," *Denver Times*, August 16, 1915; Melissa Homestead, "Willa Cather in the Denver Times in 1915 and New Evidence of the Origins of The Professor's House," *Legacy: A Journal of American Women Writers* 35, no. 2 (2018): 187–209.
36. David Harrell, *From Mesa Verde to The Professor's House* (University of New Mexico Press, 1992), 43.

37. Lewis, *Willa Cather Living*, 95.

38. Lewis, *Willa Cather Living*, 95–98.

39. "Lost in Colorado Canon: Women Editors Suffer as Result of Trip with Inexperienced Guide," *New York Times*, August 26, 1915.

40. Willa Cather, "#0323: Willa Cather to Elizabeth Shepley Sergeant, September 21 [1915]," *Complete Letters*.

41. Cather, "Mesa Verde Wonderland."

42. In her memoir, Lewis stated that they stayed in Taos for a month, when in fact it was a week. Lewis, *Willa Cather Living*, 99.

43. Willa Cather, "#0320: Willa Cather to Elizabeth Shepley Sergeant, August 31 [1915]," *Complete Letters*.

44. Stephen Fried, *Appetite for America: Fred Harvey and the Business of Civilizing the Wild West—One Meal at a Time* (Bantam, 2010), xvii–xviii.

45. Lesley Poling-Kempes, *The Harvey Girls: Women Who Opened the West* (Da Capo Press, 1989), xii.

46. Will Rogers, "Back to Babbitts, Booze, and Bankrolls," in *A Will Rogers Treasury*, ed. Bryan B. Sterling and Frances N. Sterling (Crown, 1982), 46.

47. Willa Cather, "#0322: Willa Cather to Ferris Greenslet, September 13 [1915]," *Complete Letters*.

48. Willa Cather, "#0351: Willa Cather to Dorothy Canfield Fisher, March 15 [1916]," *Complete Letters*.

49. Willa Cather, "#2073: Willa Cather to Roscoe Cather, July 8 [1916]," *Complete Letters*.

50. Cather, "Willa Cather to Roscoe Cather, July 8 [1916]."

51. Lewis, Willa Cather Living, 100; Willa Cather, "A Letter from Willa Cather," *Commonweal*, November 23, 1927, 713.

52. Willa Cather, "#0363: Willa Cather to Elizabeth Shepley Sergeant, August 3 [1916]," *Complete Letters*.

53. Lewis, *Willa Cather Living*, 101.

54. Melissa J. Homestead, "Willa Cather, Edith Lewis, and Collaboration: The Southwestern Novels of the 1920s and Beyond," *Studies in the Novel* 45, no. 3 (2013): 410.

55. Melissa Homestead, *The Only Wonderful Things: The Creative Partnership of Willa Cather and Edith Lewis* (Oxford University Press, 2021), 115.

56. Lewis, *Willa Cather Living*, 70.

57. Willa Cather, "The Enchanted Bluff," in *Willa Cather: Stories, Poems, and Other Writings* (Library of America, 1982), 69, 70.

58. Cather, "The Enchanted Bluff," 73.

59. Willa Cather, *The Song of the Lark* (Houghton Mifflin, 1988), 259.

60. Cather, *Song of the Lark*, 267.

61. Cather, *Song of the Lark*, 271.

62. Cather, *Song of the Lark*, 273.

63. Cather, *Song of the Lark*, 275.

64. Cather, *Song of the Lark*, 276.

65. Cather, *Song of the Lark*, 297.

66. Cather, "Willa Cather to Elizabeth Shepley Sergeant, April 26, 1912"; Andrew Jewell and Janis Stout, eds. *The Selected Letters of Willa Cather* (Knopf, 2013), 155.
67. Janis P. Stout, *Picturing a Different West: Vision, Illustration, and the Tradition of Austin and Cather* (Texas Tech University Press, 2007), 140.
68. Lewis, *Willa Cather Living*, 137.
69. Harrell, *From Mesa Verde to The Professor's House*, 163.
70. Willa Cather, *The Professor's House* (Vintage Classics, 1990), 179–80.
71. Cather, *Professor's House*, 191.
72. Cather, *Professor's House*, 199.
73. Cather, *Professor's House*, 219.
74. Harrell, *From Mesa Verde to The Professor's House*, 14–20.
75. Tom Mashberg, "Secret Bids Guide Hopi Indians' Spirits Home," *New York Times*, December 16, 2013.
76. Mary Hudetz, "Native American Shield Returned to New Mexico from France," *Santa Fe New Mexican*, November 18, 2019.
77. Cather, *Professor's House*, 55.
78. Fanny Butcher, "Willa Cather Tells Purpose of New Novel," *Chicago Tribune*, September 12, 1925.
79. Guy Reynolds, *Willa Cather in Context: Progress, Race, Empire* (St. Martin's Press, 1996), 133.
80. Willa Cather, "#0798: Willa Cather to Dorothy Canfield Fisher, October 22 [1925]," *Complete Letters*.

Chapter 3

1. Paul R. Reynolds, *The Middle Man: The Adventures of a Literary Agent* (William Morrow, 1972), 18; Matthew Lavin, "It's Mr. Reynolds Who Wishes It," *Cather Studies*, volume 9, Willa Cather Archive, available at www.cather.unl.edu.
2. Willa Cather, "#0798: Willa Cather to Dorothy Canfield Fisher, October 22 [1925]," *Complete Letters*.
3. Willa Cather, *My Ántonia* (Houghton Mifflin, 1918), 1.
4. Dorothy Canfield Fisher, "Willa Cather: Daughter of the Frontier," *New York Herald*, May 28, 1933.
5. Cather, *My Ántonia*, 7.
6. Willa Sibert Cather, "Nebraska: The End of the First Cycle," *Nation*, September 5, 1923, 237.
7. Willa Cather to Carl Van Vechten, January 30, 1937, box 1, folder 18, MS-1, Carl Van Vechten–Mark Lutz Collection, Book Arts, Archives, & Rare Books, Boatwright Memorial Library, University of Richmond, Richmond, Virginia.
8. Cather, *My Ántonia*, 60.
9. Melissa Homestead, *The Only Wonderful Things: The Creative Partnership of Willa Cather and Edith Lewis* (Oxford University Press, 2021), 17.
10. Willa Sibert Cather, "The Novel Démeublé," *New Republic*, April 12, 1922, 5–6.

11. Cather, "Novel Démeublé," 6; John P. Anders, "Something Soft and Wild and Free," *Cather Studies*, vol. 4., Willa Cather Archive.
12. Flora Merrill, "A Short Story Course Can Only Delay, It Cannot Kill an Artist, Says Willa Cather," *New York World*, April 19, 1925.
13. Alice Booth, "Willa Cather Who Believes There Is Nothing in the World Finer to Write About Than Life, Just as It Is, and People, Just as They Are," *Good Housekeeping*, September 1931, 34, 196–98.
14. H. L. Mencken, "Fiction Good and Bad," *American Mercury* 6 (1925): 379.
15. Alfred Knopf, "Publishing Then and Now: 1912–1964," *Bulletin of the New York Public Library* 68, no. 9 (1964): 560.
16. Willa Cather, "Not Under Forty," in *Willa Cather: Stories, Poems, and Other Writings* (Library of America, 1982), 812.
17. Joan Acocella, *Willa Cather and the Politics of Criticism* (University of Nebraska Press, 2000), 20.
18. Willa Cather, "#0601: Willa Cather to Dorothy Canfield Fisher, June 17, 1922," *Complete Letters*.
19. Willa Cather, "#3021: Willa Cather to Ellery Sedgwick, November 17, 1922," *Complete Letters*.
20. Lavin, "It's Mr. Reynolds Who Wishes It."
21. Rose C. Feld, "Restlessness Such as Ours Does Not Make for Beauty," *New York Times*, December 21, 1924.
22. Willa Cather, "#0105: Willa Cather to Witter Bynner, June 7, 1905," *Complete Letters*.

Chapter 4

1. Willa Cather, "#0782: Willa Cather to Zoë Akins, May 9 [1925]," *Complete Letters*.
2. Paul Horgan, *The Centuries of Santa Fe* (E. P. Dutton, 1956), 321.
3. Willa Cather, "#0787: Willa Cather to Elizabeth Shepley Sergeant, June 23 [1925]," *Complete Letters*; Edith Lewis to Mary Austin, April 4, 1928, mssAU 3474, Mary Hunter Austin Collection, Huntington Library, San Marino, CA.
4. Willa Cather, "#0783: Willa Cather to Mabel Dodge Luhan, May 23, 1925," *Complete Letters*.
5. Willa Cather, "#0786: Willa Cather to Mabel Dodge Luhan, June 12 [1925]," *Complete Letters*.
6. Willa Cather, "#0787: Willa Cather to Elizabeth Shepley Sergeant, June 23 [1925]," *Complete Letters*.
7. Willa Cather to Harriet Fox Whicher, October 16 [1925], in *The Selected Letters of Willa Cather*, ed. Andrew Jewell and Janis Stout (Alfred A. Knopf, 2013), 374.
8. Willa Cather, "#0788: Willa Cather to Mabel Dodge Luhan, June 26, 1925," *Complete Letters*.
9. Willa Cather, "#0789: Willa Cather to Paul Revere Reynolds, June 28 [1925]," *Complete Letters*.
10. Mabel Dodge Luhan, *Edge of Taos Desert: An Escape to Reality* (University of New Mexico Press, 1987), 6.
11. Lew Wallace, *An Autobiography*, vol. 2 (Harper & Brothers, 1906), 921–22.

12. Luhan, *Edge of Taos Desert*, 14.
13. Luhan, *Edge of Taos Desert*, 141–46.
14. Lois Palken Rudnick, *Utopian Vistas: the Mabel Dodge Luhan House and the American Counterculture* (University of New Mexico Press, 1996), 30–31.
15. Luhan, *Edge of Taos Desert*, 261.
16. Lois Palken Rudnick, *The Suppressed Memoirs of Mabel Dodge Luhan: Sex, Syphilis, and Psychoanalysis in the Making of Modern American Culture* (University of New Mexico Press, 2012), 157–65.
17. Rudnick, *Suppressed Memoirs*, 20.
18. Hutchins Hapgood, *A Victorian in the Modern World* (Harcourt, Brace, 1939), 349.
19. Max Eastman, *Venture* (Boni and Liveright, 1927), 24–25.
20. Lesley Poling-Kempes, *Ladies of the Canyon: A League of Extraordinary Women and Their Adventures in the American Southwest* (University of Arizona Press, 2015), 52.
21. Edith Lewis, *Willa Cather Living: A Personal Record* (Knopf, 1953), 142.
22. Lewis, *Willa Cather Living*, 143.
23. Elizabeth Shepley Sergeant, *Willa Cather: A Memoir* (J. B. Lippincott, 1953), 206.
24. Rudnick, *Utopian Vistas*, 134.
25. Blue Jay notebook, Charles E. Cather Collection, Archives & Special Collections, University of Nebraska–Lincoln.
26. Lewis, *Willa Cather Living*, 143.
27. Willa Cather, "#1118: Willa Cather to Carrie Miner Sherwood, August 4 [1932]," *Complete Letters*.
28. Melissa J. Homestead, "Willa Cather, Edith Lewis, and Collaboration: The Southwestern Novels of the 1920s and Beyond," *Studies in the Novel* 45, no. 3 (2013): 419.
29. Willa Cather, "#0791: Willa Cather to Wilton Graff, July 19 [1925]," *Complete Letters*.
30. Willa Cather, "#0790: Willa Cather to Mabel Dodge Luhan, July 20, 1925," *Complete Letters*.
31. Edith Lewis to Mabel Dodge Luhan, July 20, 1925, Mabel Dodge Luhan Papers, Beinecke Library, Yale University, New Haven, CT.
32. In French, Machebeuf is pronounced with three syllables: MASH-uh-boof. In Denver, where he served as the first bishop, locals pronounce the name as MATCH-buff.
33. Willa Cather, "A Letter from Willa Cather," *Commonweal*, November 23, 1927, 713.
34. In her July 20, 1925 letter to Mabel Dodge Luhan, Edith described Cather as buying books at the museum (the Palace of the Governors); however, in her memoir from 1953, she wrote that Cather checked books out of the library. I put more credence in the immediacy of the letter, rather than a memoir written nearly three decades later. Lewis, *Willa Cather Living*, 140.
35. Willa Cather, "#1741: Willa Cather to E. K. Brown, October 7, 1946," *Complete Letters*.
36. Harold Small, "Willa Cather Tells 'Secret' Novel's Title," *San Francisco Chronicle*, March 23, 1931.
37. Lewis, *Willa Cather Living*, 139.
38. Heather McClure, Fray Angélico Chávez Library, e-mail, December 23, 2019. The books that she and her staff dug up from the pre-1925 acquisition records included: William

Howlett's *Life of the Right Reverend Joseph P. Machebeuf, D.D.* (1908), Jean-Baptiste Salpointe's *Soldiers of the Cross* (1898), the Abbé Domenech's *Missionary Adventures in Texas and Mexico* (1858), Zephyrin Engelhardt's *The Franciscans in Arizona* (1899), and Elizabeth Hughes's *The California of the Padres* (1875). The Spanish quotes derived from John Baptist Salpointe, *Soldiers of the Cross: Notes on the Ecclesiastical History of New Mexico, Arizona and Colorado* (St. Boniface's Industrial School, 1898), 200.

39. Edward A. Bloom and Lillian D. Bloom, *Willa Cather's Gift of Sympathy* (Southern Illinois University Press, 1962), 211–12.

40. John J. Murphy, "Historical Essay," in Willa Cather, *Death Comes for the Archbishop*, historical essay and explanatory notes by John J. Murphy, ed. Charles W. Mignon, Frederick M. Link, and Kari A. Ronning (University of Nebraska Press, 1999) (hereafter cited as *Archbishop*, scholarly edition).

41. Willa Cather, "#2862: Willa Cather to Louise Guerber, November 11, 1925," *Complete Letters*.

42. Willa Cather, "#2863: Willa Cather to Louise Guerber, December 5, 1925," *Complete Letters*. The three book titles that Cather check-marked were E. G. Cattermole, *Famous Frontiersmen, Pioneers and Scouts*, Emerson Hough, *Way to the West*, and Henry Inman, *Old Santa Fe Trail*. Louise Guerber to Willa Cather, December 1925, Willa Cather Collection, Drew University Library Special Collections, Madison, NJ.

43. Ralph Emerson Twitchell, *The History of the Military Occupation of the Territory of New Mexico from 1846 to 1851* (Smith-Brooks, 1909), 285–308. In the scholarly edition of *Death Comes for the Archbishop*, John Murphy dissected the story of Manuel Chaves, noting it could have come from either Twitchell or Charles Lummis's *A New Mexico David*. After reading the Blue Jay notebook, it become clear that Cather was repeating the details from Twitchell, rather than Lummis. Cather, *Archbishop*, scholarly edition, 464.

44. John J. Murphy, "Explanatory Notes," in Cather, *Archbishop*, scholarly edition, 381–82.

45. "Flood Sweeps Trinidad, Colorado," *Santa Fe New Mexican*, July 23, 1925; Lewis, *Willa Cather Living*, 144–45; Willa Cather, "#0792: Willa Cather to Mabel Dodge Luhan, August 7 and 8 [1925]," *Complete Letters*.

46. Lewis, *Willa Cather Living*, 146.

47. Cather, "#0792: Willa Cather to Mabel Dodge Luhan, August 7 and 8 [1925]."

48. "The Gossip Shop," *Bookman*, October 1925, 231.

49. Louise Guerber, journal, November 1, 1925, Burroughs 25, Willa Cather Collection, Drew University Special Collections, Madison, NJ.

50. Willa Cather to Louise Guerber Burroughs, August 1, 1925, Willa Cather Collection, Drew University Special Collections, Madison, NJ.

51. Lewis, *Willa Cather Living*, 144.

Chapter 5

1. Willa Cather, "#2086: Willa Cather to Roscoe Cather, [December 29, 1925 or January 9, 1926]," *Complete Letters*.

2. Willa Cather, "#0827: Willa Cather to Ferris Greenslet [May 1 to 4, 1926]," *Complete Letters*.

3. Willa Cather, "#2867: Willa Cather to Louise Guerber, May 25 [1926]," *Complete Letters*.

4. Willa Cather, "#0832: Willa Cather to Mabel Dodge Luhan, May 26 [1926]," *Complete Letters*.

5. Cather, "#0832: Willa Cather to Mabel Dodge Luhan, May 26 [1926]."

6. Willa Cather, "#0834: Willa Cather to Blanche Wolf Knopf, May 28 [1926]," *Complete Letters*.

7. Willa Cather, "#0826: Willa Cather to Paul Revere Reynolds [April 19 to 26, 1926]," *Complete Letters*.

8. Willa Cather, "#0833: Willa Cather to Ellery Sedgwick, May 28 [1926]," *Complete Letters*.

9. According to Reynolds, Ellery Sedgwick asked Cather, "Why was the novel offered to the Atlantic? What did Miss Cather think of the Atlantic?" Cather supposedly responded that *The Atlantic* was a fine publication, but she had no time to read magazines, and thus Sedgwick declined, his ego bruised. This doesn't entirely square with Cather's letter to the man, in which she deflected blame to her agent. Paul R. Reynolds, *The Middle Man: The Adventures of a Literary Agent* (William Morrow, 1972), 26–27.

10. Edith Lewis, *Willa Cather Living: A Personal Record* (Knopf, 1953), 140–41; "Mrs. Ickes Dies in Crash of Auto Near Santa Fe," *New York Times*, September 1, 1935.

11. Willa Cather, "#0836: Willa Cather to Mabel Dodge Luhan [June 5, 1926]," *Complete Letters*.

12. Willa Cather, "#0835: Willa Cather to Alfred A. Knopf, June 3, 1926," *Complete Letters*.

13. Cather, "#0836: Willa Cather to Mabel Dodge Luhan [June 5, 1926]."

14. Willa Cather, "#0838: Willa Cather to Paul Revere Reynolds [June 4 to 9, 1926]," *Complete Letters*; Willa Cather, "#0840: Willa Cather to Mary Hunter Austin, June 26 [1926]," *Complete Letters*.

15. Sister Blandina Segale, *At the End of the Santa Fe Trail* (Kessinger Publishing, 2010), 83, 86.

16. Bruce Ellis, *Bishop Lamy's Santa Fe Cathedral* (University of New Mexico Press, 1985), 5.

17. Chris Wilson, *The Myth of Santa Fe: Creating a Modern Regional Tradition* (University of New Mexico Press, 1997), 4.

18. John Nieto-Phillips, *The Language of Blood: The Making of Spanish-American Identity in New Mexico, 1880s–1930s* (University of New Mexico Press, 2004), 108.

19. Elizabeth Shepley Sergeant, "New Mexico: A Relic of Ancient America," *Nation*, November 21, 1923, 579.

20. R. W. Birdseye, "The Indian Detour," *Santa Fe New Mexican*, January 29, 1926; "Indian Detour Ready to Go on Saturday," *Santa Fe New Mexican*, May 14, 1926; Victoria E. Dye, *All Aboard for Santa Fe: Railway Promotion of the Southwest, 1890s to 1930s* (University of New Mexico Press, 2005), 53; Diane H. Thomas, *The Southwestern Indian Detours* (Hunter Publishing, 1978), 58; Marta Weigle, "Exposition and Mediation: Mary Colter, Erna Fergusson, and the Santa Fe/Harvey Popularization of the Native Southwest, 1902–1940," *Frontiers: A Journal of Women's Studies* 12, no. 3 (1992): 133.

21. Erna Fergusson, *New Mexico: A Pageant of Three Peoples* (University of New Mexico Press, 1973), ix; Thomas, *Southwestern Indian Detours*, 44.
22. Louise Lowber Cassidy, "A 'Delight Maker,'" *Sunset Magazine*, January 1925, 38.
23. "Three Weeks' Cramming to Keep Clever Couriers Busy," *Santa Fe New Mexican*, April 16, 1926; Weigle, "Exposition and Mediation," 143; Caroline M. Woidat, "The Indian-Detour in Willa Cather's Southwestern Novels," *Twentieth-Century Literature* 48, no. 1 (2002): 32.
24. Cather, "#0836: Willa Cather to Mabel Dodge Luhan [June 5, 1926]"; "Biggest Fire in History of City," *Santa Fe New Mexican*, January 5, 1922.
25. Edith Lewis was all too often described as Cather's secretary, which in fact she was not.
26. Paul Horgan, "In Search of the Archbishop," *Catholic Historical Review* 46 (1961): 412–13.
27. "Among the Literati," *Santa Fe New Mexican*, June 14, 1926.
28. Cather, "#0836: Willa Cather to Mabel Dodge Luhan [June 5, 1926]."
29. "People Coming and Going in Santa Fe," *Santa Fe New Mexican*, June 23, 1926. The newspaper also erroneously reported on June 9 that Cather had departed Santa Fe to spend a week at Luhan's in Taos. "People Coming and Going in Santa Fe," *Santa Fe New Mexican*, June 9, 1926.
30. Willa Cather, "#2087: Willa Cather to Roscoe Cather [June 26, 1926]," *Complete Letters*.
31. Willa Cather, "#0840: Willa Cather to Mary Hunter Austin, June 26 [1926]," *Complete Letters*.
32. Willa Cather, "#1963: Willa Cather to Mary Virginia Boak Cather [June 28, 1926]," *Complete Letters*.
33. Willa Cather, "#2290: Willa Cather to Elizabeth Cather, Margaret Cather, and Virginia Cather [July 1, 1926]," *Complete Letters*.
34. "Artists Object, Statue Is Forfeited; Mrs. Austin, Applegate Protest," *Santa Fe New Mexican*, October 12, 1927.
35. Mary Austin, *Earth Horizon* (Riverside Press, 1932), 359.
36. Willa Cather, "#1135: Willa Cather to Mabel Dodge Luhan, November 22 [1932]," *Complete Letters*.
37. Elizabeth Shepley Sergeant, *Willa Cather: A Memoir* (J. B. Lippincott, 1953), 226.
38. Wheelwright had earlier purchased Los Luceros near Alcalde, New Mexico, near the San Gabriel dude ranch where Cather and Lewis vacationed in 1925. In 1937 she founded the Wheelwright Museum of the American Indian in Santa Fe.
39. Willa Cather, "#1741: Willa Cather to E. K. Brown, October 7, 1946," *Complete Letters*.
40. T. M. Pearce, ed., *Literary America 1903–1934: The Mary Austin Letters* (Greenwood Press, 1979), 205.
41. Erna Fergusson, *Our Southwest* (Alfred A. Knopf, 1940), 276.
42. "Opposition to Club Cultural Colony Holds Meeting and Petitions the City Council," *Santa Fe New Mexican*, April 24, 1926.
43. "Sentiment Grows Against Culture Center," *Santa Fe New Mexican*, May 17, 1926.
44. "Cultural Colony Would Make City 'Flimsy Fair Ground,'" *Santa Fe New Mexican*, June 5, 1926.

45. "Among the Writing Folk," *Santa Fe New Mexican*, July 3, 1926; "Willa Cather Is Not Sold on the Culture Colony Plans, States," *Albuquerque Journal*, July 4, 1926.
46. R. L. Duffus, "Santa Fe, Aloof, Clings to Its Heritage," *New York Times*, May 19, 1929.
47. Willa Cather, "#0841: Willa Cather to Zoë Akins, July 4 [1926]"; Willa Cather, "#2868: Willa Cather to Louise Guerber, July 4 [1926]," *Complete Letters*.
48. Willa Cather, "#2869: Willa Cather to Louise Guerber [August 22, 1926]," *Complete Letters*.
49. Sergeant, *Willa Cather*, 225.
50. Willa Cather, "#0845: Willa Cather to Mabel Dodge Luhan, September 26 [1926]," *Complete Letters*; Melissa J. Homestead, *The Only Wonderful Things: The Creative Partnership of Willa Cather and Edith Lewis* (Oxford University Press, 2021), 135–37.
51. Willa Cather, "#0844: Willa Cather to Blanche Wolf Knopf [September 19, 1926]"; "#0847: Willa Cather to Blanche Wolf Knopf [October 6, 1926]," *Complete Letters*.
52. Willa Cather, "#2870: Willa Cather to Louise Guerber, October 2 [1926]," *Complete Letters*.
53. Willa Cather, "#0901: Willa Cather to Eunice Chapin, September 24 [1926]"; "#2972: Willa Cather to Henry Godard Leach, October 7 [1926]," *Complete Letters*.
54. Willa Cather, "#2871: Willa Cather to Louise Guerber, October 15 [1926]"; "#3153: Willa Cather to Henry Godard Leach, October 15 [1926]," *Complete Letters*.
55. Willa Cather, "#2291: Willa Cather to Virginia Cather [December 5, 1926]," *Complete Letters*.
56. Willa Cather, "#0875: Willa Cather to Mary Virginia Auld [February 19, 1927]," *Complete Letters*.
57. Willa Cather, "#0888: Willa Cather to Blanche Wolf Knopf [June 11, 1927]"; "#2877: Willa Cather to Louise Guerber [July 15, 1927]," *Complete Letters*.
58. Lewis, *Willa Cather Living*, 148.
59. Willa Cather, "#0890: Willa Cather to Dorothy Canfield Fisher, August 17 [1927]," *Complete Letters*.
60. Willa Cather, "#1622: Willa Cather to Miss Masterson, March 15, 1943," *Complete Letters*.

Chapter 6

1. Alfred A. Knopf, "Miss Cather," *The Art of Willa Cather*, ed. Bernice Slote and Virginia Faulkner (University of Nebraska–Lincoln, 1974), 209–10.
2. Willa Cather, "#1229: Willa Cather to Alfred A. Knopf, July 25, 1934," *Complete Letters*.
3. Willa Cather, "#0909: Willa Cather to Ferris Greenslet, November 8, 1927," *Complete Letters*.
4. Alfred A. Knopf, "Willa Cather," unpublished memoir, Harry Ransom Humanities Research Center, University of Texas at Austin; Knopf, "Miss Cather," 210.
5. Willa Cather, "#0894: Willa Cather to Carl Van Vechten, September 16 [1927]," *Complete Letters*.
6. James R. Thorpe to Willa Cather, October 3, 1927, Archives & Special Collections, University of Nebraska–Lincoln.

7. Willa Cather, "#2579: Willa Cather to M. Manley Aaron, October 15 [1927]," *Complete Letters.*

8. Willa Cather to Ida Tarbell, Friday [probably October 1927], in *The Selected Letters of Willa Cather*, ed. Andrew Jewell and Janis Stout (Alfred A. Knopf, 2013), 398–99.

9. Willa Cather, "#0913: Willa Cather to Blanche Wolf Knopf [November 13, 1927]," *Complete Letters.*

10. Willa Cather, "#2880: Willa Cather to Louise Guerber [September 26, 1927]," *Complete Letters.*

11. Edith Lewis, *Willa Cather Living: A Personal Record* (Knopf, 1953), 147.

12. Willa Cather, "#0914: Willa Cather to Fanny Butcher, November 21 [1927]," *Complete Letters.*

13. Mildred R. Bennett, *The World of Willa Cather* (University of Nebraska Press, 1961), 132–33.

14. Willa Cather, "A Letter from Willa Cather," *Commonweal*, November 23, 1927, 713.

15. Cather mistakenly identified the artist as Albrecht Dürer, when in fact it was Hans Holbein the Younger. Cather, "Letter from Willa Cather," 714.

16. Cather, "Letter from Willa Cather," 714.

17. Cather, "Letter from Willa Cather," 714.

18. Willa Cather, "#0910: Willa Cather to Harriet Fox Whicher [November 8, 1927]," *Complete Letters.*

19. Willa Cather, "#0916: Willa Cather to Blanche Wolf Knopf, December 31 [1927]"; "#0921: Willa Cather to Blanche Wolf Knopf, December 31 [1928]"; "#0923: Willa Cather to Dorothy Canfield Fisher, January 18 [1928]"; "#0924: Willa Cather to Ferris Greenslet, January 21 [1928]"; "#2585: Willa Cather to Alfred A. Knopf, February 10 [1928]"; "#0926: Willa Cather to Blanche Wolf Knopf, February 14, 1928." All in *Complete Letters.*

20. Willa Cather, "#0928: Willa Cather to Dorothy Canfield Fisher, April 3 [1928]," *Complete Letters.*

21. Willa Cather, "#0934: Willa Cather to Mary Hunter Austin, May 9, 1928," *Complete Letters.*

22. Willa Cather, "#1844: Willa Cather to Mary Virginia Boak Cather, April 27 [1928]"; "#2423: Willa Cather to Mary Virginia Boak Cather, November 15 [1928]." Both in *Complete Letters.*

23. Willa Cather, "#1036: Willa Cather to Mabel Dodge Luhan, January 17 [1931]," *Complete Letters.*

24. Harold Small, "Willa Cather Tells 'Secret' Novel's Title," *San Francisco Chronicle*, March 23, 1931.

25. Harold Small, "Willa Cather Raps 'Sincerity Heresy,'" *San Francisco Chronicle*, March 29, 1931.

26. Small, "Willa Cather Raps 'Sincerity Heresy.'"

27. Willa Cather, "#0972: Willa Cather to Dorothy Canfield Fisher [April 7, 1929]," *Complete Letters.*

28. Willa Cather, "#1018: Willa Cather to Dorothy Canfield Fisher, September 30 [1930]," *Complete Letters.*

29. Willa Cather, "#1132: Willa Cather to Zoë Akins, November 21 [1932]," *Complete Letters*.
30. Knopf, "Willa Cather," unpublished memoir; John J. Murphy, "Textual Essay," in Willa Cather, *Archbishop*, scholarly edition, 519, 522.
31. Willa Cather, "#2585: Willa Cather to Alfred A. Knopf, February 10 [1928]," *Complete Letters*.
32. Murphy, "Textual Essay," 531.
33. Willa Cather, "#2609: Willa Cather to George M. Stimson, October 17 [1929]," *Complete Letters*.
34. Knopf, "Willa Cather," unpublished memoir.
35. Knopf, "Willa Cather," unpublished memoir.
36. Walt Reed, *Harold von Schmidt Draws and Paints the Old West* (Northland Press, 1972), 206–7.
37. Willa Cather, "#2652: Willa Cather to Alfred A. Knopf, August 3 [1933]," *Complete Letters*.
38. Reed, *Harold von Schmidt Draws and Paints*, 206–7.
39. Melissa J. Homestead, *The Only Wonderful Things: The Creative Partnership of Willa Cather and Edith Lewis* (Oxford University Press, 2021), 168; Charles W. Mignon, "Cather's Copy of Death Comes for the Archbishop," *Cather Studies*, vol. 4, Willa Cather Archive, available at www.cather.unl.edu.
40. Willa Cather, "#1130: Willa Cather to Ferris Greenslet, October 31, 1932," *Complete Letters*.
41. Lise Jaillant, "Canonical in the 1930s: Willa Cather's *Death Comes for the Archbishop* in the Modern Library Series," *Studies in the Novel* 45, no. 3 (2013): 478.
42. Willa Cather, "#1130: Willa Cather to Ferris Greenslet, October 31, 1932," *Complete Letters*; Sharon O'Brien, "Becoming Noncanonical: The Case Against Willa Cather," *American Quarterly* 40, no. 1 (1988): 122; Mark J. Madigan, "Willa Cather and the Book-of-the-Month Club," *Cather Studies*, vol. 7, Willa Cather Archive.
43. Henry Longan Stuart, "A Vivid Page of History in Miss Cather's New Novel," *New York Times Book Review*, September 4, 1927.
44. Michael Williams, "Willa Cather's Masterpiece," *Commonweal*, September 28, 1927, 490–92.
45. "Willa Cather Builds a Novel Around a Historical Theme," *Milwaukee Journal Sentinel*, September 10, 1927.
46. George Grimes, "Willa Cather Writes of Early New Mexico," *Omaha World Herald*, September 18, 1927.
47. Rebecca West, "Miss Cather's Business as an Artist," *New York Herald Tribune Books*, September 11, 1927.
48. Fanny Butcher, "Willa Cather's New Novel Is Simply, Beautifully Told," *Chicago Tribune*, September 3, 1927; idem, "Willa Cather Writes Another Splendid Novel," *Seattle Daily Times*, September 11, 1927.
49. Robert O. Ballou, "The Story of the West Which Willa Cather Sees," *Chicago Daily News*, September 7, 1927.

50. Lillian C. Ford, "A Santa Fe Novel!" *Santa Fe New Mexican*, September 23, 1927.
51. William Whitman III, "Eminence Comes for Miss Cather," *Independent*, September 17, 1927, 283.
52. Dorothy Foster Gilman, "Willa Cather Writes a Fictional Biography," *Boston Evening Transcript*, September 10, 1927.
53. Robert Morss Lovett, "A Death in the Desert," *New Republic*, October 26, 1927, 266–67.
54. H. L. Mencken, "The Desert Epic," *American Mercury* 12, no. 4. (1927): 508–9.
55. Charles A. Fecher, ed., *The Diary of H. L. Mencken* (Alfred A. Knopf, 1989), 33.
56. Willa Cather to Mary Hunter Austin, November 9 [1927], in Jewell and Stout, *Selected Letters of Willa Cather*, 399–400.
57. Cather, "Letter from Willa Cather," 714. See also Willa Cather to Alice Corbin Henderson, November 8, 1927, in Jane Pope Geske Heritage Room of Nebraska Authors, Bennett Martin Public Library, Lincoln, NE.
58. Willa Cather to Fanny Butcher, Thursday [probably early September 1927], in Jewell and Stout, *Selected Letters of Willa Cather*, 395–96; Cather, "Letter from Willa Cather," 714.
59. Willa Cather, "#0896: Willa Cather to Fanny Butcher, September 17 [1927]," *Complete Letters*.
60. Willa Cather, "#1066: Willa Cather to Mary Virginia Boak Cather, August 10 [1931]," *Complete Letters*.
61. Alice Booth, "Willa Cather Who Believes There Is Nothing in the World Finer to Write About Than Life, Just as It Is, and People, Just as They Are," *Good Housekeeping*, September 1931, 34, 196–98.
62. Knopf, "Willa Cather," unpublished memoir.
63. Knopf, "Willa Cather," unpublished memoir.
64. Murphy, "Textual Essay," 524–25; Mary Chinery, "Wartime Fictions: Willa Cather, the Armed Services Editions, and the Unspeakable Second World War," *Cather Studies*, vol. 6, Willa Cather Archive.
65. David G. Wittels, "What the G.I. Reads," *Saturday Evening Post*, June 23, 1945, 11.
66. Joan Acocella, *Willa Cather and the Politics of Criticism* (University of Nebraska Press, 2000), 29.
67. Hermione Lee, *Willa Cather: Double Lives* (Pantheon, 1989), 12.
68. Clifton Fadiman, "Willa Cather: The Past Recaptured," *Nation*, December 7, 1932, 564.
69. Lionel Trilling, "Willa Cather," *New Republic*, February 10, 1937, 10.
70. V. F. Calverton, *The Liberation of American Literature* (Octagon Books, 1973), 424.
71. Harlan Hatcher, *Creating the Modern American Novel* (Farrar & Rinehart, 1935), 59, 71.
72. Granville Hicks, "Bright Incidents," *Forum*, September 1931, 6–8.
73. Willa Cather, "#1842: Henry Goddard Leach, September 1 [1931]," *Complete Letters*.
74. Willa Cather, "#1841: Willa Cather to Henry Goddard Leach, May 25, 1932," *Complete Letters*.
75. Granville Hicks, "The Case Against Willa Cather," *English Review* 22, no. 9 (1933), 704, 708, 710.
76. Hicks, "Case Against Willa Cather," 708–9.

77. Willa Cather, "Escapism: A Letter from Willa Cather," *Commonweal*, April 17, 1936, 677–78.
78. John H. Randall III, *The Landscape and the Looking Glass: Willa Cather's Search for Value* (Houghton Mifflin, 1960), 306–10.
79. Randall, *Landscape and the Looking Glass*, 309–10; Willa Sibert Cather, "The Novel Démeublé," *New Republic*, April 12, 1922, 5–6.
80. Patricia Clark Smith, "Achaeans, Americanos, Prelates and Monsters: Willa Cather's *Death Comes for the Archbishop*," in *Padre Martínez: New Perspectives from Taos*, ed. E. A. Mares (Millicent Rogers Museum, 1988), 107, 121; Ray John de Aragón, "Padre Antonio José Martínez: The Man and the Myth," in Mares, *Padre Martínez*, 148; E. A. Mares, "The Many Faces of Padre Antonio José Martínez: A Historiographic Essay," in Mares, *Padre Martínez*, 42.
81. Willa Cather, "#1075: Willa Cather to Mr. Meromichey, October 5, 1931," *Complete Letters*.
82. E. K. Brown, "Homage to Willa Cather," *Yale Review* 36 (1946): 85.
83. Cather, "Novel Démeublé," 5–6.
84. Cather, "Letter from Willa Cather," 714.
85. Janis P. Stout, *Willa Cather: The Writer and Her World* (University Press of Virginia, 2000), 188.
86. Willa Cather, "#0890: Willa Cather to Dorothy Canfield Fisher, August 17 [1927]," *Complete Letters*.
87. Bette S. Weidman, "Willa Cather's Art in Historical Perspective: Reconsidering Death Comes for the Archbishop," in Mares, *Padre Martínez*, 55.
88. L. Brent Bohlke, ed., *Willa Cather in Person: Interviews, Speeches, and Letters* (University of Nebraska Press, 1986), 24.
89. John J. Murphy, "Postlude: The Green Vase, the Yellow Orange, and the White Chapel," *Cather Studies*, vol. 8, Willa Cather Archive.
90. Fanny Butcher, *Many Lives—One Love* (Harper & Row, 1972), 359.

Chapter 7

1. Louis H. Warner, *Archbishop Lamy: An Epoch Maker* (Santa Fe New Mexican Publishing, 1936), 27.
2. William J. Howlett, *Life of the Right Reverend Joseph P. Machebeuf, D.D.* (Franklin Press, 1908), 50, 77.
3. Howlett, *Life of the Right Reverend Joseph P. Machebeuf*, 40.
4. Howlett, *Life of the Right Reverend Joseph P. Machebeuf*, 42–43, 44.
5. As Cather used both fictional and historical figures for her novel, I have opted to address scenes from the novel in the present tense, while historical events are addressed in the past tense. This will help the reader sort through the fictional episodes set against factual events.
6. Paul Horgan, *Lamy of Santa Fe: His Life and Times* (Farrar, Strauss and Giroux, 1975), 92.
7. Howlett, *Life of the Right Reverend Joseph P. Machebeuf*, 154.

8. James S. Calhoun, *The Official Correspondence of James S. Calhoun* (Government Printing Office, 1915), 148.
9. Howlett, *Life of the Right Reverend Joseph P. Machebeuf*, 165.
10. "Triangular Fight Between the Military, the Judiciary and the Catholic Church," *Santa Fe Gazette*, August 30, 1851; Calhoun, *Official Correspondence*, 406–11.
11. Mary J. Straw Cook, *Doña Tules: Santa Fe's Courtesan and Gambler* (University of New Mexico Press, 2007), 101.
12. Josiah Gregg, *Commerce of the Prairies*, 2nd ed. (J. & H. G. Langley, 1845), 219.
13. William W. H. Davis, *El Gringo; or, New Mexico and Her People* (Harper, 1857), 220–22.
14. Angélico Chávez, *But Time and Chance: The Story of Padre Martínez of Taos, 1793–1867* (Sunstone, 1981), 97; Angélico Chávez and Thomas E. Chávez, *Wake for a Fat Vicar: Father Juan Felipe Ortiz, Archbishop Lamy, and the New Mexican Catholic Church in the Middle of the Nineteenth Century* (LPD Press, 2004), 83–91.
15. Chávez and Chávez, *Wake for a Fat Vicar*, 95.
16. James DeFouri, *Historical Sketch of the Catholic Church in New Mexico* (McCormick Bros., 1887), 28.
17. Howlett, *Life of the Right Reverend Joseph P. Machebeuf*, 164.
18. Chávez, *But Time and Chance*, 95, 101.
19. Howlett, *Life of the Right Reverend Joseph P. Machebeuf*, 190.
20. Howlett, *Life of the Right Reverend Joseph P. Machebeuf*, 20.
21. Nancy Hanks, *Lamy's Legion: The Individual Histories of Secular Clergy Serving in the Archdiocese of Santa Fe from 1850 to 1912* (HRM Books, 2000), xiii.
22. Angélico Chávez, *My Penitente Land: Reflections on Spanish New Mexico* (University of New Mexico Press, 1974), 257, 258.
23. John Baptist Salpointe, *Soldiers of the Cross: Notes on the Ecclesiastical History of New Mexico, Arizona and Colorado* (St. Boniface's Industrial School, 1898), 211.
24. Salpointe, *Soldiers of the Cross*, 219.
25. DeFouri, *Historical Sketch*, 58.
26. Howlett, *Life of the Right Reverend Joseph P. Machebeuf*, 257–58.
27. John O'Sullivan, "Annexation," *United States Magazine and Democratic Review*17 (1845): 5, 9.
28. Janis P. Stout, *Willa Cather: The Writer and Her World* (University Press of Virginia, 2000), 343.
29. Astrid Haas, "Borderlands Identities and Borderlands Ideologies in Willa Cather's *Death Comes for the Archbishop*," *American Studies Journal* 57 (2012). Web.
30. Sister Blandina Segale, *At the End of the Santa Fe Trail* (Kessinger, 2010), 213.
31. Warner, *Archbishop Lamy*, 252.
32. Warner, *Archbishop Lamy*, 216–17.
33. Salpointe, *Soldiers of the Cross*, 236.
34. DeFouri, *Historical Sketch*, 79.
35. Howlett, *Life of the Right Reverend Joseph P. Machebeuf*, 238–39.
36. "Bishop Lamy," *Santa Fe New Mexican*, January 23, 1864.

37. "Bishop Lamy's Account of His Adventures with the Indians," *New York Times*, September 9, 1867.
38. DeFouri, *Historical Sketch*, 112.
39. Angélico Chávez, *Très Macho—He Said: Padre Gallegos of Albuquerque, New Mexico's First Congressman* (William Gannon, 1985), 99.
40. Andrés Reséndez, *The Other Slavery: The Uncovered Story of Indian Enslavement in America* (Houghton Mifflin Harcourt, 2016), 277.
41. *Condition of the Indian Tribes* (Government Printing Office, 1867), 326.
42. Hampton Sides, *Blood and Thunder: An Epic of the American West* (Doubleday, 2006), 386.
43. "Navajo Captives," *Santa Fe New Mexican*, August 5, 1868; Oliver LaFarge, *Santa Fe: The Autobiography of a Southwestern Town* (University of Oklahoma Press, 1959), 63.
44. Reséndez, *Other Slavery*, 313.
45. Segale, *At the End of the Santa Fe Trail*, 86.
46. "Attempted Murder," *Santa Fe Gazette*, December 30, 1865.
47. Segale, *At the End of the Santa Fe Trail*, 144–45.
48. "The Bishop's Garden," *Weekly New Mexican*, September 14, 1875; Warner, *Archbishop Lamy*, 151–3.
49. Warner, *Archbishop Lamy*, 173–79.
50. Warner, *Archbishop Lamy*, 173–79.
51. Horgan, *Lamy of Santa Fe*, 369.
52. DeFouri, *Historical Sketch*, 135–37.
53. *Weekly New Mexican*, October 4, 1879; "Bonds Carried," *Weekly New Mexican*, October 11, 1879.
54. Segale, *At the End of the Santa Fe Trail*, 155.
55. "Santa Fe's Triumph," *Weekly New Mexican*, February 14, 1880.
56. DeFouri, *Historical Sketch*, 152–53.
57. Elizabeth Shepley Sergeant, *Willa Cather: A Memoir* (J. B. Lippincott, 1953), 214.
58. Thomas J. Steele, *Archbishop Lamy: In His Own Words* (LPD Press, 2000), 14.
59. Howlett, *Life of the Right Reverend Joseph P. Machebeuf*, 128–29.
60. Howlett, *Life of the Right Reverend Joseph P. Machebeuf*, 411–12.
61. Howlett, *Life of the Right Reverend Joseph P. Machebeuf*, 29.
62. Howlett, *Life of the Right Reverend Joseph P. Machebeuf*, 237.

Chapter 8

1. Kali Fajardo-Anstine, "Introduction," Willa Cather, *Death Comes for the Archbishop* (Penguin Books, 2023), ix.
2. For decades, the Ancestral Puebloans were known as Anasazi (or Násaazí). The word derives from the Navajo language and means "enemy ancestors." You can see why the Pueblo Indians are not fond of the term. But some Navajos say that the word means "ancestors who lived around us" and isn't intended to be derogatory.
3. Samuel Duwe, *Tewa Worlds: An Archaeological History of Being and Becoming in the Pueblo Southwest* (University of Arizona Press, 2020), 25–26.

4. Robert P. Powers, ed., *The Peopling of Bandelier: New Insights from the Archaeology of the Pajarito Plateau* (School of American Research Press, 2005), 4–7; David E. Stuart, *Pueblo People on the Pajarito Plateau: Archaeology and Efficiency* (University of New Mexico Press, 2010), 102–3.

5. David Treuer, *The Heartbeat of Wounded Knee: Native America from 1890 to the Present* (Riverhead, 2019), 51–55.

6. Klara Kelley and Harris Francis, *A Diné History of Navajoland* (University of Arizona Press, 2019), 40–43.

7. Kelley and Francis, *Diné History of Navajoland*, 104.

8. Ramón A. Gutiérrez, *When Jesus Came, the Corn Mothers Went Away* (Stanford University Press, 1991), xxvii–xxix.

9. Joe S. Sando and Herman Agoyo, eds., *Po'pay: Leader of the First American Revolution* (Clear Light Publishing, 2005), xvi.

10. Elizabeth Shepley Sergeant, *Willa Cather: A Memoir* (J. B. Lippincott, 1953), 164.

11. Sergeant noted that this took place in 1926, but she was wrong: Cather did not go to Taos that year, but rather the year before. Sergeant, *Willa Cather*, 207.

12. Mabel Dodge Luhan, *Edge of Taos Desert: An Escape to Reality* (University of New Mexico Press, 1987), 199.

13. Lois Palken Rudnick, *The Suppressed Memoirs of Mabel Dodge Luhan: Sex, Syphilis, and Psychoanalysis in the Making of Modern American Culture* (University of New Mexico Press, 2012), 143.

14. Willa Cather, *My Ántonia* (Houghton Mifflin, 1918), 7.

15. Willa Cather, "A Letter from Willa Cather," *Commonweal*, November 23, 1927, 714.

16. Charles F. Lummis, *The Land of Poco Tiempo* (Scribner, 1893), 67.

17. Ralph Emerson Twitchell, *The Leading Facts of New Mexico*, vol. 1 (Torch, 1911), 362; George W. James, *New Mexico: The Land of the Delight Makers* (Page, 1920), 151.

18. John Baptist Salpointe, *Soldiers of the Cross: Notes on the Ecclesiastical History of New Mexico, Arizona and Colorado* (St. Boniface's Industrial School, 1898), 64–65; William Watts Hart Davis, *The Spanish Conquest of New Mexico* (no publisher available), 304.

19. George B. Anderson, *History of New Mexico, Its Resources and People* (Pacific States Publishing, 1907), 362, 372–73.

20. William J. Howlett, *Life of the Right Reverend Joseph P. Machebeuf, D.D.* (Franklin Press, 1908), 298.

21. Willa Cather, "#2293: Willa Cather to Virginia Cather [August 10, 1927]," *Complete Letters*.

22. Blue Jay notebook, Charles E. Cather Collection, Archives & Special Collections, University of Nebraska–Lincoln.

23. Mabel Dodge Luhan, *Winter in Taos* (Sunstone Press, 2007), 90.

24. Mabel Dodge Luhan, *Lorenzo in Taos: D. H. Lawrence and Mabel Dodge Luhan* (Sunstone Press, 2007), 209.

25. Luhan, *Winter in Taos*, 86; D. H. Lawrence, "The Woman Who Rode Away," in *Selected Short Stories of D. H. Lawrence*, ed. James Wood (Modern Library, 1999), 365–98.

26. Luhan, *Edge of Taos Desert*, 303.

27. Charles H. Lange and Carroll L. Riley, eds., *The Southwestern Journals of Adolph F. Bandelier: 1880–1882* (University of New Mexico Press, 1966), 78.

28. J. W. Abert, *Report of Lieut. J. W. Abert of His Examination of New Mexico, in the Years 1846–47*. 30th Cong., 1st sess., House Ex. Doc. no. 41. (Wendell and Van Benthuysen, 1848), 446–47.
29. Josiah Gregg, *Commerce of the Prairies*, 2nd ed. (J. & H. G. Langley, 1845), 271–72.
30. John L. Kessell, *The Missions of New Mexico Since 1776* (University of New Mexico Press, 1980), 225.
31. Gutiérrez, *When Jesus Came*, 27–28.

Chapter 9

1. John J. Murphy, "Willa Cather's Archbishop: A Western and Classical Perspective," *Western American Literature* 13 (1978): 143.
2. William J. Howlett, *Life of the Right Reverend Joseph P. Machebeuf, D.D.* (Franklin Press, 1908), 192–94, 196–97; Angélico Chávez, *Très Macho—He Said: Padre Gallegos of Albuquerque, New Mexico's First Congressman* (William Gannon, 1985), 60–61.
3. Chávez, *Très Macho*, vii, 33.
4. Chávez, *Très Macho*, 45, 47.
5. Chávez, *Très Macho*, vii–viii.
6. *Santa Fe Gazette*, May 28, 1853.
7. Chávez, 49–50, 56; Fray Angelico Chavez, *But Time and Chance: The Story of Padre Martínez of Taos, 1793–1867* (Sunstone, 1981), 105–7.
8. Chávez, *Très Macho*, 81–82.
9. Thomas J. Steele, *Archbishop Lamy: In His Own Words* (LPD Press, 2000), 13.
10. Angélico Chávez, *My Penitente Land: Reflections on Spanish New Mexico* (University of New Mexico Press, 1974), xiii, 218–22; idem, Chávez, *But Time and Chance*, 35–36; Ray John de Aragón, *The Penitentes of New Mexico: Hermanos de la Luz / Brothers of the Light* (Sunstone Press, 2006), 30–33.
11. Charles F. Lummis, *The Land of Poco Tiempo* (Scribner, 1893), 24; his detailed description of observing a Penitente ritual in San Mateo is pp. 81–108.
12. Chávez, *My Penitente Land*, 179, 206.
13. Mabel Dodge Luhan, *Edge of Taos Desert: An Escape to Reality* (University of New Mexico Press, 1987), 81–82.
14. William J. Howlett, *Life of Bishop Machebeuf*, ed. Thomas J. Steele and Ronald S. Brockway (Regis College, 1987), 450.
15. Oliver LaFarge, *Santa Fe: The Autobiography of a Southwestern Town* (University of Oklahoma Press, 1959), 44–45.
16. William W. H. Davis, *El Gringo; or, New Mexico and Her People* (Harper, 1857), 97.
17. George B. Anderson, *History of New Mexico, Its Resources and People* (Pacific States Publishing, 1907), 95.
18. Anderson, *History of New Mexico*, 96.
19. Anderson, *History of New Mexico*, 94, 96; Ralph Emerson Twitchell repeated this statement nearly verbatim two years later in *The History of the Military Occupation of the Territory of New Mexico from 1846 to 1851* (Smith-Brooks, 1909), 133.

20. Anderson, *History of New Mexico*, 96.

21. Luhan, *Edge of Taos Desert*, 85–86.

22. Chávez, *My Penitente Land*, 259.

23. Chávez, *But Time and Chance*, 160.

24. Chávez, *But Time and Chance*, 83–85.

25. E. A. Mares, "The Many Faces of Padre Antonio José Martínez: A Historiographic Essay," in *Padre Martínez: New Perspectives from Taos* (Millicent Rogers Museum, 1988), 27.

26. Chávez, *But Time and Chance*, 40, 99; idem, *Très Macho*, 36–37.

27. Chávez, *But Time and Chance*, 48–50.

28. Chávez, *But Time and Chance*, 37–39.

29. Ray John de Aragón, "Padre Antonio José Martínez: The Man and the Myth," in Mares, *Padre Martínez*, 146.

30. Chávez, *But Time and Chance*, 90.

31. Howlett, *Life of the Right Reverend Joseph P. Machebeuf*, 229.

32. "El Cura de Taos," *Santa Fe Gazette*, May 24, 1856.

33. *Santa Fe Gazette*, October 25, 1856.

34. *Santa Fe Gazette*, November 22, 29, 1856.

35. Chávez, *But Time and Chance*; "Para la Geseta de Santa Fe," *Santa Fe Gazette*, October 30, 1858.

36. Paul Horgan, *Lamy of Santa Fe* (Farrar, Strauss and Giroux, 1975), 241.

37. *Santa Fe Gazette*, February 14, 1857.

38. Thomas J. Steele, "The View from the Rectory," in Mares, *Padre Martínez*, 98–99.

39. "Kit Carson and W. W. H. Davis," *Santa Fe Gazette*, August 15, 1857.

40. "Politics in New Mexico," *Santa Fe Gazette*, September 30, 1857.

41. John Baptist Salpointe, *Soldiers of the Cross: Notes on the Ecclesiastical History of New Mexico, Arizona and Colorado* (St. Boniface's Industrial School, 1898), 235.

42. Chávez, *But Time and Chance*, 142.

43. Steele, "View from the Rectory," 85.

44. Howlett, *Life of the Right Reverend Joseph P. Machebeuf*, 232; Blue Jay notebook, Charles E. Cather Collection, Archives & Special Collections, University of Nebraska–Lincoln.

45. Anderson, *History of New Mexico*, 99.

46. Father Steele laid out the timeline leading to the excommunications in April 1858. Steele, "View from the Rectory," 99–100.

47. Howlett, *Life of the Right Reverend Joseph P. Machebeuf*, 233; Blue Jay notebook.

48. Ray John de Aragón, *Padre Martínez and Bishop Lamy* (Sunstone, 2006), 97.

49. Howlett, *Life of Bishop Machebeuf*, 435.

50. Aragón, "Padre Antonio José Martínez," 148.

51. Horgan, *Lamy of Santa Fe*, 244.

52. Anderson, *History of New Mexico*, 97–99.

53. Horgan, *Lamy of Santa Fe*, 250–51.

54. "Death of Padre Martines," *Santa Fe New Mexican*, August 3, 1867.

55. The weighted treasure could be myth. Anderson placed Lucero's death in 1882 or 1882, but he was wrong about that fact: Lucero died in 1870. Anderson, *History of New Mexico*, 100.
56. Chávez, *But Time and Chance*, 158.

Chapter 10

1. John March, *A Reader's Companion to the Fiction of Willa Cather* (Greenwood, 1993), 546.
2. *Weekly New Mexican*, June 7, 1880.
3. Blue Jay notebook, Charles E. Cather Collection, Archives & Special Collections, University of Nebraska–Lincoln.
4. Blue Jay notebook; Ralph Emerson Twitchell, *The History of the Military Occupation of the Territory of New Mexico from 1846 to 1851* (Smith-Brooks, 1909), 285–99.
5. William J. Howlett, *Life of the Right Reverend Joseph P. Machebeuf, D.D.* (Franklin Press, 1908), 287.
6. Howlett, *Life of the Right Reverend Joseph P. Machebeuf*, 287, 295, 296.
7. Bruce Ellis, *Bishop Lamy's Santa Fe Cathedral* (University of New Mexico Press, 1985), 10.
8. "Inscription," *Santa Fe New Mexican*, October 8, 1869; "Vandalism–Robberies," *Santa Fe New Mexican*, October 18, 1869.
9. "The New Cathedral," *Santa Fe New Mexican*, January 3, 1873.
10. Sister Blandina Segale, *At the End of the Santa Fe Trail* (Kessinger Publishing, 2010), 130.
11. Segale, *At the End of the Santa Fe Trail*, 114.
12. "Murder of Francis Mallet," *Weekly New Mexican*, September 6, 1879; "The Shooting of Mallet," *Weekly New Mexican*, September 13, 1879; "The Lamy Case," *Santa Fe New Mexican*, September 25, 1880.
13. Ralph Emerson Twitchell, *The Leading Facts of New Mexican History*, vol. 2 (Torch, 1911), 344.

Chapter 11

1. Joseph Machebeuf to Marie Philomène Machebeuf, January 28, 1854, Denver Archdiocese Archives.
2. Deed of sale of Natividad Romero and Maria Vitalia Garcia to Juan B. Lamy, October 23, 1874, Santa Fe County Clerks Office, document no. 1874000170. Retrieved December 7, 2023, on the 150th anniversary of Willa Cather's birth.
3. *Weekly New Mexican*, November 17, 1874.
4. Fanny Butcher, *Many Lives—One Love* (Harper & Row, 1972), 359.
5. Marian Sloan Russell, *Land of Enchantment: Memoirs of Marian Russell Along the Santa Fe Trail* (University of New Mexico Press, 1997), 44.

6. "Round About Town," *Santa Fe New Mexican*, September 23, 1885.

7. John Baptist Salpointe, *Soldiers of the Cross: Notes on the Ecclesiastical History of New Mexico, Arizona and Colorado* (St. Boniface's Industrial School, 1898), 275.

8. Louis H. Warner, *Archbishop Lamy: An Epoch Maker* (Santa Fe New Mexican Publishing, 1936), 150.

9. "He Is at Rest," *Santa Fe New Mexico*, February 13, 1888.

10. "Round About Town," *Santa Fe New Mexican*, January 17, 1888.

11. Janis P. Stout, *Willa Cather: The Writer and Her World* (University Press of Virginia, 2000), 246.

12. Gary Ferguson, *The Great Divide: The Rocky Mountains in the American Mind* (W. W. Norton, 2004), 185.

13. Willa Cather, "#1741: Willa Cather to E. K. Brown, October 7, 1946," *Complete Letters*.

14. Edith Lewis, *Willa Cather Living: A Personal Record* (Knopf, 1953), 150.

15. E. K. Brown, *Willa Cather: A Critical Biography* (University of Nebraska Press, 1987), 254.

16. Francisco Palóu, *Life and Apostolic Labors of the Venerable Father Junípero Serra* (George Wharton James, 1913), 47–48.

17. John J. Murphy, "Postlude: The Green Vase, the Yellow Orange, and the White Chapel," *Cather Studies*, vol. 8, Willa Cather Archive, available in www.cather.unl.edu.

18. Willa Cather, "A Letter from Willa Cather," *Commonweal*, November 23, 1927, 714.

19. Rose C. Feld, "Restlessness Such as Ours Does Not Make for Beauty," *New York Times*, December 21, 1924.

20. Ann Neumann, *The Good Death: An Exploration of Dying in America* (Beacon Press, 2016), 210.

21. "He Is at Rest."

22. "The Beloved Dead," *Santa Fe New Mexican*, February 15, 1888.

23. William J. Howlett, *Life of the Right Reverend Joseph P. Machebeuf, D.D.* (Franklin Press, 1908), 404.

24. "Monument to His Memory," *Santa Fe New Mexican*, February 21, 1888.

25. Willa Cather, "#1741: Willa Cather to E. K. Brown, October 7, 1946," *Complete Letters*.

26. Willa Cather, "#1392: Willa Cather to Sinclair Lewis, January 14, 1938," *Complete Letters*.

27. Yehudi Menuhin, *Unfinished Journey* (Alfred A. Knopf, 1976), 128–31.

28. Willa Cather, "#1360: Willa Cather to E. K. Brown, April 9, 1937," *Complete Letters*.

29. Willa Cather, "#1622: Willa Cather to Miss Masterson, March 15, 1943," *Complete Letters*.

30. Willa Cather, "#2137: Willa Cather to Roscoe Cather, November 6 [1938]," *Complete Letters*.

31. Willa Cather, "#2359: Willa Cather to Margaret Cather Shannon, [November 9, 1938]," *Complete Letters*.

32. Edith Lewis, *Willa Cather Living: A Personal Record* (Knopf, 1953), 189.

33. Letter from Erna Fergusson to Willa Cather, 1928-07-29, 1981.010.2, Miscellaneous literary manuscripts, correspondence and photographs, 1981-010, The University of Tulsa, McFarlin Library, Department of Special Collections & University Archives.

34. Willa Cather, "#1622: Willa Cather to Miss Masterson, March 15, 1943," *Complete Letters*.

35. Willa Cather, "#2197: Willa Cather to Roscoe Cather, August 15 [1942]," *Complete Letters*.

36. Lewis, *Willa Cather Living*, 197.

37. Melissa Homestead, *The Only Wonderful Things: The Creative Partnership of Willa Cather and Edith Lewis* (Oxford University Press, 2021), 298.

38. Willa Cather, *My Ántonia* (Houghton Mifflin, 1918), 14.

39. Willa Cather, "#1741: Willa Cather to E. K. Brown, October 7, 1946," *Complete Letters*.

Bibliography

Archives and Museum Collections

Archdiocese of Santa Fe Museum and Archives, Santa Fe, NM

Archives & Special Collections, University of Nebraska–Lincoln

Beinecke Rare Book Room & Manuscript Library, Yale University

Belen Harvey House Museum, NM

Boatwright Memorial Library, University of Richmond, VA

Brooke Russell Astor Reading Room for Rare Books and Manuscripts, New York Public Library

Denver Archdiocesan Archives, Denver, CO

Fort Sumner Historic Site/Bosque Redondo Memorial, NM

Fray Angélico Chávez History Library, New Mexico History Museum, Santa Fe, NM

H. L. Mencken Room at the Enoch Pratt Free Library, Baltimore, MD

Harry Ransom Humanities Research Center, University of Texas at Austin

Indian Pueblo Cultural Center, Albuquerque, NM

Jane Pope Geske Heritage Room of Nebraska Authors, Bennett Martin Public Library, Lincoln, NE

Mary Hunter Austin Collection, Huntington Library, San Marino, CA

McFarlin Library, University of Tulsa

National Willa Cather Center, Red Cloud, NE

New Mexico History Museum, Santa Fe, NM

New Mexico Museum of Art, Santa FE, NM

New Mexico State Library, Santa Fe, NM

New Mexico State Records & Archives, Santa Fe, NM

Palace of the Governors Photo Archives, Santa Fe, NM

Prints & Photographs Division, Library of Congress, Washington, DC

Santa Fe Historical Foundation

Willa Cather Archive, Lincoln, NE

Willa Cather Collection, Drew University Special Collections, Madison, NJ

Books

Abert, J. W. *Report of Lieut. J. W. Abert of His Examination of New Mexico, in the Years*

1846–47. 30th Cong., 1st sess., House Ex. Doc. no. 41.Wendell and Van Benthuysen, 1848.

Acocella, Joan. *Willa Cather and the Politics of Criticism*. University of Nebraska Press, 2000.

Anderson, George B. *History of New Mexico, Its Resources and People*. Pacific States Publishing, 1907.

Aragón, Ray John de. "Padre Antonio José Martínez: The Man and the Myth." In Mares, *Padre Martínez*.

Aragón, Ray John de. *Padre Martínez and Bishop Lamy*. Sunstone Press, 2006.

Aragón, Ray John de. *The Penitentes of New Mexico: Hermanos de la Luz / Brothers of the Light*. Sunstone Press, 2006.

Austin, Mary. *Earth Horizon*. Riverside Press, 1932.

Bancroft, Hubert Howe. *History of Arizona and New Mexico 1530–1888*. San Francisco: History Company, 1889.

Bandelier, Adolph. *The Gilded Man (El Dorado) and Other Pictures of the Spanish Occupancy of America*. Appleton, 1893.

Bandelier, Adolph. *The Southwestern Journals of Adolph F. Bandelier: 1880–1882*. Charles H. Lange and Carroll L. Riley, eds. University of New Mexico Press, 1966.

Bennett, Mildred R. *The World of Willa Cather*. University of Nebraska Press, 1961.

Bloom, Edward A., and Lillian D. Bloom. *Willa Cather's Gift of Sympathy*. Southern Illinois University Press, 1962.

Bohlke, L. Brent, ed. *Willa Cather in Person: Interviews, Speeches, and Letters*. University of Nebraska Press, 1986.

Burke, Flannery. *A Land Apart: The Southwest and the Nation in the Twentieth Century*. University of Arizona Press, 2017.

Butcher, Fanny. *Many Lives—One Love*. Harper & Row, 1972.

Calhoun, James S. *The Official Correspondence of James S. Calhoun While Indian Agent at Santa Fé and Superintendent of Indian Affairs in New Mexico*. Government Printing Office, 1915.

Calverton, V. F. *The Liberation of American Literature*. Octagon Books, 1973.

Cather, Willa. *Death Comes for the Archbishop*. Alfred A. Knopf, 1927.

Cather, Willa. *Death Comes for the Archbishop*. Historical essay and explanatory notes by John J. Murphy. Edited by Charles W. Mignon, Frederick M. Link, and Kari A. Ronning. University of Nebraska Press, 1999.

Cather, Willa. "The Enchanted Bluff." In *Stories, Poems, and Other Writings*. Library of America, 1982.

Cather, Willa. *My Ántonia*. Houghton Mifflin, 1918.

Cather, Willa. "My First Novels (There Were Two)." *The Colophon*, 1931. Repr. *Willa Cather on Writing: Critical Studies on Writing as an Art*. University of Nebraska Press, 1988.

Cather, Willa. "Not Under Forty." In *Willa Cather: Stories, Poems, and Other Writings*. Library of America, 1982.

Cather, Willa. *The Professor's House*. Vintage Classics, 1990.

Cather, Willa. *The Song of the Lark*. Houghton Mifflin, 1988.

Cather, Willa. "A Wagner Matinée." *Willa Cather Collected Stories*. Vintage Books, 1992.

Chávez, Angélico. *But Time and Chance: The Story of Padre Martínez of Taos, 1793–1867*. Sunstone Press, 1981.

Chávez, Angélico. *My Penitente Land: Reflections on Spanish New Mexico*. University of New Mexico Press, 1974.

Chávez, Angélico. *Très Macho—He Said: Padre Gallegos of Albuquerque, New Mexico's First Congressman*. William Gannon, 1985.

Chávez, Angélico, and Thomas E. Chávez. *Wake for a Fat Vicar: Father Juan Felipe Ortiz, Archbishop Lamy, and the New Mexican Catholic Church in the Middle of the Nineteenth Century*. LPD Press, 2004.

Condition of the Indian Tribes. Government Printing Office, 1867.

Cook, Mary J. Straw. *Doña Tules: Santa Fe's Courtesan and Gambler*. University of New Mexico Press, 2007.

Davis, William Watts Hart. *El Gringo; or, New Mexico and Her People*. Harper, 1857.

Davis, William Watts Hart. *The Spanish Conquest of New Mexico*. No publisher listed, 1869.

DeFouri, James. *Historical Sketch of the Catholic Church in New Mexico*. McCormick Bros., 1887.

Duwe, Samuel. *Tewa Worlds: An Archaeological History of Being and Becoming in the Pueblo Southwest*. University of Arizona Press, 2020.

Dye, Victoria E. *All Aboard for Santa Fe: Railway Promotion of the Southwest, 1890s to 1930s*. University of New Mexico Press, 2005.

Eastman, Max. *Venture*. Boni and Liveright, 1927.

Ellis, Bruce. *Bishop Lamy's Santa Fe Cathedral*. University of New Mexico Press, 1985.

Fajardo-Anstine, Kali. "Introduction." In Willa Cather, *Death Comes for the Archbishop*. Penguin Books, 2023.

Fecher, Charles A., ed. *The Diary of H. L. Mencken*. Alfred A. Knopf, 1989.

Ferguson, Gary. *The Great Divide: The Rocky Mountains in the American Mind*. W. W. Norton, 2004.

Fergusson, Erna. *New Mexico: A Pageant of Three Peoples*. University of New Mexico Press, 1973.

Fergusson, Erna. *Our Southwest*. Alfred A. Knopf, 1940.

Fields, Annie, ed. *Letters of Sarah Orne Jewett*. Houghton Mifflin, 1911.

Fried, Stephen. *Appetite for America: Fred Harvey and the Business of Civilizing the Wild West—One Meal at a Time*. Bantam, 2010.

Gregg, Josiah. *Commerce of the Prairies*. 2nd ed. J. & H. G. Langley, 1845.

Gunn, John M. *Schat-Chen: History, Traditions, and Narratives of the Queres Indians of Laguna and Acoma*. Albright & Anderson, 1917.

Gutiérrez, Ramón A. *When Jesus Came, the Corn Mothers Went Away: Marriage, Sexuality, and Power in New Mexico, 1500–1846*. Stanford University Press, 1991.

Hanks, Nancy. *Lamy's Legion: The Individual Histories of Secular Clergy Serving in the Archdiocese of Santa Fe from 1850 to 1912*. HRM Books, 2000.

Hapgood, Hutchins. *A Victorian in the Modern World*. Harcourt, Brace, 1939.

Harrell, David. *From Mesa Verde to The Professor's House*. University of New Mexico Press, 1992.

Hatcher, Harlan. *Creating the Modern American Novel*. Farrar & Rinehart, 1935.

Homestead, Melissa. *The Only Wonderful Things: The Creative Partnership of Willa Cather and Edith Lewis*. Oxford University Press, 2021.

Horgan, Paul. *The Centuries of Santa Fe*. E. P. Dutton, 1956.

Horgan, Paul. *Lamy of Santa Fe: His Life and Times*. Farrar, Straus and Giroux, 1975.

Howlett, W. J. *The Life of the Right Reverend Joseph P. Machebeuf, D.D.* Franklin Press, 1908.

Howlett, W. J. *Life of Bishop Machebeuf*, edited by Thomas J. Steele and Ronald S. Brockway. Regis College, 1987.

James, George W. *New Mexico: The Land of the Delight Makers*. Page, 1920.

Jewell, Andrew, and Janis Stout, eds. *The Selected Letters of Willa Cather*. Knopf, 2013.

Kelley, Klara, and Harris Francis. *A Diné History of Navajoland*. University of Arizona Press, 2019.

Kessell, John L. *The Missions of New Mexico Since 1776*. University of New Mexico Press, 1980.

Knopf, Alfred A. "Miss Cather." In *The Art of Willa Cather*, edited by Bernice Slote and Virginia Faulkner. University of Nebraska Press, 1974.

Ladd, Horatio O. *The Story of New Mexico*. D. Lothrop, 1891.

LaFarge, Oliver. *Santa Fe: The Autobiography of a Southwestern Town*. University of Oklahoma Press, 1959.

Lawrence, D. H. "The Woman Who Rode Away." In *Selected Short Stories of D. H. Lawrence*, edited by James Wood. Modern Library, 1999.

Lee, Hermione. *Willa Cather: Double Lives*. Pantheon, 1989.

Lewis, Edith. *Willa Cather Living: A Personal Record*. Alfred A. Knopf, 1953.

Luhan, Mabel Dodge. *Edge of Taos Desert: An Escape to Reality*. University of New Mexico Press, 1987.

Luhan, Mabel Dodge. *Lorenzo in Taos: D. H. Lawrence and Mabel Dodge Luhan*. Sunstone Press, 2007.

Luhan, Mabel Dodge. *Winter in Taos*. Sunstone Press, 2007.

Lummis, Charles F. *The Land of Poco Tiempo*. Scribner, 1893.

Lummis, Charles F. *A New Mexico David and Other Stories and Sketches of the Southwest*. Scribner, 1891.

Lummis, Charles F. *Some Strange Corners of Our Country: The Wonderland of the Southwest*. Century, 1911.

March, John. *A Reader's Companion to the Fiction of Willa Cather*. Greenwood, 1993.

Mares, E. A. "The Many Faces of Padre Antonio José Martínez: A Historiographic Essay." In Mares, *Padre Martínez*.

Mares, E. A., ed. *Padre Martínez: New Perspectives from Taos*. Millicent Rogers Museum, 1988.

Menuhin, Yehudi. *Unfinished Journey*. Alfred A. Knopf, 1976.

Murphy, John J. "Explanatory Notes." In Cather, *Death Comes for the Archbishop*, essay and explanatory notes by John J. Murphy, edited by Mignon, Link, and Ronning.

Murphy, John J. "Historical Essay." In Cather, *Death Comes for the Archbishop*, historical essay and explanatory notes by John J. Murphy, edited by Mignon, Link, and Ronning.

Murphy, John J. "Textual Essay." In Cather, *Death Comes for the Archbishop*, historical essay and explanatory notes by John J. Murphy, edited by Mignon, Link, and Ronning.

Neumann, Ann. *The Good Death: An Exploration of Dying in America*. Beacon Press, 2016.

Nieto-Phillips, John. *The Language of Blood: The Making of Spanish-American Identity in New Mexico, 1880s–1930s*. University of New Mexico Press, 2004.

Palmer, Daryl W. *Becoming Willa Cather: Creation and Career*. University of Nevada Press, 2009.

Palóu, Francisco. *Life and Apostolic Labors of the Venerable Father Junípero Serra*. George Wharton James, 1913.

Pearce, T. M., ed. *Literary America 1903–1934: The Mary Austin Letters*. Greenwood Press, 1979.

Poling-Kempes, Lesley. *The Harvey Girls: Women Who Opened the West*. Da Capo Press, 1989.

Poling-Kempes, Lesley. *Ladies of the Canyon: A League of Extraordinary Women and Their Adventures in the American Southwest*. University of Arizona Press, 2015.

Powell, David McKay. *Cather and Opera*. Louisiana State University Press, 2022.

Powers, Robert P., ed. *The Peopling of Bandelier: New Insights from the Archaeology of the Pajarito Plateau*. School of American Research Press, 2005.

Randall, John H., III. *The Landscape and the Looking Glass: Willa Cather's Search for Value*. Houghton Mifflin, 1960.

Reed, Walt. *Harold von Schmidt Draws and Paints the Old West*. Northland Press, 1972.

Reséndez, Andrés. *The Other Slavery: The Uncovered Story of Indian Enslavement in America*. Houghton Mifflin Harcourt, 2016.

Reynolds, Guy J. *Willa Cather in Context: Progress, Race, Empire*. St. Martin's Press, 1996.

Reynolds, Paul R. *The Middle Man: The Adventures of a Literary Agent*. William Morrow, 1972.

Rogers, Will. "Back to Babbitts, Booze, and Bankrolls." In *A Will Rogers Treasury*, edited by Bryan B. Sterling and Frances N. Sterling. Crown, 1982.

Rudnick, Lois Palken. *The Suppressed Memoirs of Mabel Dodge Luhan: Sex, Syphilis, and Psychoanalysis in the Making of Modern American Culture*. University of New Mexico Press, 2012.

Rudnick, Lois Palken. *Utopian Vistas: the Mabel Dodge Luhan House and the American Counterculture*. University of New Mexico Press, 1996.

Russ, Joanna. *To Write Like a Woman: Essays in Feminism and Science Fiction*. Indiana University Press, 1995.

Russell, Marian Sloan. *Land of Enchantment: Memoirs of Marian Russell Along the Santa Fe Trail*. University of New Mexico Press, 1997.

Salpointe, John Baptist. *Soldiers of the Cross: Notes on the Ecclesiastical History of New Mexico, Arizona and Colorado*. St. Boniface's Industrial School, 1898.

Sando, Joe S., and Herman Agoyo, eds. *Po'pay: Leader of the First American Revolution*. Clear Light Publishing, 2005.

Segale, Sister Blandina. *At the End of the Santa Fe Trail*. Kessinger Publishing, 2010.

Sergeant, Elizabeth Shepley. *Willa Cather: A Memoir*. J. B. Lippincott, 1953.

Sides, Hampton. *Blood and Thunder: An Epic of the American West*. Doubleday, 2006.

Slote, Bernice, and Virginia Faulkner, eds. *The Art of Willa Cather*. University of Nebraska–Lincoln, 1974.

Smith, Patricia Clark. "Achaeans, Americanos, Prelates and Monsters: Willa Cather's *Death Comes for the Archbishop*." In Mares, *Padre Martínez*.

Steele, Thomas J. *Archbishop Lamy: In His Own Words*. LPD Press, 2000.

Steele, Thomas J. "The View from the Rectory." In Mares, *Padre Martínez*.

Stout, Janis P. *Cather Among the Moderns*. University of Alabama Press, 2019.

Stout, Janis P. *Picturing a Different West: Vision, Illustration, and the Tradition of Austin and Cather*. Texas Tech University Press, 2007.

Stout, Janis P. *Willa Cather: The Writer and Her World*. University Press of Virginia, 2000.

Stuart, David E. *Pueblo People on the Pajarito Plateau: Archaeology and Efficiency*. University of New Mexico Press, 2010.

Swift, John N., and Joseph R. Urgo. *Willa Cather and the American Southwest*. University of Nebraska Press, 2002.

Taylor, Benjamin. *Chasing Bright Medusas: A Life of Willa Cather*. New York: Viking, 2023.

Thomas, Diane H. *The Southwestern Indian Detours*. Hunter Publishing, 1978.

Treuer, David. *The Heartbeat of Wounded Knee: Native America from 1890 to the Present*. Riverhead, 2019.

Twain, Mark. *The Innocents Abroad, or The New Pilgrim's Progress*. American Publishing Company, 1869.

Twitchell, Ralph Emerson. *The History of the Military Occupation of the Territory of New Mexico from 1846 to 1851 by the Government of the United States Together with Biographical Sketches in the Conduct of the Government During That Period*. Smith-Brooks, 1909.

Twitchell, Ralph Emerson. *Leading Facts of New Mexican History*. 2 vols. Torch, 1911.

Wallace, Lew. *An Autobiography*. Vol. 2. Harper & Brothers, 1906.

Warner, Louis H. *Archbishop Lamy: An Epoch Maker*. Santa Fe New Mexican Publishing, 1936.

Weidman, Bette S. "Willa Cather's Art in Historical Perspective: Reconsidering *Death Comes for the Archbishop*." In Mares, *Padre Martínez*.

Wilson, Chris. *The Myth of Santa Fe: Creating a Modern Regional Tradition*. University of New Mexico Press, 1997.

Magazines and Periodicals

Booth, Alice. "Willa Cather Who Believes There Is Nothing in the World Finer to Write About Than Life, Just as It Is, and People, Just as They Are." *Good Housekeeping* (September 1931): 34, 196–98.

Brown, E. K. "Homage to Willa Cather." *Yale Review* 36 (1946): 77–92.

Brown, E. K. "Willa Cather and the West." *University of Toronto Quarterly* 5, no. 5 (1936): 544–66.

Carroll, Latrobe. "Willa Sibert Cather." *Bookman*, May 3, 1921, 212–16.

Cassidy, Louise Lowber. "A 'Delight Maker.'" *Sunset Magazine*, January 1925, 38–39.

Cather, Willa. "Escapism: A Letter from Willa Cather," *Commonweal*, April 17, 1936, 677–79.

Cather, Willa. "A Letter from Willa Cather." *Commonweal*, November 23, 1927, 713–14.

Cather, Willa. "Nebraska: The End of the First Cycle." *Nation*, September 5, 1923, 236–38.

Cather, Willa. "The Novel Démeublé." *New Republic*, April 12, 1922, 5–6.

Fadiman, Clifton. "Willa Cather: The Past Recaptured." Nation, December 7, 1932, 563–65.

"The Gossip Shop." *Bookman* 42, no. 2 (1925): 231.

Haas, Astrid. "Borderlands Identities and Borderlands Ideologies in Willa Cather's *Death Comes for the Archbishop*." *American Studies Journal* 57 (2012). Web.

Hicks, Granville. "Bright Incidents." *Forum*, September 1931, vi–viii.

Hicks, Granville. "The Case Against Willa Cather." *English Journal* 22, no. 9 (1933): 703–10.

Homestead, Melissa J. "Willa Cather, Edith Lewis, and Collaboration: The Southwestern Novels of the 1920s and Beyond." *Studies in the Novel* 45, no. 3 (2013): 408–41.

Homestead, Melissa J. "Willa Cather in the Denver Times in 1915 and New Evidence of the Origins of The Professor's House." *Legacy: A Journal of American Women Writers* 35, no. 2 (2018): 187–209.

Horgan, Paul. "In Search of the Archbishop." *Catholic Historical Review* 46 (1961): 409–27.

Jaillant, Lise. "Canonical in the 1930s: Willa Cather's *Death Comes for the Archbishop* in the Modern Library Series." *Studies in the Novel* 45, no. 3 (2013): 476–99.

Knopf, Alfred. "Publishing Then and Now: 1912–1964." *Bulletin of the New York Public Library* 68, no. 9 (1964): 555–73.

Lovett, Robert Morss. "A Death in the Desert." *New Republic*, October 26, 1927, 266–67.

Mencken, H. L. "The Desert Epic." *American Mercury* 12, no. 4. (1927): 508–9.

Mencken, H. L. "Fiction Good and Bad." *American Mercury*, 6 (1925): 379–81.

Murphy, John J. "Willa Cather's Archbishop: A Western and Classical Perspective." *Western American Literature* 13 (1978): 141–50.

O'Brien, Sharon. "Becoming Noncanonical: The Case Against Willa Cather." *American Quarterly* 40, no. 1 (1988): 110–26.

O'Sullivan, John. "Annexation." *United States Magazine and Democratic Review* vol. 17 (1845): 5–10.

Ross, Alex. "Cather People," *New Yorker*, October 2, 2017, 32–37.

Sergeant, Elizabeth Shepley. "New Mexico: A Relic of Ancient America." *Nation*, November 21, 1923, 577–79.

Trilling, Lionel. "Willa Cather." *New Republic*, February 10, 1937, 10–13.

Weigle, Marta. "Exposition and Mediation: Mary Colter, Erna Fergusson, and the Santa Fe/Harvey Popularization of the Native Southwest, 1902–1940." *Frontiers: A Journal of Women's Studies* 12, no. 3 (1992): 116–50.

Whitman, William III. "Eminence Comes for Miss Cather." *Independent*, September 17, 1927, 283.

Williams, Michael. "Willa Cather's Masterpiece." *Commonweal*, September 28, 1927, 490–92.

Wittels, David G. "What the G.I. Reads," *Saturday Evening Post*, June 23, 1945, 11, 91–92.

Woidat, Caroline M. "The Indian-Detour in Willa Cather's Southwestern Novels," *Twentieth-Century Literature* 48, no. 1 (2002): 22–49.

Newspaper Articles

"Additional Data." *Santa Fe New Mexican*, February 22, 1888.

"Among the Literati." *Santa Fe New Mexican*, June 14, 1926.

"Among the Writing Folk." *Santa Fe New Mexican*, July 3, 1926.

"Announcement!." *Santa Fe New Mexican*, June 5, 1926.

"Artists Object, Statue Is Forfeited; Mrs. Austin, Applegate Protest." *Santa Fe New Mexican*, October 12, 1927.

"Attempted Murder." *Santa Fe Gazette*, December 30, 1865.

Ballou, Robert O. "The Story of the West Which Willa Cather Sees." *Chicago Daily News*, September 7, 1927.

"The Beloved Dead." *Santa Fe New Mexican*, February 15, 1888.

"Biggest Fire in History of City." *Santa Fe New Mexican*, January 5, 1922.

Birdseye, R. W. "The Indian Detour." *Santa Fe New Mexican*, January 29, 1926.

"Bishop Lamy." *Santa Fe New Mexican*, January 23, 1864.

"Bishop Lamy's Account of His Adventures with the Indians." *New York Times*, September 9, 1867.

"The Bishop's Garden." *Weekly New Mexican*, September 14, 1875.

"Bonds Carried." *Weekly New Mexican*, October 11, 1879.

Butcher, Fanny. "Willa Cather Tells Purpose of New Novel." *Chicago Tribune*, September 12, 1925.

Butcher, Fanny. "Willa Cather Writes Another Splendid Novel." *Seattle Daily Times*, September 11, 1927.

Butcher, Fanny. "Willa Cather's New Novel Is Simply, Beautifully Told." *Chicago Tribune*, September 3, 1927.

Cather, Willa Sibert. "Mesa Verde Wonderland Is Easy to Reach." *Denver Times*, January 31, 1916.

"Cultural Colony Would Make City 'Flimsy Fair Ground.'" *Santa Fe New Mexican*, June 5, 1926.

"Death of Padre Martines." *Santa Fe New Mexican*, August 3, 1867.

Duffus, R. L. "Santa Fe, Aloof, Clings to Its Heritage." *New York Time*, May 19, 1929.

"El Cura de Taos." *Santa Fe Gazette*, May 24, 1856.

Feld, Rose C. "Restlessness Such as Ours Does Not Make for Beauty." *New York Times*, December 21, 1924.

Fisher, Dorothy Canfield, "Willa Cather: Daughter of the Frontier." *New York Herald*, May 28, 1933.

"Flood Sweeps Trinidad, Colorado." *Santa Fe New Mexican*, July 23, 1925.

Ford, Lillian C. "A Santa Fe Novel!" *Santa Fe New Mexican*, September 23, 1927.

Gilman, Dorothy Foster. "Willa Cather Writes a Fictional Biography." *Boston Evening Transcript*, September 10, 1927.

Grimes, George. "Willa Cather Writes of Early New Mexico." *Omaha World Herald*, September 18, 1927.

"Ha Vuelto." *Santa Fe Gazette*, September 12, 1863.

Harvey, Margaret. "Willa Sibert Cather Thanks the West for Her Success as a Writer of Stories." *Denver Times*, August 16, 1915.

"He Is at Rest." *Santa Fe New Mexican*, February 13, 1888.

Hudetz, Mary. "Native American Shield Returned to New Mexico from France." *Santa Fe New Mexican*, November 18, 2019.

"Indian Detour Ready to Go on Saturday." *Santa Fe New Mexican*, May 14, 1926.

"Inscription." *Santa Fe New Mexican*, October 8, 1869.

"Kit Carson and W. W. H. Davis." *Santa Fe Gazette*, August 15, 1857.

"The Lamy Case." *Santa Fe New Mexican*, September 25, 1880.

"Lost in Colorado Canon: Women Editors Suffer as Result of Trip with Inexperienced Guide." *New York Times*, August 26, 1915.

Mashberg, Tom. "Secret Bids Guide Hopi Indians' Spirits Home." *New York Times*, December 16, 2013.

Merrill, Flora. "A Short Story Course Can Only Delay, It Cannot Kill an Artist, Says Willa Cather." *New York World*, April 19, 1925.

"Monument to His Memory." *Santa Fe New Mexican*, February 21, 1888.

"Mrs. Ickes Dies in Crash of Auto Near Santa Fe." *New York Times*, September 1, 1935.

"Murder of Francis Mallet." *Weekly New Mexican*, September 6, 1879.

"Navajo Captives." *Santa Fe New Mexican*, August 5, 1868.

"The New Cathedral." *Santa Fe New Mexican*, January 3, 1873.

"A Noticeable Difference." *Santa Fe New Mexican*, October 13, 1873.

"Opposition to Club Cultural Colony Holds Meeting and Petitions the City Council." *Santa Fe New Mexican*, April 24, 1926.

"Para la Geseta de Santa Fe," *Santa Fe Gazette*, October 30, 1858.

"People Coming and Going in Santa Fe." *Santa Fe New Mexican*, June 9, 1926.

"People Coming and Going in Santa Fe." *Santa Fe New Mexican*, June 23, 1926. "Politics in New Mexico." *Santa Fe Gazette*, September 30, 1857.

"Round About Town." *Santa Fe New Mexican*, January 17, 1888.

"Round About Town." *Santa Fe New Mexican*, September 23, 1885.

"Santa Fe's Triumph." *Weekly New Mexican*, February 14, 1880.

"Sentiment Grows Against Culture Center." May 17, 1926.

"The Shooting of Mallet." *Weekly New Mexican*, September 13, 1879.

Simmons, Marc. "Trail Dust: Building Cathedral Became Lifelong Project for Lamy," *Santa Fe New Mexican*, May 1, 2015.

Small, Harold. "Willa Cather Raps 'Sincerity Heresy.'" *San Francisco Chronicle*, March 29, 1931.

Small, Harold. "Willa Cather Tells 'Secret' Novel's Title." *San Francisco Chronicle*, March 23, 1931.

Stuart, Henry Longan. "A Vivid Page of History in Miss Cather's New Novel." *New York Times Book Review*, September 4, 1927.

"Three Weeks' Cramming to Keep Clever Couriers Busy." *Santa Fe New Mexican*, April 16, 1926.

"Triangular Fight Between the Military, the Judiciary and the Catholic Church." *Santa Fe Gazette*, August 30, 1851.

"Vandalism–Robberies." *Santa Fe New Mexican*, October 18, 1869.

West, Rebecca. "Miss Cather's Business as an Artist." *New York Herald Tribune Books*, September 11, 1927.

"Will Shuster." *Santa Fe New Mexican*, March 12, 1950.

"Willa Cather Builds a Novel Around a Historical Theme." *Milwaukee Journal Sentinel*, September 10, 1927.

"Willa Cather Is Not Sold on the Culture Colony Plans, States." *Albuquerque Journal*, July 4, 1926.

"Willa Cather Talks of Work." *Philadelphia Record*, August 10, 1913.

Online Resources

Ammons, Elizabeth. "Cather and the New Canon: 'The Old Beauty' and the Issue of Empire." *Cather Studies*, vol. 3. Willa Cather Archive. Available at www.cather.unl.edu.

Anders, John P. "Something Soft and Wild and Free." *Cather Studies*, vol. 4. Willa Cather Archive. Available at www.cather.unl.edu.

Chinery, Mary. "Wartime Fictions: Willa Cather, the Armed Services Editions, and the Unspeakable Second World War." *Cather Studies*, vol. 6. Willa Cather Archive. Available at www.cather.unl.edu.

"The Great American Novels." *The Atlantic*, March 14, 2024. www.theatlantic.com.

Harrell, David. "Willa Cather's Mesa Verde Myth." *Cather Studies*, vol. 1. Willa Cather Archive. Available at www.cather.unl.edu.

Lavin, Matthew. "It's Mr. Reynolds Who Wishes It." *Cather Studies*, vol. 9. Willa Cather Archive. Available at www.cather.unl.edu.

Madigan, Mark J. "Willa Cather and the Book-of-the-Month Club." *Cather Studies*, vol. 7. Willa Cather Archive. Available at www.cather.unl.edu.

Mignon, Charles W. "Cather's Copy of *Death Comes for the Archbishop*." *Cather Studies*, vol. 4. Willa Cather Archive. Available at www.cather.unl.edu.

Murphy, John J. "Postlude: The Green Vase, the Yellow Orange, and the White Chapel."

Cather Studies, vol. 8. Willa Cather Archive, available atwww.cather.unl.edu.
Reynolds, Guy. "The Ideology of Cather's Catholic Progressivism." *Cather Studies*, vol. 3. Willa Cather Archive. www.cather.unl.edu.
Swift, John. "Cather's Archbishop and the 'Backward Path.'" *Cather Studies*, vol. 1. Willa Cather Archive. www.cather.unl.edu.
The Willa Cather Archive, University of Nebraska–Lincoln. Ed. Andrew Jewell. www.cather.unl.edu.
Williams, Deborah Lindsay. "Losing Nothing, Comprehending Everything." *Cather Studies*, vol. 4. Willa Cather Archive. www.cather.unl.edu.

Unpublished Material

Baumann, Gustave. "Fiesta History." Gustave Baumann Collection (AC523), Fray Angélico Chávez History Library/New Mexico History Museum, Santa Fe, NM.
Knopf, Alfred A. "Willa Cather," unpublished memoir. Harry Ransom Humanities Research Center, University of Texas at Austin.

Index

Note: Page numbers in italic text indicate figures.

About the Author

GARRETT PECK is an author, historian, and tour guide in Santa Fe. He leads the Willa Cather's Santa Fe tour and many other excursions around New Mexico, the Land of Enchantment. www.garrettpeck.com.